| DATE | | | |
|---|---|---|---|
|  |  |  |  |
|  |  |  |  |
|  |  |  |  |
|  |  |  |  |
|  |  |  |  |
|  |  |  |  |
|  |  |  |  |
|  |  |  |  |
|  |  |  |  |
|  |  |  |  |
|  |  |  |  |
|  |  |  |  |
|  |  |  |  |
|  |  |  |  |

# Social choice and public decision making
Essays in honor of Kenneth J. Arrow, Volume I

# Social choice and public decision making

## Essays in honor of Kenneth J. Arrow, Volume I

*Edited by*

**WALTER P. HELLER**
*University of California, San Diego*

**ROSS M. STARR**
*University of California, San Diego*

**DAVID A. STARRETT**
*Stanford University*

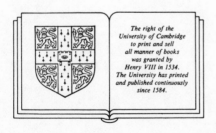

*The right of the
University of Cambridge
to print and sell
all manner of books
was granted by
Henry VIII in 1534.
The University has printed
and published continuously
since 1584.*

**CAMBRIDGE UNIVERSITY PRESS**
*Cambridge*
*London   New York   New Rochelle*
*Melbourne   Sydney*

Published by the Press Syndicate of the University of Cambridge
The Pitt Building, Trumpington Street, Cambridge CB2 1RP
32 East 57th Street, New York, NY 10022, USA
10 Stamford Road, Oakleigh, Melbourne 3166, Australia

First published 1986

Printed in the United States of America

*Library of Congress Cataloging in Publication Data*
Social choice and public decision making.
(Essays in honor of Kenneth J. Arrow ; v. 1)
Includes index.
1. Social choice.  2. Decision-making.  3. Equilibrium
(Economics)  4. Macroeconomics.  5. Uncertainty.
6. Arrow, Kenneth Joseph, 1921- .  I. Heller,
Walter P.  II. Starr, Ross M.  III. Starrett,
David A.  IV. Arrow, Kenneth Joseph, 1921- .
V. Series.
HB846.8.S59  1986     339     86-8580

*British Library Cataloguing in Publication Data*
Social choice and public decision making :
essays in honor of Kenneth J. Arrow, volume I.
1. Social choice
I. Heller, Walter P.  II. Starr, Ross M.
III. Starrett, David A.  IV. Arrow, Kenneth J.
302.1'3     HB846.8

ISBN 0 521 30454 7

# Contents

Essays in honor of Kenneth J. Arrow, Volumes I, II, III

# Contributors

Yves Balasko
Université de Genève

Theodore Bergstrom
University of Michigan

David F. Bradford*
Woodrow Wilson School of Public
   and International Affairs
Princeton University

Graciela Chichilnisky
Columbia University

John D. Geanakoplos
Yale University

Louis Gevers*
Faculté Notre Dame de la Paix
Namur, Belgium

W. M. Gorman
Nuffield College
Oxford

Jerry R. Green
Harvard University

Frank Hahn
Churchill College
Cambridge

Peter J. Hammond*
Stanford University

John C. Harsanyi*
University of California, Berkeley

Walter P. Heller
University of California, San Diego

Leonid Hurwicz*
University of Minnesota

Michael D. Intriligator*
University of California, Los Angeles

Takatoshi Ito
University of Minnesota

Heinz Koenig
University of Mannheim

Mordecai Kurz
Stanford University

Jean-Jacques Laffont
Université des Sciences Sociales
Toulouse

Robert C. Lind*
Cornell University

Thomas Marschak
University of California, Berkeley

Eric S. Maskin
Harvard University

Roger B. Myerson
Northwestern University

Marc Nerlove
University of Pennsylvania

Hajime Oniki
Osaka University

Heraklis M. Polemarchakis
Columbia University

Roy Radner
AT&T Bell Laboratories

Michael Rothschild
University of California, San Diego

Herbert E. Scarf*
Yale University

Amartya Sen*
All Souls College
Oxford

*Contributors to Volume I.

ix

x     **Contributors**

Karl Shell
University of Pennsylvania

Eytan Sheshinski*
Hebrew University
Jerusalem

Robert M. Solow
Massachusetts Institute of Technology

Ross M. Starr
University of California, San Diego

David A. Starrett*
Stanford University

Nancy L. Stokey
Northwestern University

Laurence Weiss
University of California, San Diego

Menahem E. Yaari
Hebrew University
Jerusalem

# Editors' preface

This three-volume work is composed of essays written by many of Kenneth Arrow's students and collaborators. Although it is impossible to cover the entire range of his contributions to economics, we have organized the presentation around the major topics of his research career: Volume I treats "Social Choice and Public Decision Making," Volume II covers "Equilibrium Analysis," and Volume III deals with "Uncertainty, Information, and Communication."

We would like to thank all contributors to these volumes not only for their cooperation in helping expedite on-time production but also for voluntary efforts contributed in reading and commenting on each other's essays. In addition, we acknowledge with thanks the help of the following outside referees: Chuck Blackorby, Mark Johnson, Mark Machina, John McMillan, and Joel Sobel.

Special thanks go to Deborah Bailey who coordinated our (sometimes chaotic) correspondence among authors, editors, and publisher; she cheerfully dealt with potential disasters and enabled us to deliver the completed manuscript as scheduled. Also, we would like to thank Colin Day and his staff at Cambridge University Press for a highly professional effort at their end.

Finally, and most importantly, we speak for all contributors in thanking Kenneth Arrow for being an inspirational teacher and colleague over the years. The intellectual standards he set and the enthusiasm with which he approaches our subject are surely part of all of us. We can only hope that these essays convey some sense of our appreciation and esteem.

# Kenneth J. Arrow

The impact of Kenneth Arrow's work on twentieth century economics has been to change fundamentally economists' understanding of their discipline and their view of several major classes of problems.[1] Arrow was a leader in the post–World War II push to bring the full power of mathematics and statistics to bear on economic analysis. The fields of general equilibrium, social choice and welfare economics, mathematical programming, and economics of uncertainty have been fundamentally altered by his contributions. In addition, Arrow is a man of wide learning, refreshing spontaneity, personal warmth, and remarkable absence of pretension.

Born in 1921 to Harry and Lillian Arrow of New York City, Kenneth Arrow was raised in and around New York. He pursued his undergraduate studies at City College of New York. On graduation from CCNY in 1940, he was awarded the Gold Pell Medal for highest grades in the graduating class. He studied then at Columbia, in particular with Harold Hotelling, and received an M.A. in mathematics in 1941.

Arrow's studies were interrupted by World War II. He served with the Weather Division of the Army Air Force and there wrote his first scientific paper ("On the use of winds in flight planning"). However, his other professional activities in the division almost prevented this line of research. The new young group of statisticians in the Weather Division subjected the prevailing prediction techniques to statistical test against a simple null hypothesis based on historical averages for the date in question. Finding that prevailing techniques were not significantly more reliable, several junior officers sent a memo to the general in charge suggesting that the unit be disbanded and the manpower reallocated. After a succession of such memos, the general's secretary is reported to have replied brusquely on his behalf, "The general is well aware that your division's forecasts are worthless. However, they are required for planning purposes." The division remained intact.

---

[1] Arrow has a rich personal intellectual history. This is best summarized in the headnotes to his research papers in the *Collected papers of Kenneth J. Arrow*. We have borrowed freely from this material. Discussions of Arrow's contributions to each of the topics treated in this collection appear in the introductions to the individual sections.

In 1946, Arrow returned to Columbia for doctoral study with Hotelling. In 1947, he joined the Cowles Commission at the University of Chicago, then under the direction of Jacob Marschak. Cowles was then virtually synonymous with mathematical economics and econometrics in North America. With Hurwicz, Klein, Koopmans, and Marschak there, it formed an active research environment. Arrow was unsure then of his vocation. He considered the possibility of pursuing a nonacademic career as an actuary. Tjalling Koopmans advised him that actuarial statistics would prove unrewarding, saying, with characteristic reticence, "There is no music in it." Fortunately for economic science, Arrow followed this advice and decided to continue a research career.

In 1947, Arrow married Selma Schweitzer, then a graduate student in economics at the University of Chicago. Jacob Marschak, in his capacity as Cowles Commission Research Director, had arranged for the Commission to administer the Sarah Frances Hutchinson Fellowship. This fellowship was held by Sonia Adelson (subsequently married to Lawrence Klein) and then by Selma Schweitzer. The succession of fellows generated some administrative scrutiny. Upon review, it was determined that the terms of the bequest establishing the fellowship required the fellows to be women of the Episcopal Church of Seneca Falls, New York, and the fellowship was withdrawn from Cowles' administration. Nevertheless, the fellowship was clearly a great social success while at Cowles.

In 1948, Arrow joined the recently formed RAND Corporation in Santa Monica, California. RAND was then an active center for fundamental research, particularly in the fast-developing area of mathematical game theory. He returned to RAND during several subsequent summers. There, in the summers of 1950 and 1951, the collaboration with Leonid Hurwicz was initiated.

In 1949, Arrow accepted an assistant professorial appointment in economics and statistics at Stanford University. The research work and publications of the next decade represent an extraordinary burst of creativity and scientific progress. In the space of four years, 1951–4, three of Arrow's most important works of economic theory appeared: *Social choice and individual values* (1951), "An extension of the basic theorems of classical welfare economics" (1951), and "Existence of equilibrium for a competitive economy" (with G. Debreu, 1954). Work on the theory of social choice, started at RAND, was a particularly distinctive act of creation, since the theory was developed with very few antecedents. Arrow describes it as "a concept that took possession of [him]...development of the theorems and their proofs...required only about three weeks, although writing them as a monograph...took many months" (Arrow, *Collected papers*).

The Ph.D. from Columbia was awarded in 1950; and the dissertation, *Social choice and individual values,* was published in 1951. "Extension of the basic theorems of classical welfare economics" was developed for the Second Berkeley Symposium on Mathematical Statistics and Probability to which Arrow was invited in his capacity as a statistician.

In the early 1950s, Arrow pursued – largely by correspondence – joint work on general equilibrium theory with Gerard Debreu, who was then at the Cowles Commission in Chicago. Abraham Wald, with whom Arrow had studied at Columbia, had written several papers in the field but had run up against fundamental mathematical difficulties. It was the recognition by Arrow and Debreu of the importance of using a fixed point theorem that led to major progress in this area.[2] Publication of Arrow and Debreu's "Existence of equilibrium for a competitive economy" represented a fundamental step in the revision of economic analysis and modeling, demonstrating the power of a formal axiomatic approach with relatively advanced mathematical techniques.

During the mid-1950s, Leonid Hurwicz was a frequent academic visitor to Stanford. In 1955–6, Hurwicz was at the Center for Advanced Study in the Behavioral Sciences at Stanford, and in 1957–8 he was a visiting faculty member in the economics department. Collaboration with Hurwicz led to papers in mathematical programming, decentralization, and classic work on the stability of competitive equilibrium. The research faculty in mathematical economics was housed in a converted residence, Serra House. Colleagues there included Herbert Scarf and Hirofumi Uzawa. The informal, quiet, and somewhat isolated setting resulted in a particularly friendly atmosphere and esprit de corps.

Arrow was rapidly promoted at Stanford: to associate professor in 1950 and to full professor in 1953. The full professorship included appointment to the new Department of Operations Research, in addition to economics and statistics. Mathematical programming is a recurrent area of Arrow's research interest, and the new department was founded with Arrow's vigorous support. Although the profession is used to it now, the mathematical complexity of the body of work was then regarded as a bit forbidding. This reputation was a source of some humor when Arrow received the 1957 John Bates Clark Award of the American Economic Association. At the presentation ceremony, introductory remarks were made by George Stigler, who reportedly advised Arrow, in a loud stage-whisper, "You should probably say, 'Symbols fail me.'"

[2] Credit for independent discovery of the importance of fixed point theorems in this context is due to Lionel McKenzie ["On equilibrium in Graham's model of world trade and other competitive systems," *Econometrica,* 22: 147–61 (1954)].

In 1962, Arrow served on the research staff of the Council of Economic Advisers. In 1963–4, he was visiting fellow at Churchill College, Cambridge. The collaboration with Frank Hahn on *General competitive analysis* was pursued there and continued at Stanford in 1967. During the late 1960s, Arrow took up a research program in continuous-time optimal control (a topic touched on twenty years earlier in his Army Air Force service). In collaboration with Mordecai Kurz of Stanford, the result was *Public investment, the rate of return, and optimal fiscal policy*.

In 1968, Arrow accepted a professorship at Harvard and moved to Cambridge, Massachusetts. For the next decade, Harvard was the center of his activity, though he returned to Stanford annually for summer-long seminar series.

When the Nobel Prize in Economics was created in the mid-1960s, a common parlor game among professional economists was to forecast the next recipient. Arrow was on virtually everyone's short list. It was hence no surprise when the 1972 Nobel Prize in Economic Sciences was announced. Arrow was the laureate, jointly with the distinguished British economic theorist, John Hicks of Oxford. Age 51 at the time of the award, he is (at this writing) by far the youngest recipient of the Nobel Prize in Economics.

In 1979, Arrow returned to Stanford; he has been on the faculty there continually since then. Arrow lives on the Stanford campus with his wife, Selma. They have two sons, David and Andrew.

At both Stanford and Harvard, Arrow has been active in the affairs of the faculty and institution. Indeed, he has sometimes advised students, "true academic freedom is freedom from committee assignments." At both institutions and within the profession at large, he has been a source of intellectual excitement and ferment. He holds honorary doctorates from a variety of universities around the globe, including his alma mater, CCNY. He is a fellow of the Econometric Society, Institute of Mathematical Statistics, and American Statistical Association and a distinguished fellow of the American Economic Association. He is past president of the Econometric Society, American Economic Association, Institute of Management Sciences, and Western Economic Association. He holds the distinction, particularly rare among non-Japanese, of membership in the Second Class Order of the Rising Sun, an award presented by the Emperor of Japan.

Arrow is personally accessible and unpretentious, addressed as Ken by students, colleagues, and staff. The student, however junior, who steels his nerve to talk with the distinguished professor discovers that he has Arrow's undivided attention. To devoted students and colleagues, Arrow is a legendary figure, larger than life. Stories abound, highlighting his abilities:

• Arrow thinks faster than he – or anyone else – can talk. Hence conversation tends to take place at an extremely rapid pace; no sentence is ever actually completed.

• The breadth of Arrow's knowledge is repeatedly a surprise, even to his friends. By the end of an evening's dinner party whose guests included a professor of art specializing in the art of China, it seemed clear to the host that Arrow was as well versed as the specialist in this subject.

• Arrow can quote passages of Shakespeare and facts of English history accurately and at length.

• Arrow's presence in seminars is legendary. He may open his (abundant) mail, juggle a pencil, or give every evidence of inattention. He will then make a comment demonstrating that he is several steps ahead of the speaker.

Those of us who have had the chance to know him well are particularly fortunate. We are far richer for the experience.

# Contents

# PART I

# Social choice

Arrow is the creator of the field of social choice. Naturally, there were precursors, but the leap from previous literature to *Social choice and individual values* (1951) was as great as any in the postwar period in economics. Arrow showed that it was impossible to find a reasonable and consistent procedure for any society to choose among conflicting alternatives. The basic properties a procedure had to satisfy to be "reasonable" were these: that all rankings (including the social ranking) be transitive, that any preferences are possible (universal domain); that the social ordering put alternative $a$ ahead of alternative $b$ if everybody prefers $a$ to $b$ (Pareto principle); that, in choosing between two alternatives, society only need consult people's preferences over those two alternatives (independence of irrelevant alternatives), and finally, that no person is a dictator.

All literature that followed had to grapple with, in some way, the basic facts behind Arrow's theorem. Indeed, much of the subsequent literature is devoted to weakening one or more of Arrow's conditions in attempting to escape from the impossibility theorem.

Hammond reexamines two attempts to escape from Arrow impossibility from the viewpoint of "consequentialism," that is, all decisions should be based solely on their feasible consequences. He finds that relaxation of either the independence of irrelevant alternatives or the ordinality of the social choice function violates consequentialism. He goes on to examine the consequentialist approach in a society of identical individuals and finds that the Arrow dictator reappears.

Sen's chapter takes up the informational constraints basic to any theory of choice, including the impossibility theorem. He argues persuasively that if there are new insights to be gained from a particular ethical framework, it must contain restrictions as to what information is relevant to the decision. This view is fruitfully applied to the impossibility theorem, where a side benefit is a remarkably concise proof.

Harsanyi's contribution relates to Arrow's work on "extended sympathy," in which he argued that people can make interpersonal judgments of the form "I am better off under alternative $x$ than you are under alternative

1

*y*." It also provides a very accessible account of Harsanyi's views on a number of issues involving utilitarianism. Harsanyi argues that utilitarian calculations based strictly on the consequences of actions leads to demonstrably worse results than utilitarian calculations based on rules or moral principles.

Hurwicz shows that the results of Maskin characterizing the social choice rules that can be implemented as Nash equilibria of an abstract game extend to models in which the underlying preferences need not be transitive. He generalizes Maskin's concepts of monotonicity and no-veto power to the case of choice correspondences and explains how existing proofs of Maskin's theorem do not depend on additional assumptions on underlying preferences.

Gevers considers afresh the connection between competitive economies and the social choice rule. He studies the Walras correspondence, which relates the distribution of endowments to equilibrium outcomes. Naturally, the Walras correspondence cannot satisfy all the conditions of the Arrow theorem. In particular, it violates the universal domain condition. Gevers shows, however, that it is the most selective rule that satisfies three reasonable axioms: individual rationality; monotonicity in the sense of Maskin, and a third rather innocuous property.

CHAPTER 1

# Consequentialist social norms for public decisions

*Peter J. Hammond*

A consequence cannot make evil an action that was good nor good an action that was evil.

St. Thomas Aquinas[1]

That the morality of actions depends on the consequences which they tend to produce, is the doctrine of rational persons of all schools; that the good or evil of these consequences is measured solely by pleasure or pain, is all of the doctrine of the school of utility, which is peculiar to it.

J. S. Mill (from Warnock, 1962, p. 120)

It must always be the duty of every agent to do that one, among all the actions which he *can* do on any given occasion, whose *total consequences* will have the greatest intrinsic value.

G. E. Moore (1912, p. 121)

## 1 Motivation and outline

### 1.1 Introduction

Ever since the publication of the first edition of Arrow's *Social choice and individual values,* controversy has surrounded several of the conditions that he showed would lead inexorably to a dictatorship. Some of the controversy was discussed in the second edition (Arrow 1963). Much has happened since then, largely reflected in Sen (1970, 1982, 1984, 1985) as well as Arrow (1983).

The research reported in this essay was supported by the National Science Foundation under Grants SES-8201372 and SES-8302460, by the Institute of Advanced Studies of the Hebrew University in Jerusalem, and by the Österreichische Länderbank. I am grateful to these institutions for their support, and to Menahem Yaari, an anonymous referee, and the members of seminars at the University of Graz, Stanford University, the California Institute of Technology, and the Southern Methodist University for their comments, especially Kenneth Arrow and Norman Schofield.

3

Two conditions in particular were often relaxed in an attempt to escape from dictatorship. One was independence of irrelevant alternatives, and a second was ordinality of the social choice function. Without independence of irrelevant alternatives, a wide class of ranking rules such as the Borda rule will satisfy all the other Arrow conditions, as discussed by Fishburn (1973), Fine and Fine (1974), and Gärdenfors (1973), for example. If ordinality is not insisted upon, the door is left open for rules such as Sen's (1970) "Pareto-extension rule," based on the Pareto quasiordering, and the transitive closure of majority rule.

One purpose of this essay is to show that both of these escapes from the Arrow theorem present fundamental difficulties of their own. Specifically, they lead to social choices that violate what is perhaps the most fundamental axiom of normative choice, that all decisions should be based solely on the consequences of decisions that are feasible. This fundamental axiom I call "consequentialism" following Anscombe (1958) and numerous succeeding moral philosophers;[2] it is an obvious generalization of the condition Arrow (1971) called "valuation of actions by consequences." Examples are presented in Sections 1.1 and 1.2 to illustrate how consequentialism is violated by the Pareto-extension rule and by the Borda rule.

A much more fundamental objection to utilitarianism in particular and to most of social choice theory in general is expressed in the introduction to Sen and Williams (1982). Indeed, their objections apply to any consequentialist theory of ethics, as Williams (1973) earlier made clear. Related objections are considered by Sen (1984) and, in particular, by Parfit (1984), Scheffler (1984), and Slote (1984). They seem to carry most force, however, in the field of personal ethics, where one is asking what constitutes moral behavior for an individual. Arrow and his many successors in social choice theory were more concerned with the making and evaluation of public policy, especially but not exclusively economic policy. Although one looks (all too often in vain) for high standards of personal morality among public policymakers, personal ethics is obviously a very inadequate guide to the public policymaker. Nor is it obvious that the kind of objections Sen and Williams and others have made to consequentialist ethics carry over with much force from personal morality to public choice. In all probability, some such objections will be advanced, though it is unclear that most of them cannot be met by allowing enough relevant ethical considerations to be counted within the space of "consequences." Nevertheless, in this chapter I shall investigate the implications of assuming that anybody responsible for a public decision of any kind

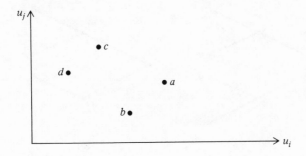

Figure 1. Utility possibilities.

makes it solely on the basis of its social consequences. I shall say a little more about the issues raised by this assumption in Sections 1.4 and 4.1.

After the examples of Sections 1.2 and 1.3, Section 1.4 argues why a much simplified model of public choice suffices to explore the implications of consequentialism. Section 1.5 then gives an outline of the heart of this essay.

## 1.2   *Inconsequentialism of the Pareto rule*

Allowing anything that is Pareto efficient into the social choice set is Sen's (1970) Pareto-extension social choice rule, which I shall call the *Pareto rule*. It is not consequentialist, as the following example shows.

Suppose there are two individuals $i$ and $j$ and four social states, or consequences, $a$, $b$, $c$, and $d$. Let the two individuals have strict preference rankings such that

$$a P_i b P_i c P_i d \quad \text{and} \quad c P_j d P_j a P_j b.$$

Corresponding utility possibilities are illustrated in Figure 1. Consider first a decision tree in which society chooses between nodes $n_1$ and $n_2$ at the initial node $n_0$. At $n_1$, $a$ and $d$ are still available, whereas at $n_2$, $b$ and $c$ are available, as shown in Figure 2(a). Then the Pareto choice set at node $n_0$ is $\{a, c\}$, since this pair is Pareto efficient whereas $b$ and $d$ are inefficient. Thus the Pareto rule allows the first decision at node $n_0$ to take the society either to $n_1$, planning to go on to $a$, or to $n_2$, planning to go on to $c$.

Consider, however, the second decision in the tree. Suppose society does make its first move from $n_0$ to $n_1$. Then, at $n_1$, the choice is between

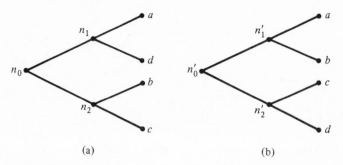

*a* and *d*, both of which are Pareto efficient because *c*, which Pareto dominated *d* originally, is no longer available. To exclude *d*, society has to
remember that *c* was available previously and Pareto dominated *d*. Or it
has to precommit itself somehow to choosing only *a* at node $n_1$. In either
case, one is led to wonder what past alternatives no longer available at
node $n_0$ might have Pareto dominated *a* or *c*, or else what past commitments had been entered into. Moreover, the choice at $n_1$ of *a* over *d* depends not just on the pair of consequences *a* and *d*, which society faces
then; it also depends on other consequences or on other considerations
and so violates consequentialism according to the definition I shall give
of this term.

Nor can the problem be avoided by moving to $n_2$ first, intending to
continue on to *c*, which is Pareto efficient. For, at $n_2$, both *b* and *c* are
Pareto efficient because *a*, which Pareto dominated *b* originally, is no
longer available. Thus an exactly similar problem arises at $n_2$ as at $n_1$. At
$n_1$, the Pareto rule chooses both *a* and *d*; at $n_2$, it chooses both *b* and *c*;
therefore, the outcome of following it throughout could be *a*, *b*, *c*, or *d* –
nothing whatsoever is ruled out.

Suppose now that the decision tree changes but the four consequences
*a*, *b*, *c*, and *d* do not. Specifically, suppose that society chooses between
the two nodes $n_1'$, $n_2'$ at the initial node $n_0'$ of the new tree. Suppose now
that *a* and *b* are available at node $n_1'$, but at node $n_2'$, *c* and *d* are available, as shown in Figure 2(b). Then, since *a*, *c* are Pareto efficient and
*b*, *d* are Pareto dominated, society's first decision could take it to $n_1'$ or to
$n_2'$. Now, however, at $n_1'$, *b* is Pareto dominated by *a* so that only *a* will
be chosen, and at $n_2'$, *d* is Pareto dominated by *c* so that only *c* will be
chosen. For this new decision tree, the Pareto rule leads only to *a* or to *c*;
*b* and *d* are excluded. Thus, by changing the structure of the decision

tree, the social choice set has been changed from $\{a, b, c, d\}$ to just $\{a, c\}$. There is now no danger of choosing a consequence that was originally Pareto inefficient. In particular, the choice of consequences has been shown to depend on the structure of the decision tree rather than just on the set of available consequences. This shows that the Pareto rule does indeed violate consequentialism.

In this simple example, it is easy to construct other decision trees that lead the Pareto rule to the choice set $\{a, b, c\}$ or to the choice set $\{a, c, d\}$, as the reader will easily verify. Of course, a Pareto-efficient consequence can never be rejected by applying the Pareto rule within a decision tree.

To avoid such inconsequentialist choices, there must be a social preference ordering rather than just a quasiordering such as the Pareto rule applies. This was already shown implicitly in Hammond (1977) and explicitly in Hammond (1985b) and is discussed in Section 3.2.

### 1.3 Inconsequentialism of the Borda rule

Next I shall consider the Borda rule, which does indeed maximize a social ordering and has a number of other desirable properties, such as Pareto efficiency, anonymity, and so on. The Borda rule, however, violates Arrow's independence of irrelevant alternatives condition and this, we shall see, leads to inconsequentialism.

Suppose that there are two individuals, $i$ and $j$ as before, but that there are now five possible consequences $a$, $b$, $c$, $d$, and $e$. Suppose that the two individuals have strict preference rankings given by

$$a P_i b P_i c P_i d P_i e \quad \text{and} \quad d P_j e P_j a P_j b P_j c.$$

According to the Borda rule, each consequence is given a Borda count equal to the sum of the ranks given to it by both the individuals, with preferred consequences ranking higher. Thus $i$ gives $a$ a rank of 4 and $j$ gives $a$ a rank of 2, for a total Borda count $B(a) = 4 + 2 = 6$. Similarly, $B(b) = 3 + 1 = 4$, $B(c) = 2 + 0 = 2$, $B(d) = 1 + 4 = 5$, and $B(e) = 0 + 3 = 3$. Since $a$ has the highest Borda count, it is the consequence chosen by the Borda rule.

Suppose, however, there is a decision tree in which the choice of $a$ leads to a second decision node $n$ at which $d$ and $e$ are still available as alternatives to $a$, but $b$ and $c$ are no longer possible. Then, applying the Borda rule once again and ignoring the irrelevant consequences $b$ and $c$, the preference rankings are

$$a P_j d P_i e \quad \text{and} \quad d P_j e P_j a$$

so the total Borda counts are

$$B(a) = 2 + 0 = 2, \qquad B(d) = 1 + 2 = 3, \qquad B(e) = 0 + 1 = 1.$$

This leads to the social choice of $d$ rather than $a$. Clearly, then, the Borda rule gives rise to a dynamic inconsistency in the sense of Strotz (1956). If $d$ is indeed the final outcome, it also shows that the Borda rule is inconsequentialist. If the decision tree only has one decision node so that the society is forced to choose at once between $a$, $b$, $c$, $d$, and $e$ without any chance to revise the choice at a later node, the choice is $a$. But for the decision tree just considered, the choice is $d$ even though the available consequences are exactly the same.

## 1.4     Modeling normative public choice

Since Arrow's *Social choice and individual values* appeared in 1951, normative social choice theory has concerned itself with devising good rules for deciding public policy questions. Arrow and most of his successors considered feasible sets of possible *social states* and examined various ways of choosing from such sets. Then a policy would be chosen, presumably, that led to good social states. This, however, is an intrinsically static model of social choice and also one that allows no uncertainty, imperfect information, and so forth, of the kind that besets most practical public policy questions. To allow fully for all such considerations, public choice needs to be modeled in an extensive game in which both individual members of the society and the public policymaker have moves to make. In fact, not even the usual von Neumann and Morgenstern (1953) apparatus of an extensive game or the generalization due to Kuhn (1953) are really quite sufficient; as Dubey and Kaneko (1982) and others have noticed, an extensive game in which two or more players really do move simultaneously may not be the same as one that uses the standard representation of *simultaneous* moves, with players moving in sequence but in ignorance of what other players have chosen. Allowing such simultaneous moves leads to consideration of *generalized* extensive games.

A complete model of a public decision problem, then, is likely to be an immensely complicated generalized extensive game whose players are the individual members of the society as well as at least one public agent whose behavior is the ultimate subject of our normative analysis. That is, we are particularly interested in recommendations or evaluations concerning the decisions of this public agent. A complete theory will specify how the public agent should behave in each and every possible society and extensive game, taking full account of all the strategic considerations that arise in such a game. In particular, such a theory requires a complete theory of solutions to extensive games; such a theory is lacking even in the standard but perhaps rather special case where all players are known to be expected utility maximizers, as von Neumann and Morgenstern originally assumed.

In this chapter, I shall circumvent the major difficulties such general extensive games present by restricting attention to trivial games under complete certainty in which all moves are made by the public agent whose behavior is the object of our normative analysis. Such games are, of course, one person games. Assuming that the public agent has perfect recall, the game can then be represented by a certain decision tree of the kind discussed in Hammond (1976a, 1977), for instance.

This is, of course, a very serious restriction indeed, which will have to be relaxed later on if any significant public decisions at all are to fall within the scope of the theory. Nevertheless, I shall show that considering only such a severely restricted class of public decision problems, consequentialism has very strong implications. These will be implications concerning the implicit choice of consequences in any such public decision tree. Later on, when the theory can be extended to broader classes of public decision problems under uncertainty in which also individuals other than the public agent have strategic choices to make, these results for such restricted decision problems will still be of use. In effect, they will tell us about the objectives the public agent should pursue subject to the constraints that arise because of individuals' strategic behavior. However, this last observation rather anticipates results concerning the likely nature of consequentialist behavior in extensive games – results in a theory yet to be developed. So it should be viewed with caution if not skepticism for the time being.

## 1.5    *Outline of chapter*

I hope the reader is convinced that a reexamination of the axiomatic foundations of social choice theory is still worthwhile. That, at any rate, is what I shall present in the remaining sections. Section 2 prepares the ground by presenting a formal description of general social norms for behavior in certain public decision trees. A new feature will be the definition of an individual's welfare norm in Section 2.3 as the norm for a society of identical individuals. This makes the concept of individual welfare explicitly normative and removes many of the usual objections to the Pareto criterion or to utilitarianism. An Arrow social norm is defined in Section 2.4

as one whose prescriptions in any decision tree depend only on the prescriptions of individuals' welfare norms in the same tree.

Section 3 then considers the implications of consequentialism for Arrow social norms. Assuming only consequentialism and an otherwise unrestricted domain of possible individual welfare norms, all the conditions of Arrow's general possibility theorem are shown to follow, which implies that there must be a dictator. That is, the social norm must always prescribe behavior that is acceptable to the individual welfare norm of a single dictator; the society is essentially treated as though all individuals had the same welfare norm as the dictator.

Section 4 discusses three important limitations and possible extensions of these results. First are the limitations of consequentialism itself. Second is the assumption of an unrestricted domain of individual norms and its inapplicability in economics. The third limitation discussed is the exclusion of interpersonal comparisons.

## 2    General social norms for certain decision trees

### 2.1    *Certain decision trees and behavior*

Certain decision trees describe decision problems in the absence of uncertainty. A *finite certain decision tree* $T = (N, N^{+1}, X)$ consists of a set of nodes $N$, a set of terminal nodes (or outcomes) $X$, and a successor correspondence $N^{+1}: N \twoheadrightarrow N$ defined so that $N^{+1}(n)$ is the set of nodes that immediately succeed $n$ in the tree $T$. The set $N$ includes an initial node $n_0$. The correspondence $N^{+1}$ has to be suitably restricted so that $T$ really is a tree (cf. Hammond 1976a, 1977, 1983, 1985b).

An *intended behavior* in the decision tree $T$ is a *behavior strategy correspondence* $B: N \twoheadrightarrow N$ that determines at every node $n$ a nonempty *behavior set* $B(n)$ that is a subset of $N^{+1}(n)$. Thus an intended behavior selects a set of acceptable moves at each decision node. Notice that any selection $\beta: N \to N$ from the correspondence $B$ is a behavior strategy satisfying $\beta(n) \in B(n) \subset N^{+1}(n)$ for all $n \in N$.

However, intended behavior may easily depart from actual behavior, as the literature on naive choice certainly testifies (see, e.g., Strotz 1956; Hammond 1976a; Elster 1979). It is reasonable to assert that actual behavior matches intended behavior only at the initial node $n_0$ of the tree $T$. At any node $n$ other than $n_0$, the agent no longer faces the decision tree $T$ but only the *continuation decision tree* $T(n)$ whose initial node is $n$

itself and whose set of nodes $N(n)$ consists exactly of those nodes in $N$ that eventually succeed $n$ in $T$ (including $n$ itself).

Whereas intended behavior is of psychological interest, a normative theory of behavior is concerned with prescribing actual behavior rather than mere intentions. An agent's actual behavior in the choice tree $T$ is described by the behavior set $B_{T(n)}(n)$ at the initial node of $T(n)$ for each decision node $n \in N$. So we naturally *define* $B_T(n) := B_{T(n)}(n)$ (all $n \in N$). In other words, an agent's actual behavior is described not by original intentions but by the intentions the agent has later on when he or she is about to make a move at the initial node $n$ of the continuation tree $T(n)$. Then the agent's actual behavior must be *dynamically consistent* in the sense that whenever $n \in N$ for a decision tree $T$ and $n' \in N(n)$ is a decision node of the continuation tree $T(n)$, then $B_{T(n)}(n') = B_T(n')$ because both must be equal to $B_{T(n')}(n')$.

Before coming to the definition of a behavior rule, two preliminary definitions are required. First, if $T$ is a decision tree, say that $T'$ is a *subtree* of $T$, and write $T' \subset T$ if (i) the set of nodes of $N'$ of the tree $T'$ is a subset of $N$, the set of nodes of $T$ and (ii) $T'$ is the decision tree with the same initial node $n_0$ whose successor correspondence $N_{T'}^{+1}$ is the obvious restriction of $N^{+1}$ to the set of nodes $N'$. Second, a collection $\Im$ of finite decision trees is *complete* if

   (i)   whenever $T' \subset T$, then $T' \in \Im$, and
   (ii)  whenever $T \in \Im$ and $n \in N_T$, then $T(n) \in \Im$;

that is, a complete collection of decision trees includes all subtrees and continuation trees of its member trees.

A *behavior rule or norm* $B$ is mapping whose domain $\Im$ is a complete set of decision trees, such that

   (i)   for each $T \in \Im$, $B_T$ is a behavior in the decision tree $T$ and
   (ii)  $B$ is dynamically consistent (as defined above).

## 2.2   Social norms for public decision trees

A membership $M$ is a finite set of individuals. For each individual member $i \in M$, assume there is a set $\Theta_i$ of possible characteristics $\theta_i$ of $i$. Let $\Theta^M$ denote the Cartesian product space $X_{i \in M} \Theta_i$ of possible *profiles* of individual characteristics, with typical member $\theta^M = (\theta_i)_{i \in M}$. A *society S* then consists of a pair $(M, \theta^M)$. I shall assume throughout this essay that the society is *exogenous* in the sense that it cannot be affected by behavior within the public decision tree. Where behavior does affect the society, the society itself becomes a matter for public decision. Such *endogenous* societies are considered in Hammond (1985a; in press). Here, I assume that $M$ is fixed and that a society is sufficiently described by the profile $\theta^M$.

A *social norm* is then a mapping $B(\theta^M)$ defined on a domain of societies $S$ such that in each society $\theta^M$ of $S$, $B(\theta^M)$ is a behavior rule for a complete collection of decision trees $\mathfrak{I}$. Then $B_T(\theta^M)$ will denote behavior in decision tree $T$ when the profile is $\theta^M$.

## 2.3    *Individuals' welfare norms*

A general social norm $B(\theta^M)$ will have no regard for the behavior, intentions, choices, or preferences of the individual members of $M$. Such preferences may be part of the characteristic profile $\theta^M$, but this has not yet been postulated. I shall now do so, but by an indirect route that enables the ethical value judgment of consumers' sovereignty so common in welfare economics to be dispensed with when it is appropriate to do so. It will also circumvent all the usual objections to the Pareto criterion. Since our concern is normative behavior, it is appropriate to have a normative concept of individual behavior too, and this is what I shall assume that we have.

First, I assume that there is a fixed set of possible individual characteristics $\Theta$ such that, for each individual $i$ in $M$, $\Theta^i = \Theta$. This really amounts to assuming that the set of possible societies $S$ is broad enough to allow any individual to have any possible characteristic.

Next, given any membership $M$ and any characteristic $\theta$ of $\Theta$, write $\theta 1^M$ for the society whose membership is $M$ all of whom share the same characteristic $\theta$. In other words, $\theta 1^M$ is a society of individuals with identical characteristics. Define the *welfare behavior rule* of an individual with characteristic $\theta$ in a membership $M$ as $B(\theta 1^M)$. Notice that, by definition, individuals with the same characteristic have the same welfare behavior rule. This is not unreasonable; two individuals with different welfare behavior rules should be described by different characteristics, after all. Notice, however, that an individual's welfare behavior rule may depend on the membership $M$. In particular, the size of the membership may be important. For example, if all individuals are identical, equality of treatment is appealing unless there is so much scarcity that equality precludes survival. In any case, the very specification of behavior may depend on the membership $M$ – one cannot ask fifty people to perform a certain task unless the society includes at least fifty people.

In the following, I shall write $B(\theta)$ for the welfare behavior rule of an individual with characteristic $\theta$, treating the membership $M$ as fixed throughout.

## 2.4 *Arrow social norms and unanimity*

Let $M$ be any membership and $T$ any decision tree in the domain $\mathfrak{I}$ of the social norm $B$. Then $B_T(\cdot)$ describes how social behavior within the tree $T$ varies as society varies, with its membership fixed at $M$, however. Say that $B_T(\cdot)$ is *based purely on individuals' welfare behavior* within the subtrees of $T$ if, whenever in the two societies $\theta^M$, $\bar{\theta}^M$ all the individuals' welfare behavior is identical for all subtrees $T'$ of the tree $T$, so that

$$B_{T'}(\theta_i) = B_{T'}(\bar{\theta}_i) \qquad \text{(all } i \in M; \text{ all } T' \subset T),$$

then social behavior in the tree $T$ in the two societies is the same too, so $B_T(\theta^M) = B_T(\bar{\theta}^M)$. Thus, within the tree $T$, each individual $i \in M$ is characterized just by welfare behavior $B_T(\theta_i)$ in all subtrees $T' \subset T$ for any profile $\theta^M$.

As will be seen in Section 3.3, Arrow's original theory of social choice involves a social norm based purely on individuals' (welfare) behavior (or "values," though perhaps in a different sense from the one propounded here) within each tree in precisely this way. Thus I shall refer to such norms as *Arrow social norms*.

Let $T$ be any decision tree and $\theta^M$ any profile. Say that individuals' welfare behavior is *unanimous within the subtrees of $T$* if, for every $T' \subset T$, $B_{T'}(\theta_i)$ is the same for all $i \in M$.

**Lemma 1 (Unanimity).** Let $B$ be an Arrow social norm, $T$ any decision tree, and $\theta^M$ any profile in which individuals' welfare behavior is unanimous within the subtrees $T$. Then $B_T(\theta^M) = B_T(\theta_i)$ (all $i \in M$); that is, social behavior within the tree $T$ is identical to the individuals' unanimous behavior.

*Proof:* Because of unanimity, there is at least one characteristic $\bar{\theta} \in \Theta$ such that $B_{T'}(\theta_i) = B_{T'}(\bar{\theta})$ for every $i \in M$ and $T' \subset T$. Define $\bar{\theta}^M := \bar{\theta}1^M$. Then $B_{T'}(\theta_i) = B_{T'}(\bar{\theta}_i)$ for every $i \in M$ and $T' \subset T$. Because $B$ is an Arrow social norm, it follows that $B_T(\theta^M) = B_T(\bar{\theta}^M)$. But $B_T(\bar{\theta}^M) = B_T(\bar{\theta}1^M) = B_T(\bar{\theta})$, where the last equality follows from the definition of an individual's behavior norm. Also, by definition of $\bar{\theta}$, $B_T(\bar{\theta}) = B_T(\theta_i)$ (all $i \in M$). So

$$B_T(\theta^M) = B_T(\bar{\theta}^M) = B_T(\bar{\theta}) = B_T(\theta_i) \qquad \text{(all } i \in M). \qquad \text{Q.E.D.}$$

## 3    Consequentialist Arrow social norms and dictatorship

### 3.1    *Consequential decision trees and the consequences of behavior*

Suppose that there is a set $Y$ of possible *consequences*. Set $Y$ should be sufficiently comprehensive to include everything that is relevant to any public decision. In ethics, many criticisms of utilitarianism in particular and of consequentialism in general take the form of introducing pertinent considerations that, it is alleged, do not affect utility or else are not consequences. Obviously, such criticisms lose much of their force if the space of consequences is expanded to accommodate *all* relevant considerations, though at the risk of having a theory so general that it loses virtually all empirical content [cf. the discussion in Broome (1984)]. Such grand issues are best left for discussion elsewhere; however, I shall say a little bit more about them in Section 4.1.

A decision tree $T = (N, N^{+1}, X)$ in a society with membership $M$ is *consequential* if there is a *consequence mapping* $\gamma \colon X \to Y$ from terminal nodes to consequences. In future, it will be assumed that $\mathfrak{I}$, the domain of the Arrow social norm, consists of all such consequential decision trees. For each $T$ of $\mathfrak{I}$, the existence of the consequence mapping $\gamma$ will be implicitly assumed. Notice that $\mathfrak{I}$ is then a complete set of decision trees.

Given any consequential decision tree $T$ in $\mathfrak{I}$, which is the domain of the Arrow social norm $B(s)$ for all societies $s$ in $S$, the value of the norm in tree $T$ is $B_T(s)$. This behavior norm leads to a set of nodes $N_T^B(s)$ in $T$ that can be constructed recursively according to the rules

(i)    $n_0 \in N_T^B(s)$ and

(ii)    if $n \in N_T^B(s)$ and $n' \in B_T(s)(n)(\subset N^{+1}(n))$, then $n' \in N_T^B(s)$.

Ultimately, there is a set of terminal nodes,

$$X_T^B(s) := N_T^B(s) \cap X_T,$$

to which the norm gives rise. Corresponding to these terminal nodes are the consequences of the set $\gamma(X_T^B(s))$. These are the consequences that the norm $B$ recommends, effectively, given the tree $T$ and the society $s$.

### 3.2    *Consequentialist social norms and social welfare orderings*

As in Hammond (1985b), behavior is said to be consequentialist when it can be predicted solely on the basis of consequences, no matter what the decision tree may be. More specifically, knowledge of the set of consequences $\gamma(X_T)$ available in the decision tree should suffice to determine the consequences of behavior. Consequentialism is intended as a normative standard of behavior, and it retains its appeal for social norms as well as for individual behavior.

Two consequential decision trees $T, T'$ are said to be *consequentially equivalent* if $\gamma(X_T) = \gamma'(X_{T'})$, so that the set of available consequences is the same in both trees, given the respective consequence mappings $\gamma, \gamma'$. The social norm $B$ is said to be *consequentialist* if (i) whenever $T, T'$ are two consequentially equivalent decision trees with consequence mappings $\gamma, \gamma'$ and for any fixed society $s$, the sets of consequences $\gamma(X_T^B(s))$ and $\gamma'(X_{T'}^B(s))$ of the norm $B$ are identical and (ii) the same is true whenever $T$ or $T'$ are continuations of consequential decision trees (as defined in Section 2.1). This is the obvious extension to social norms of the concept of consequentialist individual behavior. As with individual behavior, it has far-reaching implications, as will now be seen.

First, it is at once evident from the inclusion of all consequential decision trees in the domain $\Im$ that, given any nonempty finite subset $Z$ of the set of consequences $Y$, there exists a decision tree $T$ in $\Im$ and a consequence mapping $\gamma \colon X_T \to Y$ such that $\gamma(X_T) = Z$. Moreover, from the definition of consequentialism above, for each society $s$, there is a uniquely specified *consequence choice set* $C(s)(Z)$ whenever the decision tree $T$ and consequence mapping $\gamma$ together satisfy $\gamma(X_T) = Z$. So the consequentialist social norm $B$ induces and indeed corresponds to a *consequence social choice function* $C(s)(\cdot)$ in each society $s$ of $S$. The choice function $C(s)(\cdot)$ is defined on the set of all nonempty finite subsets of $Y$ in the society $s$ with membership $M$ and takes values $C(s)(Z)$ that are nonempty subsets of $Z$ for all such $Z$. In fact, $B(s)$ and $C(s)(\cdot)$ are related by the identity

$$\gamma(X_T^B(s)) = C(s)[\gamma(X_T)]$$

for all consequential decision trees $T$ with consequence mappings $\gamma \colon X_T \to Y$.

The crucial implications of consequentialism discussed in Hammond (1977, 1983, 1985b) come about because of the application of consequentialism to each continuation decision tree $T(n)$ of a given tree $T$. It has been suggested that this represents an extra assumption, since, in principle, continuation trees (as defined in Section 2.1) could be treated quite differently from decision trees. If this were conceded, consequentialism would lose nearly all its force.

Continuation decision trees, however, *are* very obviously decision trees. In the absence of precommitment, decisions have to be taken sequentially at successive nodes of the tree, and the continuation decision tree describes the decision problem that is then faced. If precommitment is possible, then it really ought to be modeled *within* the decision tree – Odysseus' opportunity to precommit himself and his crew before confronting the Sirens is a wonderful example of this, as Strotz (1956) recognized (see also Elster 1979). Once all possibilities for precommitment are modeled as available decisions within the tree, then the sequence of decisions remains exactly as I have described it.

What may still be true, however, is that behavior within a continuation tree depends on consequences available from the *whole* tree and not just on consequences available within the continuation. Then continuation trees would have to be regarded as different from entire decision trees in formulating the consequentialist hypothesis, even though they may be consequentially equivalent according to the above definition. Put more simply, counterfactual consequences that past decisions made infeasible are still allowed to count.

I want to argue that such counterfactual consequences are not relevant to choices in continuation decision trees. Here, I feel that I can claim support from Arrow himself, who wrote as follows:

> The social welfare function approach, whether in Bergson's version or in mine, and "populistic democracy," as Dahl terms it, both imply that the social choice at any moment is determined by the range of alternative social states available (given the preferences of individuals); there is no special role given to one alternative because it happens to be identical to or derived from a historically given one. . . .
>
> It is against this background that the importance of the transitivity condition becomes clear. Those familiar with the integrability controversy in the field of consumer's demand theory will observe that the basic problem is the same: the independence of the final choice from the path to it. Transitivity will insure this independence; from any environment, there will be a chosen alternative, and, in the absence of a deadlock, no place for the historically given alternative to be chosen by default. . . .
>
> Collective rationality in the social choice mechanism is not then merely an illegitimate transfer from the individual to society, but an important attribute of a genuinely democratic system capable of full adaptation to varying environments. (1963, pp. 119-20 *passim*)

Although admitting the relevance of counterfactual consequences is rather different in principle from allowing a "place for the historically given alternative to be chosen by default," it has an identical effect. Certainly, it flies in the face of the claim "that the social choice at any moment is determined by the range of alternative social states available." Moreover, counterfactual consequences pose problems at the start of any contemporary decision tree. That is how lawyers earn their keep, after all. Good law, however, looks forward to future consequences rather than backward to what might have been. Of course, property rights are upheld and criminals punished because of what happened in the past, in part; but the ultimate justification, as many lawyers would recognize, are the future consequences of not maintaining property rights or of failing to punish criminals (cf. Harsanyi 1986). Deterrence is preferred to retribution. Future consequences, including the consequences of upholding the law, are relevant; past consequences are not. To quote Moore (1942, p. 559),[3] "Among the consequences of $A$ nothing is included but what is the case *subsequently* to the occurrence of $A$."

Applying consequentialism to all consequential decision trees and to their continuations yields the following strong result. Its proof can be found in Hammond (1977, 1985b).

**Lemma 2 (Ordinality).** If the social norm $B_T(s)$ on the domain of profiles $S$ and of consequential decision trees $\mathfrak{I}$ is consequentialist, then there exists a preference ordering $R(s)$ (complete, reflexive, and transitive) on $Y$ for each $s \in S$ such that the consequence social choice function $C(s)$ satisfies

$$C(s)(Z) \equiv \{y \in Z \mid y' \in Z \text{ implies } yR(s)y'\}$$

for all nonempty and finite $Z \subset Y$.

Thus the consequentialist social norm must maximize a *social welfare ordering $R(s)$* on $Y$ in every society $s$ of $S$.

### 3.3 Consequentialist Arrow social norms and social welfare functions

An Arrow social norm was defined in Section 2.4 so that in all societies $s$ with membership $M$ and for all decision trees $T$ in the complete domain $\mathfrak{I}$, social behavior $B_T(s)$ in tree $T$ depends only on individuals' welfare behavior $B_T(\theta_i)$ $(i \in M)$ within all subtrees $T' \subset T$ of the same tree. An individual's welfare behavior $B_T(\theta_i)$ was defined to be $B_T(\theta_i 1^M)$ where $\theta_i 1^M$ denotes a society with membership $M$ all of whom have the identical characteristic $\theta_i$.

If an Arrow social norm is also consequentialist, and if the domain $\mathfrak{I}$ consists of all consequential decision trees, then the conclusion of Section 3.2 implies that in any society $s$ with membership $M$, the behavior

$B_T(s)$ corresponds to a preference ordering $R(s)$ on the space of consequences $Y$. Since $B_T(\theta) = B_T(\theta 1^M)$ for all possible $T$ and $\theta$, it follows too that every possible individual welfare behavior corresponds to a preference ordering $R(\theta)$ determined by the individual characteristic $\theta$.

In Section 3.6 I shall show that a consequentialist Arrow social norm with a suitably large domain of possible societies $s$ must be dictatorial. I shall do this by showing that such a norm satisfies all the conditions of Arrow's impossibility (or "general possibility") theorem. In particular, a consequentialist Arrow social norm can be represented by a "consequence" Arrow social welfare function (or "constitution") that satisfies the controversial independence of irrelevant alternatives condition as well as the Pareto criterion.

A *consequence Arrow social welfare function* (ASWF) is a mapping $f$ whose domain is the space $\mathfrak{R}^M(\Theta^M)$ of possible profiles of individual welfare orderings on $Y$, whose typical member is

$$R^M(\theta^M) \equiv (R(\theta_i))_{i \in M}.$$

Here $\Theta^M$ denotes the range of possible characteristic profiles $\theta^M$ in societies with membership $M$.

Because consequentialism implies that both the social norm and all individual welfare norms correspond to preference orderings, and because an Arrow social norm depends only on individual welfare norms, the following is immediate.

**Lemma 3 (Existence of a consequence Arrow social welfare function).**
Corresponding to any consequentialist Arrow social norm $B_T(s)$ defined on a set of societies $S$ and the set of all consequential decision trees $\mathfrak{I}$, there exists a unique consequence ASWF $f$ on the domain $\mathfrak{R}^M(\Theta^M)$ such that whenever $B_T(\theta_i)$ $(T \in \mathfrak{I})$ corresponds to $R(\theta_i)$ for all $i \in M$, then $B_T(\theta^M)$ $(T \in \mathfrak{I})$ corresponds to $f(R^M(\theta^M))$.

### 3.4     *Independence of irrelevant alternatives*

The example of Borda's rule was discussed in Section 1.3 and was used to suggest that consequentialism implies that a consequence ASWF must satisfy independence of irrelevant alternatives. This will now be claimed formally, though the proof is sufficiently close to proofs given elsewhere that I will omit it.

Say that the consequence ASWF $f$ satisfies *condition I* (independence of irrelevant alternatives) if, for any set of consequences $Z \subset Y$ and for any pair of individual welfare profiles $R^M, \bar{R}^M$ of the domain $\mathfrak{R}^M(\Theta^M)$

that meet the requirement that for all pairs of consequences $y^1, y^2 \in Z$ and for all members $i \in M$,

$$y^1 R_i y^2 \quad \text{iff} \quad y^1 \bar{R}_i y^2,$$

it must be true that for all pairs of consequences $y^1, y^2 \in Z$,

$$y^1 f(R^M) y^2 \quad \text{iff} \quad y^1 f(\bar{R}^M) y^2.$$

As already shown in Hammond (1977) in effect and more especially in Hammond (1983, pp. 184–6), consequentialism actually implies that this consequence ASWF must indeed satisfy condition I. Of course, the argument of Section 1.3 also suggests this. Thus:

**Lemma 4 (Independence of irrelevant alternatives).** The consequence Arrow social welfare function that corresponds to a consequentialist Arrow social norm in societies with a fixed membership must satisfy condition I.

### 3.5    The Pareto and Pareto indifference conditions

In addition, the consequence ASWF that corresponds to a consequentialist Arrow social norm can be shown to satisfy not just the ordinary Pareto condition but also the extra Pareto indifference condition, which has sometimes been invoked in social choice theory. This will be an implication of the unanimity Lemma 1 of Section 2.4. First, however, a few preliminaries, followed by a statement of the two Pareto conditions.

In accordance with standard practice, let $P(\theta_i)$ and $I(\theta_i)$ denote, respectively, the strict preference and the indifference relations determined by the weak preference relation $R(\theta_i)$. Similarly, write $R(\theta^M)$ for the preference ordering $f(R^M(\theta^M))$ that corresponds to the Arrow social norm for the profile $\theta^M$, and let $P(\theta^M)$ and $I(\theta^M)$ denote the corresponding strict social preference and indifference relations.

Now, say that the consequence ASWF $f$ satisfies *condition P* (Pareto) if, whenever $y^1, y^2$ is a pair of consequences in $Y$ and $\theta^M$ is a profile of individual characteristics in $\Theta^M$ with the property $y^1 P(\theta_i) y^2$ (all $i \in M$), then $y^1 P(\theta^M) y^2$. And say that the consequence ASWF $f$ satisfies *condition $P^0$* (Pareto indifference) if, whenever instead $y^1 I(\theta_i) y^2$ (all $i \in M$), then $y^1 I(\theta^M) y^2$.

**Lemma 5 (Pareto and Pareto indifference).** The consequence Arrow social welfare function that corresponds to a consequentialist Arrow social norm must satisfy conditions P and $P^0$.

The proof is rather obvious; for any pair of consequences $y^1, y^2$ of $Y$, consider a consequential decision tree $T$ with just one decision at the initial node and just two terminal nodes, which give rise to the pair of consequences $y^1, y^2$. For this tree $T$, the unanimity Lemma 1 of Section 2.4 gives the result immediately.

### 3.6     *Unrestricted domain and dictatorship*

Lemmas 2–5 have shown that a consequentialist Arrow social norm corresponds, for each fixed membership $M$, to a consequence ASWF $f$ that satisfies conditions I, P, and $P^0$. The only remaining conditions of Arrow's theorem that remain unsatisfied are the nondictatorship condition and condition U (unrestricted domain). I want to prove that any consequentialist Arrow social norm is dictatorial. So it remains only to ensure that condition U is indeed satisfied. Yet obviously it will not be satisfied unless a rich enough domain of possible individual characteristics and of individual welfare norms is allowed in each society. Indeed, as Arrow himself pointed out, should the domain of individuals' characteristics be suitably restricted – for example, if their welfare orderings are single peaked – then there will be a nondictatorial ASWF such as majority rule (provided the number of individuals happens to be odd so that the social weak preference relation is indeed transitive). Thus, apart from consequentialism, one other assumption is required, as follows.

Say that *individual welfare norms are unrestricted* in the domain of societies $S$ if, for any preference ordering $R$ on the space of consequences $Y$, there exists an individual characteristic $\theta$ and a society $\theta 1^M$ of identical individuals such that the consequential behavior rule $B_T(\theta 1^M)$ on the domain $\Im$ of consequential decision trees $T$ corresponds to the preference ordering $R$. Then the following is immediate.

**Lemma 6 (Unrestricted domain).** The consequence Arrow social welfare function that corresponds to a consequentialist Arrow social norm must have an unrestricted domain of individual preference profiles provided that individual welfare norms are unrestricted.

Finally, say that an Arrow social norm $B_T(s)$ on a domain of societies $S$ and of decision trees $\Im$ is *dictatorial* if there exists $d \in M$ such that, given any decision tree $T$ of $\Im$ and any node $n$ of $N_T$,

$$B_T(\theta^M)(n) \subset B_T(\theta_d)(n).$$

In other words, a dictatorial social norm must always prescribe behavior that is acceptable according to the individual welfare norm of the dictator, behavior that would be acceptable if all individuals were like the dictator.

Evidently, then, Arrow's theorem, in combination with Lemmas 2–6, implies Theorem 7.

**Theorem 7 (Arrow's theorem for consequentialist social norms).** Any consequentialist Arrow social norm that leaves individual welfare norms unrestricted must be dictatorial. In fact, there must exist a consequence ASWF $f$ and a dictator $d$ with the property that, for all pairs of consequences $y^1, y^2$ in $Y$,

(a) $y^1 P(\theta_d) y^2$ implies $y^1 P(\theta^M) y^2$ and
(b) $y^1 I(\theta_i) y^2$ (all $i \in M$) implies $y^1 I(\theta^N) y^2$.

Note that conclusion (b) of Theorem 7 strengthens the usual Arrow theorem, but it is true here because of Lemma 4, which is really an implication of my definition of an Arrow social norm.

## 4 Conclusion: limitations and extensions

### 4.1 *Limitations of consequentialism*

The positive results of this essay have already been summarized in Section 1.5. In this and the next two sections, I shall discuss some of their limitations.

As I have already noted in Sections 1.1 and 3.1, many moral philosophers have produced cogent criticisms of consequentialism in general and of utilitarianism in particular. Among the criticisms, two deserve special attention. The first is the argument that is well represented (as far as I can judge) in the introduction to Sen and Williams (1982), who try to persuade us of the need to go "beyond utilitarianism" to more of a "pluralist" theory of ethics [see also Williams (1973) and Sen (1982, 1984)]. The second is the argument that consequentialism is likely to be self-defeating (see, e.g., Hodgson 1967; Parfit 1984; Scheffler 1984; Slote 1984; Harsanyi 1986).

If the consequences in any utilitarian theory of ethics are too coarsely defined, then obviously one has to go beyond these coarsely defined consequences and coarse concepts of utility in order to make consequentialism ethically acceptable. The notion of a consequence needs refining until all ethically relevant distinctions are accommodated. Sen and Williams view utilitarianism as a "monist" theory of ethics in which everything is reduced to consequences and their utilities. They argue instead for a more pluralist theory. My counterargument is that all considerations of plurality should already be taken into account when consequences are being defined and refined. An advantage of this approach is that we can replace abstruse arguments regarding the validity of consequentialism and of utilitarianism with much more practical arguments concerning what should count as a consequence in a theory of ethics.

A similar counterargument may, I believe, treat the objection that consequentialism is self-defeating. Parfit (1984) considers the self-defeating argument in its most subtle and sophisticated form, including one that recognizes the need for a refined notion of consequences (pp. 26–7). In one of its simpler forms, the objection is that if one tells lies or breaks promises in order to produce good consequences, the ultimate outcome may be bad because a liar or defaulter loses his credibility and his capacity to do good. Hodgson (1967) already recognizes that in fact such arguments are no threat to a broad enough conception of consequentialism; after all, certain acts are being condemned for their bad consequences. All such examples show is that the concept of a relevant consequence may be very subtle, including people's reputations and also the reputation of certain moral rules. Rather more interesting is the possibility that in a world full of consequentialist "pure do-gooders," everybody would be so concerned with the benefits of their actions to the world in general that very few specific benefits would ever get conferred. Perhaps that is why charity begins at home, and why we should follow Sidgwick (1907) and Adams (1976) in considering even motives as part of the relevant description of consequences. Indeed, Parfit (1984, pp. 40–3) even considers the possibility that consequentialism is *self-effacing* because it ultimately requires that we believe in some other, nonconsequentialist approach to ethics; even then, however, consequentialism is effective in determining what our nonconsequentialist ethical theory should be. In fact, Parfit's arguments show just how robust is the appeal of the consequentialist approach to ethics.

## 4.2    *Economic domains*

The second limitation is the assumption in Section 3.6 of an unrestricted domain of individual norms. This is unappealing when attention is concentrated on economic environments with private goods, as has been pointed out by numerous authors. The reason is that each individual usually cares only for his own private goods (in the absence of externalities) and has monotone preferences. In the extreme example with only one private good, this suffices to determine individuals' norms uniquely. Nor is the construction of an individual's welfare norm in Section 2.3 satisfactory in economic environments because, when individuals have different private concerns, they can never be all alike in the relevant sense of having identical welfare norms. Thus, following Arrow (1950, 1963) himself, in effect, my analysis is essentially restricted to domains in which all goods are public or, to use a terminology I find preferable, in which the consequence of a public decision is the "public environment." Even when no goods are private, there are natural restrictions such as monotonicity and continuity on preferences for public goods alone (see Kalai, Muller, and Satterthwaite 1979). I hope to be able to relax the unrestricted domain assumption in later work, just as Maskin (1976); Kalai and Ritz (1980); Kalai, Muller, and Satterthwaite (1979); Border (1983); and Ritz (1983, 1985) already have done to a considerable extent. Their work suggests that for fairly rich domains with at least two private goods, Arrow's theorem will remain valid under reasonably mild conditions.[4]

### 4.3    Interpersonal comparisons

A third serious limitation has been emphasized by Sen (1977, 1982, 1985) especially. Much of the power of Arrow's theorem derives from the paucity of information about individuals that is allowed to count. Indeed, as Arrow (1950, 1963, 1983) makes perfectly clear, his original theory of social choice was formulated precisely with the purpose of excluding interpersonal comparisons of utility, since they appear to lack any relationship to behavior. Actually, as Arrow (1977), Mirrlees (1982), and others have suggested, interpersonal comparisons of utility may be interpretable as representing preferences for alternative selves. And Yaari and Bar-Hillel (1984) showed that students with a rudimentary knowledge of economics were capable of making interpersonal comparisons in a fairly reasonable manner in several simple distribution problems.

So I believe that the lack of interpersonal comparisons needs to be tackled by considering an extended consequence space of triples $(y, M, \theta^M)$ where $y \in Y^M$ is an ordinary consequence of the kind considered here, $M$ is the membership of a society, and $\theta^M$ is the profile of personal characteristics. A further extension, admitting cardinal utilities, would be to include lotteries over such triples. It can then be postulated that both individual and social norms apply to all decision trees with consequences in this extended space. The result is a form of utilitarianism due to Harsanyi (1955), at least when $M$ is fixed. However, in the absence of domain restrictions, Arrow's theorem applies to this extended domain of consequences as well, and there must be a dictator. This is an implication Arrow certainly foresaw when we discussed interpersonal comparisons in 1975. The dictatorship is considerably weaker, however, than the usual one; all individuals' norms over the space of consequences $Y$ can contribute to the social norm, in many cases, but the choice of a society $(M, \theta^M)$ and the implicit interpersonal comparisons of utility will usually have to be dictated by an "ethical" dictator (one hopes). This, at least, is my present conjecture, for which Roberts' (1980) analysis provides some support in a rather special case. [See also Pazner (1979) and Hammond (1985a).]

Even when the ethical dictator's interpersonal comparisons are admitted, however, another form of dictatorship easily arises. Consider a tree $T$ in which the society $(M, \theta^M)$ is the same in all possible consequences so that the decision problem reduces to the choice of $y$ in a fixed society, as has been considered throughout this chapter. Then it is in the spirit of this essay to have a consequentialist Arrow social norm depending only on individuals' behavior norms in the tree $T$. Thus we are back with a dictator as in Section 3.6; all the interpersonal comparisons that govern the choice of $(M, \theta^M)$ become irrelevant. In this sense, indeed, Arrow has always been right to insist that interpersonal comparisons do really violate independence of irrelevant alternatives.

So consequentialist Arrow social norms lead to a dictatorial social preference ordering, as in Arrow's general possibility theorem. Escape from dictatorship not only requires the richer information that interpersonal comparisons can provide but also the social norm within any decision tree has to depend on more than just individuals' behavior norms within the same tree, since allowing only such dependence – as in an Arrow social norm – implies independence of irrelevant alternatives in any fixed society. A weaker form of independence has to be admitted if interpersonal comparisons are to lead us away from dictatorship. Suggestions have been left for later work.[5]

NOTES

1  Attributed to St. Thomas Aquinas on p. 239 of Sayers and Reynolds' (1962) translated and annotated version of Dante's *Il Paradiso*. I am much indebted to Kenneth Arrow for this reference.
2  Actually, while Anscombe is apparently responsible for coining this particular ism, the origins of the doctrine are much older, going back to Mill in 1838 at

least and underlying the work of Moore (1903, 1912) as well as Broad (1914). See Bergström (1966). And note the quotation from St. Thomas Aquinas at the head of the chapter. For a more formal exposition of consequentialism and its implications for behavior in decision trees, see Hammond (1985b).

3 As cited in Bergström (1966, p. 63).

4 In fact, in Hammond (in press) the unrestricted domain assumption is replaced by an ethical liberalism assumption that is compatible with economic domains.

5 This contradicts what I have previously suggested in Hammond (1976b). For possible weakenings of Arrow's independence condition, see Hammond (1985a; in press).

REFERENCES

Adams, R. M. (1976), "Motive utilitarianism," *The Journal of Philosophy*, 73: 467–81.

Anscombe, G. E. M. (1958), "Modern moral philosophy," *Philosophy* 33: 1–19.

Arrow, K. J. (1950), "A difficulty in the concept of social welfare," *Journal of Political Economy*, 58: 328–46.

Arrow, K. J. (1963), *Social choice and individual values*, 2nd ed., New Haven: Yale University Press.

Arrow, K. J. (1971), *Essays in the theory of risk-bearing*, Chicago: Markham, and Amsterdam: North-Holland.

Arrow, K. J. (1977), "Extended sympathy and the possibility of social choice," *American Economic Review* (Papers and Proceedings), 67: 219–25.

Arrow, K. J. (1983), *Collected papers, Vol. 1, Social choice and justice*, Cambridge, Mass.: Harvard University Press.

Bergström, L. (1966), *The alternatives and consequences of actions: An essay on certain fundamental notions in teleological ethics*, Stockholm: Almquist and Wiksell.

Border, K. C. (1983), "Social welfare functions for economic environments with and without the Pareto principle," *Journal of Economic Theory*, 29: 205–16.

Broad, C. D. (1914), "The doctrine of consequences in ethics," *The International Journal of Ethics*, 24: 293–320.

Broome, J. (1984), "Rationality and the sure-thing principle," University of Bristol, Economics Discussion Paper No. 84/158.

Dubey, P. and M. Kaneko (1982), "Information about moves in extensive games: I and II," Yale University, Cowles Foundation Discussion Papers Nos. 625 and 629.

Elster, J. (1979), *Ulysses and the sirens: Studies in rationality and irrationality*, Cambridge: Cambridge University Press.

Fine, B. and K. Fine (1974), "Social choice and individual ranking I and II," *Review of Economic Studies*, 41: 303–22 and 459–75.

Fishburn, P. C. (1973), *The theory of social choice*, Princeton: Princeton University Press.

Gärdenfors, P. (1973), "Positionalist voting functions," *Theory and Decision*, 4: 1–24.

Hammond, P. J. (1976a), "Changing tastes and coherent dynamic choice," *Review of Economic Studies,* 43: 159–73.

Hammond, P. J. (1976b), "Equity, Arrow's conditions, and Rawls' difference principle," *Econometrica,* 44: 793–804.

Hammond, P. J. (1977), "Dynamic restrictions on metastatic choice," *Economica,* 44: 337–50.

Hammond, P. J. (1983), "Ex-post optimality as a dynamically consistent objective for collective choice under uncertainty," in P. K. Pattanaik and M. Salles (Eds.), *Social choice and welfare,* Amsterdam: North-Holland.

Hammond, P. J. (1985a), "Independence of irrelevant personal consequences," for presentation at the 5th World Congress of the Econometric Society.

Hammond, P. J. (1985b), "Consequentialist behaviour in decision trees and expected utility," Stanford University, Institute for Mathematical Studies in the Social Sciences, Economics Working Paper No. 112.

Hammond, P. J. (in press), "On reconciling Arrow's theory of social choice with Harsanyi's fundamental utilitarianism," in G. Feiwel (ed.), *Arrow and the foundations of the theory of economic policy,* New York: Macmillan.

Harsanyi, J. C. (1955), "Cardinal welfare, individualistic ethics, and interpersonal comparisons of utility," *Journal of Political Economy,* 63: 309–21.

Harsanyi, J. C. (1986), "Utilitarian morality in a world of very half-hearted altruists," this volume.

Hodgson, D. H. (1967), *Consequences of utilitarianism,* Oxford: Clarendon Press.

Kalai, E., E. Muller, and M. Satterthwaite (1979), "Social welfare functions when preferences are convex, strictly monotonic, and continuous," *Public Choice,* 34: 87–97.

Kalai, E. and Z. Ritz (1980), "Characterization of the private alternative domains admitting Arrow social welfare functions," *Journal of Economic Theory,* 22: 23–36.

Kuhn H. W. (1953), "Extensive games and the problem of information," in H. W. Kuhn and A. W. Tucker (Eds.), *Contributions to the theory of games II,* Princeton: Princeton University Press.

Maskin, E. S. (1976), "Social welfare functions on restricted domains," and "Social welfare functions for economics," mimeo.

Mirrlees, J. A. (1982), "The economic uses of utilitarianism," in A. K. Sen and B. A. O. Williams (Eds.), *Utilitarianism and beyond,* Cambridge: Cambridge University Press.

Moore, G. E. (1903), *Principia Ethica,* Cambridge: Cambridge University Press.

Moore, G. E. (1912), *Ethics,* London: Home University Library, Williams and Norgate.

Moore, G. E. (1942), "A reply to my critics," in P. A. Schlipp (Ed.), *The philosophy of G. E. Moore,* Evanston and Chicago: Northwestern University.

Parfit, D. (1984), *Reasons and persons,* Oxford: Oxford University Press.

Pazner, E. A. (1979), "Equity, nonfeasible alternatives and social choice: A reconsideration of the Concept of Social Welfare," in J.-J. Laffont (Ed.) *Aggregation and revelation of preferences,* Amsterdam: North-Holland.

Rawls, J. (1971), *A theory of justice,* Cambridge, Mass.: Harvard University Press.

Ritz, Z. (1983), "Restricted domains, Arrow social welfare functions and noncorruptible and nonmanipulable social choice corresondences: The case of private alternatives," *Mathematical Social Sciences,* 4: 155-79.

Ritz, Z. (1985), "Restricted domains, Arrow social welfare functions and noncorruptible and nonmanipulable social choice correspondences: The case of private and public alternatives," *Journal of Economic Theory,* 35: 1-18.

Roberts, K. W. S. (1980), "Possibility theorems with interpersonally comparable welfare levels," *Review of Economic Studies,* 47: 409-20.

Sayers, D. L. and B. Reynolds (translators and editors) (1962), *The divine comedy of Dante Alighieri the Florentine: Cantica III, Paradise,* Harmondsworth: Penguin Books.

Scheffler, S. (1984), *The rejection of consequentialism,* Oxford: Clarendon Press.

Sen, A. K. (1970), *Collective choice and social welfare,* San Francisco: Holden Day.

Sen, A. K. (1977), "On weights and measures: Informational constraints in social welfare analysis," *Econometrica,* 45: 1539-72.

Sen, A. K. (1982), *Choice, welfare and measurement,* Oxford: Basil Blackwell, and Cambridge, Mass.: M.I.T. Press.

Sen, A. K. (1984), "Consistency," Presidential Address to the Econometric Society.

Sen, A. K. (1985), "Information and invariance in normative choice," this volume.

Sen, A. K. and B. A. O. Williams (Eds.) (1982), *Utilitarianism and beyond,* Cambridge: Cambridge University Press.

Sidgwick, H. (1907), *The methods of ethics,* 7th. ed., London: Macmillan.

Slote, M. (1984), *Common sense morality and consequentialism,* London: Routledge and Kegan Paul.

Strotz, R. H. (1956), "Myopia and inconsistency in dynamic utility maximization," *Review of Economic Studies,* 23: 165-80.

von Neumann, J. and O. Morgenstern (1953), *Theory of games and economic behavior,* 3rd ed., Princeton: Princeton University Press.

Warnock, M. (Ed.) (1962), *Utilitarianism: Selections from the writings of Jeremy Bentham, John Stuart Mill, and John Austin,* London: Collins, the Fontana Library in Philosophy.

Williams, B. A. O. (1973), "A critique of utilitarianism," in J. J. C. Smart and B. A. O. Williams, *Utilitarianism for and against,* Cambridge: Cambridge University Press.

Yaari, M. E. and M. Bar-Hillel (1984), "On dividing justly," *Social Choice and Welfare,* 1: 1-24.

CHAPTER 2

# Information and invariance in normative choice

*Amartya Sen*

## 1    Introduction

Any principle of choice uses certain types of information and ignores others. A principle can be understood and assessed in terms of the information that it demands and the information that it "rules out" (i.e., prevents from being directly used).[1] Principles used in social choice theory, moral philosophy, rational choice under certainty and uncertainty, and studies of actual behavior can all be interpreted and analyzed in terms of the *informational constraints* that they – typically implicitly – involve (Sen 1970a, b, 1979).

The philosophical foundations of informational analysis go back at least to Kant (1788) and to his discussion of the need for universalization in categorical imperatives. The need to make similar judgments in similar circumstances is a requirement that has been used in many different forms, and the domain and scope of such a requirement depend on the way "similarity" of circumstances is interpreted and the way "similarity" of judgments is required. But the "bite" of such requirements of universalization lies in the constraint that excludes discriminations based on information *not* included in the relevant notion of similarity of circumstances.

Informational constraints are typically used implicitly. Although it is often helpful to analyze and assess principles of choice in terms of the informational constraints they involve, these constraints are usually entailed rather than explicitly stated in the formulation of these principles. An interesting and important example of an informational constraint that is *explicitly* stated is Arrow's (1951) condition of "the independence of irrelevant alternatives," ruling out any direct use of information regarding

For helpful comments on an earlier version, I am most grateful to Peter Hammond and Mark Johnson.

the placing of "irrelevant" alternatives (in individual preferences) in making social choice over a given set of ("relevant") alternatives.[2] Informational constraints are very often used without being stated in the unambiguous and formal way in which Arrow states his "independence" condition. But there is a good case for seeking explicit formulations in making the contents of the principles in question more transparent and thus easier to assess.

The object of this chapter is to analyze the procedure of using informational constraints in the form of invariance conditions (Section 2) and also to use that approach to comment on a few difficult issues in normative choice theory, dealing with social choice theory (Sections 3 and 4), rational choice behavior (Section 5), and moral philosophy (Section 6).

## 2     Informational constraints and invariance

The basic form of informational constraint is that of an invariance requirement: If two objects $x$ and $y$ belong to the same *isoinformation set* $\theta$ (that is, if they are taken to be similar in terms of relevant information), then they must be treated in the same way $(x \, J \, y)$ in the exercise of choice or judgment.

*Invariance requirement:* For all $x, y$:

$$x, y \in \theta \Rightarrow x \, J \, y. \tag{1}$$

An invariance requirement is stated in a particular "context," involving the characterization of *objects* (that is, of $x$, $y$, etc.) and the specification of the content of being *treated in the same way* $(J)$. Given the context, an invariance requirement partitions the set of objects into a class of isoinformation sets, with the interpretation that if two objects $x$ and $y$ belong to the same isoinformation set $\theta$, then they are, for the purpose in question, treated as the same.

To illustrate, consider two rather different types of invariance requirements: (1) the Pareto indifference rule $(P^0)$ in the choice over social states and (2) Arrow's condition of independence of irrelevant alternatives.

Taking the Pareto indifference rule first, in this context, the "objects" $x, y, \ldots$, represent social states, and $x \, J \, y$ stands for some notion of being "indifferent" between $x$ and $y$ in social choice. One interpretation of the latter is that $x$ and $y$ are judged to be equally good and that the social choice is based on optimization according to the relation of being at least as good. But this requires a "binary choice" format that may be rather limiting in more general contexts (though not unduly dubious in the present one), and it may be best to define $x \, J \, y$ in more direct choice-functional terms. In this format, $x \, J \, y$ may be seen as standing for the relation that

Arrow and Hurwicz (1977) call "being optimally equivalent,"[3] that is, in any set containing both $x$ and $y$, either *both* are chosen or *neither* but not just one of them without the other. Let $x \hat{P}_c y$ stand for $x$ being *revealed preferred* to $y$ in the sense of Arrow (1959),[4] that is, there exists a set $S$ from which $x$ is chosen and $y$ is not, despite $y$ belonging to $S$. Negation is denoted $\sim$. The utility vector of individual utilities in state $z$ is denoted $\mathbf{U}(z)$.

**Definitions.** *Optimal equivalence:*

$$x J y \Leftrightarrow [\sim (x \hat{P}_c y) \text{ and } \sim (y \hat{P}_c x)]. \tag{2}$$

*Paretian invariance:* For all $x, y$,

$$\mathbf{U}(x) = \mathbf{U}(y) \Rightarrow x J y, \tag{3}$$

where $J$ is the optimal equivalence relation. It may be mentioned that this way of defining Paretian invariance is different from (and, in an important way, more demanding than) taking $x J y$ to be an assertion that both $x$ and $y$ be chosen in the choice exactly over the pair $\{x, y\}$. This particular requirement is one of the implications of the requirement imposed by Paretian invariance as defined here, if the domain of the choice function includes the pair $\{x, y\}$, so that something has to be chosen from that pair.

As the second illustration, consider Arrow's original version of the independence of irrelevant alternatives. In this case, the objects $x$ and $y$ stand, respectively, for two $n$-tuples of individual preference orderings $\{R_i\}$ and $\{R_i^*\}$. The two are seen as belonging to the same isoinformation set in the context of the choice from a given subset $S$ if and only if every individual's rankings of the states in $S$ are the same in the two cases. The restriction of $R_i$ on a subset $S$ is denoted $R_i \mid^S$, and the congruence of two preference orderings $R_i$ and $R_i^*$ over a subset $S$ is shown as $R_i \mid^S = R_i^* \mid^S$. In this context, the interpretation of $x J y$ is that of the same choice being made from the given subset $S$ for preference $n$-tuples $x$ and $y$, respectively. The choice set of $S$ for any $n$-tuple of individual preferences $z$ is denoted $C(S, z)$.

**Definitions.** *Subset choice equivalence over S:*

$$x J y \Leftrightarrow C(S, x) = C(S, y). \tag{4}$$

*Arrow independence condition:* For all $x = \{R_i\}$ and $y = \{R_i^*\}$,

$$(\forall i : R_i \mid^S = R_i^* \mid^S) \Rightarrow x J y, \tag{5}$$

where $J$ is the relation of subset equivalence over $S$.

## 3    On Arrow's impossibility theorem

Arrow's (1951, 1963) general possibility theorem, which has provided so much insight into matters of social choice over many decades, uses an axiom system that combines informational constraints with other types of requirements. The independence of irrelevant alternatives (I) is, as was discussed in the last section, primarily an informational constraint. The weak Pareto principle (P), which requires that unanimous strict individual preferences over a pair must be reflected in a strict social preference[5] over that pair (a condition not to be confused with the Pareto indifference rule $P^0$), involves a "directional" feature as well (the more the better).

Unrestricted domain (U) is also *partly* an informational constraint, restricting attention to preference profiles only. Let a social scenario $z$ be the set of all things on which the social ordering of the set $X$ of social states might possibly depend: $R = R(z)$ (see Bergson 1938; Samuelson 1947). Condition U entails that two social scenarios $x$ and $y$ (no matter how richly characterized) must yield exactly the same social ordering $R$ if they happen, *inter alia,* to incorporate the same $n$-tuple of individual preference orderings (no matter how different the social scenarios may be in other respects[6]): $\{R_i^x\} = \{R_i^y\} \Rightarrow R(x) = R(y)$. But, in addition, it also requires that all possible preference $n$-tuples $\{R_i\}$ would be covered in this way (i.e., the class of social scenarios that can be considered is sufficiently rich for all preference $n$-tuples to have been covered). This is, of course, more than a purely informational constraint [in the sense of (1)]. Finally, nondictatorship (D) is not an informational constraint at all in any interesting sense. It simply rules out the existence of a person such that whenever that person strictly prefers any $x$ to any $y$, so does the society, but it does have the effect of negating the use of preference information of *one person only* (except when he or she is indifferent).

The axiom system is, thus, a mixed one. Leaving out the nondictatorship condition, the rest of the axioms, which have informational content, namely, U, I, and P, can be seen as yielding two important informational constraints *as consequences*. These "intermediate" results relate closely to Arrow's own proof but leave out the noninvariant, directional features in the intermediate results (e.g., by dropping the notion of "*almost* decisiveness"[7]) and stick only to equivalence.

**Definitions.** *Decisiveness:* A set of individuals $G$ is decisive over a pair $\{x, y\}$, denoted $D_G(x, y)$ if and only if (for all $i$ in $G$, $x P_i y$), denoted

$x P_G y$, entails $x P y$.[8] A set of individuals decisive over *all* pairs is "decisive," and $\mathfrak{D}$ is the class (possibly empty) of decisive sets of individuals.

The first lemma establishes an invariance requirement over pairs of social states, with $\{x, y\} J^1 \{a, b\}$ standing for the demand that any group can be decisive over $\{x, y\}$ if and only if it is decisive over $\{a, b\}$. Note that $J^1$ must be, by definition, reflexive, symmetric, and transitive. Let $X$ be the set of all social states figuring in the social scenarios, with $\#X \geq 3$.

**Invariant decisiveness (ID).** For any $X$,

$$\text{if } \{x, y\}, \{a, b\} \in X^2, \quad \text{then } \{x, y\} J^1 \{a, b\}. \tag{6}$$

*Proof of ID:* Suppose $D_G(x, y)$. Take $x P_G y$ and $y P_G b$, with all persons *not* in $G$, preferring $y$ to $b$ (and ranking the rest in any way they like). So $x P y$, by the decisiveness of $G$, and $y P b$, by the weak Pareto principle. Hence $x P b$ by transitivity.[9] This implies, by virtue of the independence condition, that $D_G(x, b)$. Similarly, the converse is true, and thus $\{x, y\} J^1 \{x, b\}$. By a similar argument, $\{x, y\} J^1 \{a, y\}$. These two cases combined together entail all others. If $x, y, a, b$ are all distinct, then $\{x, y\} J^1 \{a, y\}$, and $\{a, y\} J^1 \{a, b\}$, and hence $\{x, y\} J^1 \{a, b\}$. We get $\{x, y\} J^1 \{a, x\}$ from $\{x, y\} J^1 \{a, y\}$ and $\{a, y\} J^1 \{a, x\}$. And $\{x, y\} J^1 \{y, b\}$ from $\{x, y\} J^1 \{x, b\}$ and $\{x, b\} J^1 \{y, b\}$. Finally, for $\{a, b\} = \{y, x\}$, we have $\{x, y\} J^1 \{x, z\}$, $\{x, z\} J^1 \{y, z\}$ and $\{y, z\} J^1 \{y, x\}$. Thus, $\{x, y\} J^1 \{a, b\}$. Hence ID.[10]    ∎

Invariant decisiveness is an invariance condition that rules out the use of any information regarding particular *features* of social states in the context of decisiveness of a set of individuals.[11] The next invariance requirement has as its objects different sets of individuals. With $S$ and $T$ two sets of individuals, $S J^2 T$ stands for $S$ being decisive if and only if $T$ is, that is, $S \in \mathfrak{D} \Leftrightarrow T \in \mathfrak{D}$. Two such sets $S$ and $T$ are put in the same isoinformation set if and only if one is a subset of the other and the complement of the former in the latter is not itself decisive.

**Definitions.** *Excludability of the undecisive:*

$$S, T \in \theta \Leftrightarrow [S \subseteq T \text{ and } T - S \notin \mathfrak{D}]. \tag{7}$$

**Equivalent subsets (ES).** For all $S, T$,

$$S, T \in \theta \text{ in the sense of excludability of the undecisive} \Rightarrow S J^2 T.^{12} \tag{8}$$

*Proof of ES:* Consider $T \in \mathfrak{D}$, with $S \subset T$, and $T - S \notin \mathfrak{D}$. Obviously,

$$S \in \mathfrak{D} \Rightarrow T \in \mathfrak{D},$$

and it is the converse that needs to be demonstrated. Let everyone in $S$ strictly prefer $x$ to $y$ and $x$ to $z$, whereas everyone in $T - S$ strictly prefer $x$ to $y$ and $z$ to $y$. The *remaining* preferences of $S$ and $T$ are unspecified (that is, they can be anything), and *nothing at all* is required of the preferences of those not in $T$. Since $T \in \mathfrak{D}$, clearly $x P y$. If $z P y$, then $D_{T-S}(z, y)$, and by ID we would have $T - S \in \mathfrak{D}$, which is false. Hence $y R z$, and given $x P y$, we have $x P z$.[13] But then $D_S(x, z)$, and by ID, $S \in \mathfrak{D}$. So $S J^2 T$. Hence ES.     ■

Given these two invariance requirements established on the basis of Arrow's conditions U, I, and P, namely, (1) ignoring information regarding features of states (ID) and (2) ignoring information regarding the presence or absence of individuals who themselves do not form a decisive subset (ES), the rest of Arrow's theorem follows immediately.

*Proof of Arrow's theorem:* By the weak Pareto principle, the set of all individuals is decisive. Since that set is finite, by repeated partitioning, it is established through equivalent subsets (ES) that some individual must be decisive. This violates nondictatorship (D).     ■

This way of proving Arrow's theorem has the virtue of brevity, but more importantly it brings out the fact that much of the "meat" of the result consists in establishing purely informational constraints in the form of invariance requirements. Given these invariance requirements, the Pareto principle conflicts with nondictatorship.[14] Starting with the Pareto principle, by virtue of ES, we are required to ignore all information regarding the presence or absence of all but one individual in the set of individuals.

Even with infinite sets of individuals, the "equivalence" consequence continues to hold. It explains such limit results as Kirman and Sondermann's (1972) "invisible dictators." [See also Hansson (1976). On related matters, see Fishburn (1970), Blau (1972, 1979), Brown (1974), Blair and Pollak (1979), and Chichilnisky (1982).]

It is also worth remarking that the concept of *almost* decisiveness used in standard proofs (Arrow 1963; Sen 1970a) of Arrow's theorem is, in fact, redundant. Indeed, aside from complicating the proof, it distracts attention a little from the role that *purely* invariance requirements, namely ID and ES (entailed by Arrow's U, P, and I), play in taking us to Arrow's stunning and profoundly influential theorem.

## 4     Invariance conditions in social choice

Arrow's independence condition characterizes similarity in the context of choice over any given subset in terms of individual orderings being the same over that particular subset. It insists that we must ignore all other basis of discrimination. In the vast literature on social choice theory to which Arrow's contribution led, the independence condition has been often challenged. It is important in this context to distinguish between two different types of criticisms of Arrow's independence of irrelevant alternatives, and they can indeed be helpfully assessed in the format of invariance requirements, even though they have not been typically presented in that form.

One line of attack – best represented by Little (1952) and Samuelson (1967a) – rejects the need for any "interprofile" consistency condition (see also Bergson, 1966). In terms of the structure used here, this denies the need to consider isoinformation sets for different social scenarios when the scenarios involve different $n$-tuples of individual preferences $\{R_i\}$ (i.e., different *profiles*, as they are sometimes called). Interpreting the social welfare exercise in terms of what has now come to be called the single-profile Bergson–Samuelson social welfare function, they have argued for dispensing with the demand that two different $n$-tuples of individual preferences have to satisfy any invariance requirement at all (even when – as in Arrow's case – the $n$-tuples coincide over a given subset). "For Bergson," Samuelson explained, "one and only one of the. . . possible patterns of individuals' orderings is needed"; it could be "*any* one, but it is *only* one" (Samuelson 1967a, pp. 48–9). The assumption of individual tastes being given is central to Little's (1952, p. 423) presentation of the problem, and he argued that "Arrow's work has no relevance to the traditional theory of welfare economics, which culminates in the Bergson–Samuelson formulation" (p. 425). With the invariance requirement of the independence condition out of the way,[15] there is no similar impossibility,[16] and it becomes possible for Samuelson to take the view that "it is not true, as many used to believe, that Professor Kenneth Arrow of Stanford has proved 'the impossibility of a social welfare function'" (Samuelson 1967b, p. vii).

I have examined (and argued for the rejection of) this line of criticism elsewhere (Sen 1977b) and shall not repeat the arguments here. But it is hard to see why the problem of invariance is regarded as irrelevant whenever two social scenarios differ in terms of individual preference $n$-tuples over $X$ no matter how remote that difference is to the subset $S$ over which social choice is being considered. Norms of social decisions must take a view as to what information is relevant for social choice over a particular subset and what is not, and it is extraordinary to deny the need for any consistency *at all* whenever there is any change whatever in the preference of any one individual over any one pair no matter how unrelated that pair is to the subset from which choice is being made. If the Bergson–Samuelson exercise must indeed be concerned just with "only one" individual preference $n$-tuple $\{R_i\}$, then it is no great embarrassment to Arrow's approach that (in Little's words) "Arrow's work has no relevance to the traditional theory of welfare economics, which culminates in the Bergson–Samuelson formulation." The "traditional theory of welfare economics," on this interpretation,[17] does not even seriously address the basic issues of *information-based* welfare judgments and social choice.

The second line of criticism does not dispute the need for invariance conditions of the type of Arrow's independence but the particular demands that Arrow's independence condition makes. This could be because the position of apparently irrelevant alternatives may be seen as being informationally relevant in some cases (e.g., because it tells us something about intensities of preference[18]). Or, the questioning of independence may come from recognizing (as Arrow's own analysis has made clear) that combining independence with other apparently mild conditions produces quite unacceptable results [e.g., Arrow's impossibility or also such invariance results as invariant decisiveness (ID) and equivalent subsets (ES)], and it can be thus reasonably argued that something or other "has to give."[19] The criticism of Arrow's independence condition may be related to the view that the Arrow framework of social choice is informationally too restrictive, especially in ruling out the use of information regarding interpersonally comparable utilities (see Sen 1970a, b). If the framework is informationally broadened, then the independence condition would require reformulation involving differently specified isoinformation sets relevant to social choice.

The last line of reasoning leads to questioning not merely the independence condition but even the condition of unrestricted domain, since the informational constraint implicit in condition U rules out the use of interpersonally comparable utilities as well as of cardinality.[20] If the social ordering $R$ of the set of social states $X$ is required to be a function of the $n$-tuple of individual utility functions $\{U_i\}$ defined over $X$, then the independence condition has to be redefined in terms of congruence of individual utility values. Also, the specification of the social choice framework has to be completed by imposing other invariance conditions requiring that two different $n$-tuples of individual utility functions $\{U_i\}$ and

$\{U_i^*\}$ be put in the same isoinformation set when one can be derived from the other on the basis of transformations allowed by the particular measurability and interpersonal comparability framework.

A general format in which the social ordering $R$ depends on the social scenarios $x, y, \ldots$ (as discussed in Section 2) is converted into a SWFL framework by the combination of unrestricted domain $\tilde{U}$ and some notion of utility equivalence. The former requires *inter alia* that if $U_i^x = U_i^y$ for all $i$, then $R(x) = R(y)$. This permits the formulation of the SWFL: $R = F(\{U_i\})$, so that the social ordering over $X$ is a function of the $n$-tuple of individual utility functions over $x$.[21] Depending on the exact extent of measurability and comparability of individual utilities, a set $\mathfrak{I}$ of permissible $n$-tuples of transformations $\{T_i\}$ are specified for defining isoinformation regarding $n$-tuples of individual utilities (see Sen 1970a, b; Gevers 1979; Roberts 1980a, b).

**Definitions.** *Utility isoinformation:* For all $\{U_i\}$ and $\{U_i^*\}$,

$$\{U_i\}, \{U_i^*\} \in \theta \Leftrightarrow \exists \{T_i\} \in \mathfrak{I}: \forall i: U_i^* = T_i(U_i). \tag{9}$$

*Utility-based equivalence* (UE): For all $\{U_i\}$ and $\{U_i^*\}$,

$$\{U_i\}, \{U_i^*\} \in \theta \Rightarrow F(\{U_i\}) = F(\{U_i^*\}). \tag{10}$$

*SWFL independence condition* $(\tilde{I})$: For all $\{U_i\}, \{U_i^*\}$,

if for all $x$ in some $S \subseteq X: \forall i: U_i(x) = U_i^*(x)$, then
$$C(S, \{U_i\}) = C(S, \{U_i^*\}).[22] \tag{11}$$

In this framework of SWFLs, the Arrow conditions U, I, P, and D (appropriately redefined for SWFLs) are perfectly consistent if the invariance condition reflecting utility-based equivalence allow interpersonal comparability of utilities (even if only *ordinal* comparability is permitted).[23] By specifying different measurability and comparability assumptions, characterizing $\mathfrak{I}$, various possibility and impossibility results have been obtained in the literature using Arrow's conditions and other requirements, and some "distinguished" rules (such as utilitarianism, utility-based lexicographic maximum) have been firmly axiomatized (see, among other contributions, Hammond 1976a, 1977; Strasnick 1976; Arrow 1977; d'Aspremont and Gevers 1977; Sen 1977b; Deschamps and Gevers 1978, 1979; Maskin 1978, 1979; Roberts 1980a, b; Myerson 1983; Suzumura 1983; Blackorby, Donaldson and Weymark 1984).

These requirements can be fruitfully examined in terms of implied invariance restrictions and the plausibility of the corresponding informational constraints. I shall not, however, proceed further in that line in this essay. However, I would like to comment on a different way of seeing the invariance requirement that has been found to be of some use in this literature. This takes the form of dropping the requirement of completeness of the social ranking $R$ and of the corresponding social choice function. Instead of insisting on utility equivalence (UE), it is possible to demand that only the *intersection* of the set of generated social orderings be accepted.[24]

*Utility-based intersection* (UI): For any utility isoinformation set $\theta$, the appropriate social partial ordering $\bar{R}$ is given by

$$\bar{R} = \bigcap_{\{U_i\} \in \theta} F(\{U_i\}). \tag{12}$$

This is a more permissive framework, and it does not discard any noncontroversial part of the social ranking [on the grounds of the lack of *complete* congruence of the generated social rankings needed by utility-based equivalence (UE)]. On the other hand, when the utility-based equivalence condition (UE) does in fact hold, then the intersection social ranking $\bar{R}$ will indeed be the same social ordering as UE would yield. The difference lies in those cases in which UE does not hold (e.g., tryng to use the utilitarian rule with somewhat "fuzzy" information regarding interpersonal comparability of units of utility). Then the approach of utility-based equivalence will yield nothing, whereas the approach of utility-based intersection may still yield a social partial ordering, which can possibly be even quite extensive (see Sen 1970b; Blackorby 1975; Fine 1975; Basu 1979).

The choice between the "equivalence" approach and the "intersection" approach is, in fact, quite a general one and reflects two rather different views of informational constraints. The equivalence approach interprets isoinformation sets $\theta$ as definitely giving "just the same" information for the choice in question. If two objects $x$ and $y$ belong to the same isoinformation set, then any rule that does not yield the same result for both $x$ and $y$ is simply getting something "wrong." On that interpretation, the rejection of such inconsistent rules would indeed make sense.

On the other hand, the intersection approach takes a more tentative view of isoinformation sets. Two elements of $\theta$ *may well be* informationally identical. We know that informational identity cannot demand *any more* than what would be supported by every element of $\theta$. So that if any partial ranking goes through for every element of $\theta$, then that is clearly "okay." In those parts of the ranking in which different elements of $\theta$

differ, no decision is possible given what we know so far. On this approach, it may even be the case that refining $\theta$ to satisfy UE might be simply impossible if the nature of information has some inescapable ambiguity. That is, however, no reason – on this second view – to ignore what has uncontroversially emerged, confirmed by every element of $\theta$.

Thus, the "equivalence approach" and the "intersection approach" each has its own rationale. Although the contrast here has been discussed only in the context of interpersonal comparability of utility, it should be obvious that the difference between the two approaches will apply to other types of informational problems as well.[25] In this chapter, it is the equivalence approach that is being mostly used, but the intersection approach also has much scope for application.

## 5 States, utilities, and informed rationality

In this section, a few issues in the theory of rational behavior are examined in the light of invariance requirements and informational constraints. It is useful to begin by commenting on two basic concepts in the theory of rational choice, namely, states and utilities. In the discussion on social choice in the last two sections, both concepts were in fact used, but we did not pay particular attention to the relationship between states and utilities.

One important question to ask is whether the states already include the utilities of the individuals involved. The concept of "state of affairs" in moral philosophy certainly does include utility information as part of the states (see, e.g., Williams 1973; Hare 1981), and, indeed, in utilitarian moral philosophy, that turns out to be the only part of the state of affairs that ultimately counts. In contrast, in social choice theory, utility functions are defined over states of affairs $U_i(x)$ rather than being a part of it. This may look like a trivial distinction, and in many contexts it is indeed trivial. But it is quite important in some respects. There can be internal contradiction if the states "include" utilities and at the same time utilities rank the states.[26] Even if we are able to make the two parts of the story consistent by some special assumption (e.g., by associating the *same* utility function in the different states in terms of which of these states are ranked and evaluated), the condition of unrestricted domain would be hard to incorporate into such structures. It is precisely for these reasons that in the standard social choice approach it makes sense to follow the Arrow procedure of seeing social states *sans* utilities and then considering different individual orderings of these states in different scenarios. Whether a similar exclusion of utilities makes sense in the context of the theory of individual rational choice is, however, yet to be examined. This question will be taken up presently.

Another source of complexity arises from different interpretations of individual utility, for example, happiness, desire fulfillment, numerical representation of the binary relation of individual choice. It is fair to say that the standard interpretation of utility has shifted from the focus on mental states (on which Bentham, Edgeworth, Marshall, Pigou, and even Hicks largely concentrate) to the binary relation of the "choice function" (much influenced by the appeal of the theory of revealed preference). I believe the methodological foundations of this choice-based approach are deeply problematic, as I have tried to argue elsewhere (Sen 1977a), but I shall not take up that issue here. The fact remains, however, that *both* mental state utility and choice interpretation utility have meanings of their own, and though they are not by any means unrelated to each other, neither can *in general* informationally subsume the other. The question as to whether I am happier in state $x$ than in state $y$ does make sense, but it is not the same question as to which one I would choose, everything considered (see Broome 1978, Sen 1977a, 1982). The issue, therefore, is not so much which is the "correct" interpretation of utility but how the different interpretations would respectively figure in actual choice problems (no matter which one we decide to sanctify by the name of *utility*).

This range of issues is of obvious relevance to the controversies surrounding rational behavior under uncertainty and the use of such axioms as "strong independence" and "sure thing principle." Briefly, the main problem is this. If the outcomes are identified *without* specification of mental states in the respective outcomes, then it is not clear why, say, strong independence would be a requirement of rationality, since our choice may be sensibly influenced by anticipated mental states (over which we may have limited control) that would not figure in the outcome specification. If, on the other hand, outcomes do include mental states as well, then such axioms as strong independence would be almost impossible to apply in practice, since psychological variations of regret, disappointment, relief, and so on, would make states that are otherwise the same different from each other.[27]

To pursue this question further, consider the axiom of strong independence. This is another invariance requirement reflecting an informational constraint. In the format of the invariance requirement, the objects here can be seen as ordered pairs of lotteries such as $x = (L_1, L_2)$, and $y = (L_1^*, L_2^*)$. The two pairs will belong to the same isoinformation set if one pair, say $x$, can be obtained from the other, $y$, by "mixing" a third lottery with both elements of $y$ (with the same probabilities) in two respective compound lotteries. That is, $x, y \in \theta$, in this context, if and only if there exists a lottery $L^{**}$ and a number $p: 0 \le p \le 1$ such that $L_i^* = (p, L_i; 1-p, L^{**})$ for $i = 1, 2$. We shall then call $x$ and $y$ *additively iso-informative*. The content of being treated the same $(x \, J \, y)$ may be that of optimal equivalence defined earlier (Section 2). Or, less demandingly, $x \, J \, y$ may stand for $L_1$ being chosen (respectively, rejected) from the *pair* $(L_1, L_2)$ if and only if $L_1^*$ is chosen (respectively rejected) from the pair $(L_1^*, L_2^*)$. This may be called *pair choice equivalence*.

*Strong independence:* For all ordered pairs of lotteries $x$ and $y$

$x, y \in \theta$ in the sense of being additively isoinformative $\Rightarrow x \, J \, y$ in the sense of pair choice equivalence.

Consider first the case in which the mental reactions are not part of the outcomes. Considering what I would choose after reaching home for work, I choose $L_1$ over $L_2$, with $L_1$ involving the certainty of doing some rather "worthy" work (like refereeing a paper) over a bit of self-indulgence (like watching a movie). Consider now the alternative choice in which I take some big risk when coming home. I may "go under," for example, be injured and hospitalized, with probability $1-p$. If I do get home uninjured, I have the choice of the worthy work $(L_1)$ and the self-indulgent one $(L_2)$. This latter choice describes the mixed lottery $L_1^* = (p, L_1; 1-p, \text{hospitalized})$ and $L_2^* = (p, L_2; 1-p, \text{hospitalized})$. If I were now to choose $L_2^*$ over $L_1^*$, I might argue that this is sensible enough since if I come home, this would be coexistent with my having escaped the "dire consequence" of injury and hospitalization, and the feeling of great relief should be consummated in some self-indulgence rather than in doing the worthy activity. If this *is* a violation of strong independence, then so be it.

On the other hand, it could be argued that there is no violation of strong independence here. It is true that in both cases my choice between $L_1$ and $L_2$ starts when I am back home and there is no difference in the outcome space – except in terms of mental states – between my having reached home undangerously or having got home knowingly escaping a danger (a "counterfactual" that did *not* occur and is thus not part of the outcome). But my mental state, which can take note of counterfactuals, *is* different, and if the outcomes were to be seen *inclusive* of mental states, then $L_1^*$ and $L_2^*$ are not so simply related to $L_1$ and $L_2$, respectively.[28] Seeing a movie while enjoying a great relief from escaping a danger is not the same as seeing a movie in other circumstances; nor is refereeing a paper the same thing in the two cases. Strong independence would not have been violated in this way of seeing outcomes. But this is precisely because strong independence would not have demanded anything at all in this case. And there, of course, is the rub. The fuller the characterization of outcomes, and in particular the more it includes mental state information, the less the scope for any application of conditions like strong independence. But if we leave out mental states from the outcomes, strong independence (and a number of other invariance requirements of that type) could well be quite unreasonable.

Problems of this kind arise also in other ways of enriching the outcome specification, for example, including *processes,* considering *responsibility,* and admitting *regret* (as an activity and not just as an expression of opportunity forgone). There is quite an extensive literature dealing with various "counterexamples" to conditions like strong independence (see, e.g., Allais 1953; Savage 1954; Davidson, Suppes, and Siegel 1957); Diamond 1967; MacCrimmon 1968; Drèze 1974; Luce and Raiffa 1957; Tversky 1975; Allais and Hagen 1979; Machina 1981; Arrow 1982; Bell 1982; Kahneman, Slovik, and Tversky 1982; Loomes and Sugden 1982; McClennen 1983; Stigum and Wenstøp 1983; Broome 1984; Sen 1984b). They may not, in fact, be counterexamples if the outcomes are appropriately characterized, but then that is a matter of little consolation, since strong independence will win by demanding *nothing* in these cases, and the scope of application of that condition will be severely limited.

There is a genuine dilemma here and one on which I do not wish to pronounce a simple judgment. But in general the case for distinguishing between relevantly different outcomes (including processes, responsibilities, regrets, reliefs, etc.) seems clear enough. If they are *not* relevant for rational assessment, it would be good to see arguments as to why that is the case. [Such arguments may, of course, exist in many cases; see, e.g., Davidson (1980).] If, on the other hand, they *are* relevant, then they cannot be taken out of the story by artificially constructed isoinformation sets to give scope and reach to conditions like strong independence.

## 6    Universalizability and objectivity

I turn, finally, to a different type of use of invariance requirements, namely, universalization in moral philosophy. The importance of universalizability in informative judgments has been well recognized at least since Kant's (1788) *Critique of practical reason,* in which Kant argued that there was ultimately "but one categorical imperative, namely, this: Act only on that maxim whereby thou canst at the same time will that it should become a universal law" (p. 38). Although this is perhaps the most discussed form in which the requirement of universalizability has been considered, other types of universalizing requirements have also been extensively investigated in moral philosophy (see Mackie 1977; Hare 1981; Parfit 1984).

There is, however, one quite general difficulty in giving content to any particular demand of universalizability. In taking two situations as "similar" and demanding that they call for similar treatment, it is necessary to have a clear view of what being similar involves. No two situations (or states, or acts, etc.) are in fact exactly the same. Indeed, we cannot see them as two situations (states, acts, etc.) if they were in fact the same. Thus, for the principles of universalizability to have a nontrivial domain, the identification of two objects must involve both (1) *noticing* differences between the objects and (2) *ignoring* the differences in taking them to be similar. An element of discrimination in overlooking noticeable difference is clearly involved in the notion of similarity.

When Henry Sidgwick claimed (applying the principle of universalizability) that "if a kind of conduct that is right (or wrong) for me is not right (or wrong) for some one else, it must be on the ground of some difference between the two cases, other than the fact that I and he are different persons" (1907, p. 379), he was using a powerful informational constraint to rule out the use of information regarding *personal identity* in making these judgments.[29] In some context, the differences in personal identity may be important, perhaps even altogether crucial (e.g., in pursuing self-interest or in maximizing individual profits). Sidgwick's claim about universalizability can be seen as asserting that in the context of moral judgments of rightness or wrongness of conduct, the differences of personal identity must be ignored. The specification of isoinformation sets calls for taking a certain view of the appropriate notion of similarity in the context of the exercise under consideration.

It is possible to think of the specification of isoinformation sets in two different ways in the context of universalizability of moral judgments. One is to see it as reflecting some very elementary moral judgments that all "reasonable" moral systems can be expected to satisfy. The other is to see it as a *necessary* condition that *all* moral judgments must satisfy, necessitated by the discipline of moral language, without having to invoke any particular moral approach at all. It is fair to say that given the traditions in welfare economics, it is the former approach (i.e., seeing the specification of isoinformation sets as involving substantive moral claims) that would tend to appeal to most economists. On the other hand, powerful arguments have been presented for the second view, most notably by Hare (1952, 1963) in his analysis of "the language of morals." In that analysis, a class of invariance constraints are seen as being necessary because of the very nature of normative judgments and the discipline imposed by prescriptive language (including the language of morals). Hare stated, "I cannot say 'This is a good motor-car, but the one next to it, though exactly like it in all other respects is not good'" (1952, p. 135). Also, "if I call a thing a good $X$, I am committed to calling any $X$ like it good" (Hare 1963, p. 15). In a somewhat different context, Arrow (1963) too makes a statement that can be seen as being on the same general line: "Value judgements may equate empirically distinguishable phenomena, but they cannot differentiate empirically indistinguishable states" (p. 112).[30]

At one level, this issue can be seen as simply an aspect of the theory of identity, to wit: $x = y \Rightarrow f(x) = f(y)$. If $x$ and $y$ are indeed identical, then any function – even a normative one (such as a moral function) – must assert $f(x) = f(y)$, no matter what the substantive nature of the evaluation is. That is, $f(x) = f(y)$ follows simply from $f(\cdot)$ being a *function* and does not depend on what kind of a function $f(\cdot)$ happens to be. This line of interpretation has, incidentally, the implication that some moral judgments must of necessity follow from empirical judgments and thus violate the so-called "Hume's law" on the impossibility of deriving moral propositions from purely factual ones (see Sen 1966).[31] If $x$ and $y$ are *empirically* indistinguishable, then they must be *morally* equivalent.

But this way of seeing the issue is problematic in the sense that the "identity" of $x$ and $y$ already involves some selection of information and thus formally involves putting $x$ and $y$ in the same isoinformation set rather than seeing them to be really indistinguishable in every possible way. In Hare's own statement the car "next to" the already acknowledged "good" one is distinguishable in terms of its *position,* and Hare describes the two as being exactly like each other "in all *other* respects" (italics added).

There is quite a deep metaethical issue here. It is hard to argue that the concept of empirical identity is completely empty. The nature of particular classes of isoinformation sets can be such that the differences between distinct elements in the same set can be seen – even in a *premoral* context – as just trivial. The claims of universalizability based on empirical *identity* demand serious consideration and cannot be disposed of by a simple assertion of the *impossibility* of empirical identity.

The broader issue of *objectivity* is *primarily* one of the nature of beliefs (see Nagel 1980; McDowell 1981). Moral beliefs may fail to be objective in some straightforward way. Trying to distinguish between cases on the basis of arbitrary criteria, involving trivial factual variations that would not command attention in premoral assessment, is one example of the failure of objectivity of a moral outlook. (For example, "I believe *A* and *B* are indeed much the same *empirically,* but *morally A* is right whereas *B* is wrong!".) The central issue here is the "supervenient" nature of moral assessment (see Sen 1966, 1985; Nagel 1980; Hare 1981; Hurley 1985).

More specifically, one can be seen as being particularly "nonobjective" in a moral judgment if, say, one censures someone else – in a morally righteous way – for a conduct for which one would not censure oneself. These and other cases of "nonobjectivity" involve the violation of some *invariance restrictions,* which are seen to be necessary for being "objective" in moral outlook rather than being patently "subjective." If (1) moral objectivity is seen as primarily a matter of the nature of moral beliefs and (2) the possibility of greater or less objectivity is accepted (rather than treating it as a yes-or-no question), then the old issue of objectivity of morals can be seen in a different light altogether – involving different issues from those involved in the traditional rejection of *naturalism* and the old assertion of Hume's law. The central question, in this way of seeing the problem of moral objectivity, is the special status of some invariance restrictions in *moral beliefs,* related to empirical features reflected by specifications of certain classes of isoinformation sets.[32]

## 7      Concluding remarks

I have examined normative choice in terms of the informational constraints that normative principles entail. Invariance restrictions related to isoinformation sets provide a general format that can be used in different ways depending on the nature of the exercise and the types of principles to be invoked (Sections 1 and 2). Examples of use presented here come from different areas of normative choice theory.

This includes social choice theory, a discipline pioneered by Kenneth Arrow (1950, 1951). Arrow has made explicit use of some invariance restrictions related to informational constraints (e.g., in his independence condition). In fact, it can be seen that Arrow's impossibility theorem is really a corollary of two derived invariance restrictions that can be established through the use of his axiom system (Section 3). This avenue also provides, arguably, a somewhat neater way of proving Arrow's impossibility theorem, but that is rather secondary to the main purpose here of bringing out the derivation and use of informational invariance requirements entailed by the axiom system of Arrow.

The impossibility result can be removed by enriching informational use in social choice (Sen 1970a). But the modified and more permissive conditions can also be fruitfully compared and examined in terms of the corresponding invariance features and informational exclusions (Section 4).

Also, the use of invariance requirements and the underlying informational constraints provides a helpful focus for understanding and assessing some of the controversial questions in the pure theory of rational choice under uncertainty. The specification of isoinformation sets in the context of rational choice theory involves fundamental questions about the nature of utility and the contents of states, and these in turn relate to different stands taken on such axioms as strong independence (Section 5). It was also argued that utility in the sense of choice cannot be taken to be a substitute of utility in the classical sense of mental states. The relation between mind and choice is too complex to permit sensible axiomatization of rational choice in the space of "mindless states" (Section 5).

I have tried in earlier occasions to analyze specific moral principles by explicitly invoking informational constraints and invariance (Sen 1970a, 1979). This aspect of substantive moral philosophy has not been further pursued here, and instead the section on moral assessment has been devoted to some methodological questions regarding universalizability and objectivity. The principle of universalizability, much used since Kant (1788), demands rather special classes of isoinformation sets. That issue, which relates to the supervenient nature of moral assessment, turns out to be closely related to the foundational question of the objectivity of moral beliefs (Section 6).

Our willingness to use the format of invariance restrictions in one context does not, of course, force us to use it in others. But there is enough in common in the formal procedures of invariance and informational constraints to justify seeing them as different applications of one general methodological technique. However, the more important insights come from the specifics of particular applications.

NOTES

1   Note, however, that a principle can never be *fully* characterized by informational requirements and exclusions. There is also the question of *direction* of influence, which would depend on the form of some "monotonicity" condition. This is readily seen by reversing the direction of influence (e.g., replacing the utilitarian rule of choice by the rule of *minimizing* the utility sum – a rule that has exactly the same informational base as the utilitarian principle). How-

ever the direction is often obvious enough not to be a matter of serious dis-
putation once the informational base is accepted.

2  There are many different versions of the independence condition, on which
see, among others, Arrow (1963), Blau (1971), Fishburn (1973), Hansson
(1973), Ray (1973), Plott (1976), Kelly (1978), Pattanaik (1978), and Suzumura (1983).

3  Arrow and Hurwicz (1977) define the relation of being "optimally equivalent"
with respect to a *given* set of alternatives (p. 464). The definition that is used
here is a natural extension of that characterization applied to *all* sets containing both $x$ and $y$.

4  Not the same as revealed preference in the sense of Samuelson (1938), which is
perhaps more frequently used in the literature. On the distinction, see Arrow
(1959) and Sen (1971). See also Herzberger (1973) and Suzumura (1983).

5  Formally, for any $x, y$, if for all $i$, $x P_i y$, then $x P y$. This condition is stated
here in terms of social preference rather than choice, but such conditions can
be readily translated to choice requirements in the context of Arrow's (1951)
basic framework; on this see Sen (1982). See also Blair, Bordes, Kelly, and
Suzumura (1976).

6  The scenarios may also include information regarding interpersonal rankings
of welfare, intensities of preferences, histories behind the present circumstances, and so on. Unrestricted domain imposed on the Arrovian social welfare function $R = f(\{R_i\})$ rules out the use of any such additional information by making the functional relation $f(\cdot)$ apply to every possible $\{R_i\}$.

7  Arrow does not use the term *almost decisive,* but his distinction between
$x D y$ and full decisiveness $x \bar{D} y$ deals with what has later come to be called
almost decisiveness, to wit: "$x D y$ means that $x$ is socially preferred to $y$ if
individual $I$ prefers $x$ to $y$ and all other individuals have the opposite preference" (Arrow 1963, p. 98). The proof used here dispenses with that notion
and sticks to the pure equivalence of full decisiveness over different pairs.

8  Once again (see note 5), the social preference framework can be easily translated into a corresponding social choice framework.

9  The requirement of transitivity of social preference $P$ (and the corresponding exogeneously imposed *internal* consistency conditions of social choice)
can be dispensed with by tightening the external correspondence conditions
imposed by the Pareto principle and the independence condition (see Sen
1984b).

10  Note that the result established here is a *purely invariance* requirement, viz.,
the equivalence of decisiveness, rather than the more demanding lemma established by Arrow that a set of individuals *almost* decisive over any pair is
fully decisive over all pairs (Arrow 1963, pp. 98–100; see also Blau 1957).

11  The only things that matter are the placing of social states in individual preference orderings. Since the "social states" as characterized by Arrow do not include utilities or the placing of these states in individual orderings (unlike in
the usual philosophical literature on "states of affairs"), no "feature," as such,
of social states are informationally admitted for influencing social choice, by
virtue of the combination of conditions U, P, and I.

12  This is, of course, the special ultrafilter property of the class of decisive sets
(see Hansson 1976).

13   The use of transitivity here can be replaced by tightening the other conditions (see Sen 1984b).

14   This equivalence result ES, with its elementary proof, helps to give an insight into the apparently perplexing claim in the title of Chichilnisky's (1982b) interesting and important paper: "Topological equivalence of the Pareto condition and the existence of a dictator."

15   Samuelson inadvertently muddies the water a bit by insisting that he is not disputing the independence condition: "If the ordering is transitive, it *automatically* satisfies the condition called 'independence or irrelevant alternatives'" (Samuelson 1967a, p. 43). Unfortunately, internal consistency in the form of transitivity of social ordering for any profile does not guarantee any *interprofile* consistency of the kind of independence. Samuelson's assertion may have been based on a confusion between Arrow's independence condition and the independence condition of Nash (1950). On this and related matters, see Sen (1970a, 1977b) and Ray (1973).

16   Impossibility theorems with some similarity with Arrow's have been, in fact, derived for single-profile social choice by Parks (1976), Kemp and Ng (1976), Hammond (1976b), Pollak (1979), and others. But unlike the case of Arrow's independence condition, the axioms used in these exercises involve direct use of some neutrality condition [similar to invariant decisiveness (ID) but applied *within* a given profile of individual preferences]. (See Sen 1985b, Section 9.) On the general question of the relationship between single-profile and multiple-profile results, see Roberts (1980c) and Rubinstein (1981).

17   Note that the tradition referred to by Little is not the old one in welfare economics based on some form or other of utilitarianism (e.g., Edgeworth 1881; Marshall 1890; Pigou 1920). That tradition demands a great deal in terms of interprofile consistency, and indeed the independence condition in particular is fully satisfied by the utilitarian social welfare function when independence is appropriately defined for a social choice framework admitting interpersonally comparable cardinal utility. See Harsanyi (1955), Sen (1970a, 1977b), d'Aspremont and Gevers (1977), Deschamps and Gevers (1978), Maskin (1978), Roberts (1980b), and Mirrlees (1982).

18   This view is closely related to Borda's (1781) motivation in proposing what is now called the Borda rule, which makes use of information regarding *intermediately placed* alternatives to form a judgment about preference strength. A different reason for attaching importance to the position of some "irrelevant" alternative is Nash's (1950) argument for the relevance of status quo in the ranking of non-status-quo states. See also Buchanan and Tullock (1962).

19   See Wilson (1972), Fishburn (1974), Binmore (1975), and Hansson (1976), on a basic tension between "collective rationality" and Arrow's "independence" requirement.

20   As it happens, the introduction of cardinality of individual utilities in the Arrow framework does not remove Arrow's impossibility result, which is extendable to the case of noncomparable cardinal utilities (see Sen 1970a, Theorem 8*2). But interpersonal comparisons do relieve the impossibility.

21   Note that this does not by itself imply neutrality (or "welfarism"), since there is no necessity that different social states must be treated in the same way in

terms of choice whenever they yield the same utility information. It is only when unrestricted domain is combined with some other conditions imposed on the SWFL (e.g., independence and the Pareto principle) that the neutrality result follows; on this, see d'Aspremont and Gevers (1977). Note also that unrestricted domain also requires that the class of social scenarios for which $R(\cdot)$ is defined is sufficiently rich to include all possible $n$-tuples of individual utility functions over $X$, thereby making the domain of the SWFL unrestricted.

22 $C(S, \{U_i\})$ is the choice set of $S$, given the utility $n$-tuple $\{U_i\}$.

23 See Sen (1970a). Deschamps and Gevers (1979) and Roberts (1980a) have established the important result that with ordinal comparability of utilities, and the Arrow nondictatorship condition strengthened to "anonymity," the remaining Arrow conditions would tend to confine the permitted social welfare functionals to the class of "rank dictatorial" rules, i.e., giving the $k$th worst-off position a dictatorial influence (with the Rawlsian case of maximin or leximin standing for the dictatorship of the worst-off position).

24 For the underlying motivation, see Sen (1970a: Chapter 7, 1970b). On a related issue, see Levi (1974).

25 I have discussed the relationship between partial ignorance and incomplete orderings in the context of moral judgments as well as economic policymaking in Sen (1970a, 1979, 1985a and c). See also Basu (1979).

26 There are also serious conceptual issues involved in including interpersonal comparisons of utilities in the states of affairs; see Arrow (1963, 1977), Suppes (1966), Sen (1970a, 1982), Hammond (1977), Gevers (1979), Roberts (1980a), and Borglin (1982).

27 If the mental states could be obtained from other information, then this lacuna would not exist. In particular, mental states might be given by a function of other features of the state, and if two states are "otherwise the same," then they would yield the same mental states as well. But mental states may, in fact, depend also on other things, e.g., the *process* that led to the state.

28 Similarly, if *processes* leading to particular states are brought into the specification of the states, then again the simple relation is broken.

29 Rawls's (1971) "veil of ignorance" similarly provides an informational constraint for his theory of justice as fairness. Many ethical disagreements, in fact, turn on different conceptions of what information is relevant and correspondingly on the invariance restrictions that should be used. This is discussed in Sen (1974, 1979, 1985a).

30 Here Arrow is, in fact, discussing – indeed disputing – Abram Bergson's (1954) claim that "if one can advance the Utilitarian criterion with empirical comparability then it should also be possible to do so without it" (p. 251). So that indistinguishability in this case has a somewhat different meaning from that in Hare. However, Arrow's remark seems to make equally good sense even with indistinguishability interpreted in terms of being identical rather than noncomparable.

31 The point of my paper (1966) was not so much to argue that Hume's law was false but that "Hare's adherence to 'Hume's Law' conflicts with his adherence to 'universal prescriptivism'" (Sen 1966, p. 75). More formally, it was argued

(conceding the possibility of denying that "two separate objects can be exactly alike") that "either Hare's principle of universalizability is empty of content, or it conflicts with Hume's Law" (pp. 78–9). In his analysis of this point, Hare says generously: "I have later allowed, in response to examples produced by Professor Sen and others, that other qualifications are needed, in particular that which is demanded by the thesis of universalizability itself, the admission of the inference from '*A* did exactly as *B* did' to 'If *B* did wrong, then *A* did wrong'" (Hare 1981, pp. 223–4; see also Hare 1977). I have examined the scope and significance of this qualification elsewhere (Sen 1985a).

32  I have discussed these issues elsewhere (Sen 1985a) and will not further pursue them here. A crucial issue concerns the question of arbitrariness of some factual distinctions.

## REFERENCES

Allais, M. (1953), "Le comportement de l'homme rational devant le risque: Critique des postulates et axiomes de l'ecole Américaine," *Econometrica,* 21: 503–46.

Allais, M. and O. Hagen (Eds.) (1979), *Expected utility hypotheses and the Allais paradox: Contemporary discussions under uncertainty with Allais' rejoinder,* Dordrecht: Reidel.

Arrow, K. J. (1950), "A difficulty in the concept of social welfare," *Journal of Political Economy,* 58: 328–46.

Arrow, K. J. (1951), *Social choice and individual values,* New York: Wiley.

Arrow, K. J. (1959), "Rational choice functions and ordering," *Economica,* 26: 121–7.

Arrow, K. J. (1963), *Social choice and individual values,* 2nd ed., New York: Wiley.

Arrow, K. J. (1967), "Public and private values," in Sidney Hook (Ed.), *Human Values and Economic Policy,* New York: New York University Press.

Arrow, K. J. (1973), "Some ordinalist-utilitarian notes on Rawls' theory of justice," *Journal of Philosophy,* 70: 245–63.

Arrow, K. J. (1977), "Extended sympathy and the possibility of social choice," *American Economic Review,* 67: 219–25.

Arrow, K. J. (1982), "Risk perception in psychology and economics," *Economic Inquiry,* 20: 1–9.

Arrow, K. J. and L. Hurwicz (1977), "An optimality criterion for decision-making under ignorance," in K. J. Arrow and L. Hurwicz (Eds.), *Studies in resource allocation processes,* Cambridge: Cambridge University Press.

Basu, K. (1979), *Revealed preference of governments,* Cambridge: Cambridge University Press.

Bell, D. E. (1982), "Regret in decision making under uncertainty," *Operations Research,* Vol. 30.

Bergson, A. (1938), "A reformulation of certain aspects of welfare economics," *Quarterly Journal of Economics,* 52: 310–34.

Bergson, A. (1954), "On the concept of social welfare," *Quarterly Journal of Economics,* 68: 233–52.

Bergson, A. (1966), *Essays in normative economics,* Cambridge, Mass.: Harvard University Press.

Binmore, K. (1975), "An example in group preference," *Journal of Economic Theory,* 10: 377–85.

Blackorby, C. (1975), "Degrees of cardinality and aggregate partial orderings," *Econometrica,* 43: 845–52.

Blackorby, C., D. Donaldson, and J. A. Weymark (1984), "Social choice with interpersonal utility comparisons: A diagrammatic introduction," *International Economic Review,* 25: 327–56.

Blair, D. H. and R. A. Pollak (1979), "Collective rationality and dictatorship: The scope of the Arrow theorem," *Journal of Economic Theory,* 21: 186–94.

Blair, D. H., G. Bordes, J. S. Kelly, and K. Suzumura (1976), "Impossibility theorems without collective rationality," *Journal of Economic Theory,* 13: 361–79.

Blau, J. H. (1957), "The existence of a social welfare function," *Econometrica,* 25: 302–13.

Blau, J. H. (1971), "Arrow's theorem with weak independence," *Econometrica,* 38: 413–320.

Blau, J. H. (1972), "A direct proof of Arrow's theorem," *Econometrica,* 40: 61–7.

Blau, J. H. (1979), "Semiorders and collective choice," *Journal of Economic Theory,* 21: 195–206.

Borch, K. and J. Mossin (1968), *Risk and uncertainty,* London: Macmillan.

Borda, J. C. (1781), "Mémoire sur les elections au scrutin," *Mémoires des l'Academie Royale des Sciences;* English translation by A. de Grazia, *Isis,* 44 (1953).

Borglin, A. (1982), "States and persons — On the interpretation of some fundamental concepts in the theory of justice as fairness," *Journal of Public Economics,* 18: 85–104.

Broome, J. (1978), "Choice and value in economics," *Oxford Economic Papers,* 30: 313–33.

Broome, J. (1984), "Uncertainty and fairness," *Economic Journal,* 94: 624–32.

Brown, D. J. (1974), "An approximate solution to Arrow's problem," *Journal of Economic Theory,* 9: 375–83.

Buchanan, J. M. and G. Tullock (1962), *The calculus of consent,* Ann Arbor: University of Michigan Press.

Chichilnisky, G. (1982a), "Social aggregation rules and continuity," *Quarterly Journal of Economics,* Vol. 96.

Chichilnisky, G. (1982b), "Topological equivalence of the Pareto condition and the existence of a dictator," *Journal of Mathematical Economics,* 9: 223–33.

d'Aspremont, C. and L. Gevers (1977), "Equity and informational basis of collective choice," *Review of Economic Studies,* 46: 199–210.

Davidson, D. (1980), *Essays on actions and events,* Oxford: Clarendon Press.

Davidson, D., P. Suppes, and S. Siegel (1957), *Decision making: An experimental approach,* Stanford: Stanford University Press.

Deschamps, R. and L. Gevers (1978), "Leximin and utilitarian rules: A joint characterisation," *Journal of Economic Theory,* 17: 143–63.

Deschamps, R. and L. Gevers (1979), "Separability, risk-bearing and social welfare judgments," in J.-J. Laffont (Ed.), *Aggregation and revelation of preferences,* Amsterdam: North-Holland.

Diamond, P. A. (1967), "Cardinal welfare, individualistic ethics, and interpersonal comparisons of utility: Comment," *Journal of Political Economy,* 75: 765–6.

Drèze, J. H. (1974), "Axiomatic theories of choice, cardinal utility and subjective probability: A review," in J. H. Drèze (Ed.), *Allocation under uncertainty: Equilibrium and optimality,* London: Macmillan.

Edgeworth, F. Y. (1881), *Mathematical psychics: An essay on the application of mathematics to the moral sciences,* London: Kegan Paul.

Fine, B. J. (1975), "A note on 'Interpersonal aggregation and partial comparability'," *Econometrica,* 43: 173–4.

Fishburn, P. C. (1970), "Arrow's impossibility theorem: Concise proof and infinite voters," *Journal of Economic Theory,* 2: 103–6.

Fishburn, P. C. (1973), *The theory of social choice,* Princeton: Princeton University press.

Fishburn, P. C. (1974), "On collective rationality and a generalized impossibility theorem," *Review of Economic Studies,* 41: 445–59.

Gevers, L. (1979), "On interpersonal comparability and social welfare orderings," *Econometrica,* 47: 75–90.

Graaff, J. de V. (1967), *Theoretical welfare economics,* 2nd ed., Cambridge: Cambridge University Press.

Hammond, P. J. (1976a), "Equity, Arrow's conditions and Rawls' difference principle," *Econometrica,* 44: 793–804.

Hammond, P. J. (1976b), "Why ethical measures of inequality need interpersonal comparisons," *Theory and Decision,* 7: 263–74.

Hammond, P. J. (1977), "Dual interpersonal comparisons of utility and the welfare economics of income distribution," *Journal of Public Economics,* 6: 51–71.

Hansson, B. (1973), "The independence condition in the theory of social choice," *Theory and Decision,* 4: 25–49.

Hansson, B. (1976), "The existence of group preferences," *Public Choice,* 28: 89–98.

Hare, R. M. (1952), *The language of morals,* Oxford: Clarendon Press; 2nd ed., 1961.

Hare, R. M. (1963), *Freedom and reason,* Oxford: Clarendon Press.

Hare, R. M. (1977), "Geach on murder and sodomy," *Philosophy,* Vol. 52.

Hare, R. M. (1981), *Moral thinking,* Oxford: Clarendon Press.

Harsanyi, J. C. (1955), "Cardinal welfare, individualistic ethics, and interpersonal comparisons of utility," *Journal of Political Economy,* 63: 309–21.

Harsanyi, J. C. (1977), *Rational behaviour and bargaining equilibrium in games and social situations,* Cambridge: Cambridge University Press.

Herzberger, H. G. (1973), "Ordinal preference and rational choice," *Econometrica,* 41: 187–237.

Hurley, S. (1985), "Objectivity and disagreement," in T. Honderich (Ed.), *Ethics and objectivity,* London: Routledge.

Jeffrey, R. C. (1965), *The logic of decision,* New York: McGraw-Hill; 2nd ed., Chicago: University of Chicago Press, 1983.

Kahneman, D., P. Slovick, and A. Tversky (1982), *Judgment under uncertainty: Heuristics and biases,* Cambridge: Cambridge University Press.

Kant, I. (1788), *Critique of practical reason,* English translation by T. K. Abbott, *Kant's critique of practical reason,* London: Longmans; 6th ed., 1909.

Kelly, J. S. (1978), *Arrow impossibility theorems,* New York: Academic Press.

Kemp, M. C. and Y.-K. Ng (1976), "On the existence of social welfare functions, social orderings and social decision functions, *Economica,* 43: 59–66.

Kemp, M. C. and Y.-K. Ng (1977), "More on social welfare functions: The incompatibility of individualism and ordinalism," *Economica,* 44: 89–90.

Kirman, A. P. and D. Sondermann (1972), "Arrow's theorem, many agents and invisible dictators," *Journal of Economic Theory,* 5: 267–77.

Laffont, J.-J. (Ed.) (1979), *Aggregation and revelation of preferences,* Amsterdam: North-Holland.

Levi, I. (1974), "On indeterminate probabilities," *Journal of Philosophy,* 71: 391–418.

Little, I. M. D. (1952), "Social choice and individual values," *Journal of Political Economy,* 60: 422–32.

Little, I. M. D. (1957), *A critique of welfare economics,* 2nd ed., Oxford: Clarendon Press.

Loomes, G. and R. Sugden (1982), "Regret theory: An alternative theory of rational choice under uncertainty," *Economic Journal,* 92: 805–24.

Luce, R. D. and H. Raiffa (1957), *Games and decisions,* New York: Wiley.

McClennen, E. F. (1983), "Sure-thing doubts," in B. P. Stigum and F. Wenstøp (Eds.), *Foundations of utility and risk theory with applications,* Dordrecht: Reidel.

MacCrimmon, K. R. (1968), "Descriptive and normative implications of decision theory postulates," in K. Borch and J. Mossin (Eds.), *Risk and uncertainty,* London: Macmillan.

McDowell, J. (1981), "Non-cognitivism and rule-following," in S. H. Holtzman and C. M. Leich (Eds.), *Wittgenstein: To follow a rule,* London: Routledge.

Machina, M. (1981), "'Rational' decision making vs. 'rational' decision modelling?" *Journal of Mathematical Psychology,* 24.

Machina, M. (1983), "Generalized expected utility analysis and the nature of observed violations of the independence axiom," in Stigum and Wenstøp (1983).

Mackie, J. L. (1977), *Ethics,* Harmondsworth: Penguin Books.

Marshall, A. (1890), *Principles of economics,* London: Macmillan.

Maskin, E. (1978), "A theorem on utilitarianism," *Review of Economic Studies,* 45: 93–6.

Maskin, E. (1979), "Decision-making under ignorance with implications for social choice," *Theory and Decision,* 11: 319–37.

Mirrlees, J. A. (1982), "The economic uses of utilitarianism," in A. K. Sen and B. Williams (Eds.), *Utilitarianism and beyond,* Cambridge: Cambridge University Press.

Myerson, R. B. (1983), "Utilitarianism, egalitarianism, and the timing effect in social choice problems," *Econometrica,* 49: 883–97.

54    Amartya Sen

Nagel, T. (1979), *Mortal questions,* Cambridge: Cambridge University Press.
Nagel, T. (1980), "The limits of objectivity," in S. McMurrin (Ed.), *Tanner lectures on human values,* Cambridge: Cambridge University Press.
Nash, J. F. (1950), "The bargaining problem," *Econometrica,* 18: 155-62.
Parfit, D. (1984), *Reasons and persons,* Oxford: Clarendon Press.
Parks, R. P. (1976), "An impossibility theorem for fixed preferences: A dictatorial Bergson-Samuelson social welfare function," *Review of Economic Studies,* 43: 447-50.
Pattanaik, P. K. (1978), *Strategy and group choice,* Amsterdam: North-Holland.
Pigou, A. C. (1920), *The economics of welfare,* London: Macmillan.
Plott, C. R. (1976), "Axiomatic social choice theory: An overview and interpretation," *American Journal of Political Science,* 20: 511-96.
Pollak, R. A. (1979), "Bergson-Samuelson social welfare functions and the theory of social choice," *Quarterly Journal of Economics,* 93: 73-90.
Rawls, J. (1971), *A theory of justice,* Cambridge, Mass.: Harvard University Press.
Ray, P. (1973), "Independence of irrelevant alternatives," *Econometrica,* 41: 987-91.
Roberts, K. W. S. (1980a), "Possibility theorems with interpersonally comparable welfare levels," *Review of Economic Studies,* 47: 409-20.
Roberts, K. W. S. (1980b), "Interpersonal comparability and social choice theory," *Review of Economic Studies,* 47: 421-39.
Roberts, K. W. S. (1980c), "Social choice theory: The single and multiple-profile approaches," *Review of Economic Studies,* 47: 441-50.
Rubinstein, A. (1981), "The single profile analogues to multiple profile theorems: Mathematical logic's approach," mimeo, Murray Hill: Bell Laboratories.
Samuelson, P. A. (1938), "A note on the pure theory of consumer's behaviour," *Economica,* 5: 61-71.
Samuelson, P. A. (1947), *Foundations of economic analysis,* Cambridge, Mass.: Harvard University Press.
Samuelson, P. A. (1967a), "Arrow's mathematical politics," in S. Hook (Ed.), *Human values and economic policy,* New York: N.Y.U. Press.
Samuelson, P. A. (1967b), "Foreword" in J. de V. Graaff, *Theoretical welfare economics,* 2nd ed., Cambridge: Cambridge University Press.
Savage, L. J. (1954), *The foundations of statistics,* New York: Wiley.
Sen, A. K. (1966), "Hume's law and Hare's rule," *Philosophy,* 41: 75-9.
Sen, A. K. (1970a), *Collective choice and social welfare,* San Francisco: Holden Day; North-Holland, Amsterdam.
Sen, A. K. (1970b), "Interpersonal aggregation and partial comparability," *Econometrica,* 38: 393-409; "A correction," 40(1972): 959.
Sen, A. K. (1971), "Choice functions and revealed preference," *Review of Economic Studies,* 38: 307-17.
Sen, A. K. (1974), "Informational bases of alternative welfare approaches: Aggregation and income distribution," *Journal of Public Economics,* 3: 387-403.
Sen, A. K. (1977a), "Rational fools: A critique of the behavioral foundations of economic theory," *Philosophy and Public Affairs,* 6: 317-44.
Sen, A. K. (1977b), "On weights and measures: Informational constraints in social welfare analysis," *Econometrica,* 45: 1539-72.

Sen, A. K. (1979), "Informational analysis of moral principles," in R. Harrison (Ed.), *Rational action,* Cambridge: Cambridge University Press.

Sen, A. K. (1982), *Choice, welfare and measurement,* Oxford: Blackwell, and Cambridge, Mass.: M.I.T. Press.

Sen, A. K. (1984a), *Resources, values and development,* Oxford: Blackwell, and Cambridge, Mass.: Harvard University Press.

Sen, A. K. (1984b), "Consistency," Presidential Address to the Econometric Society. *Econometrica* forthcoming.

Sen, A. K. (1985a), "Well-being, agency and freedom: The Dewey lectures 1984," *Journal of Philosophy,* 82: 169–221.

Sen, A. K. (1985b), "Social choice theory," in K. J. Arrow and M. Intriligator (Eds.), *Handbook of mathematical economics,* vol. 3, Amsterdam: North-Holland.

Sen, A. K. (1985c), "Rationality and uncertainty," *Theory and Decision,* 18: 109–27.

Sen, A. K. and B. Williams (Eds.) (1982), *Utilitarianism and beyond,* Cambridge: Cambridge University Press.

Sidgwick, H. (1907), *The method of ethics,* 7th ed., London: Macmillan.

Stigum, B. P. and F. Wenstøp (Eds.) (1983), *Foundations of utility and risk theory with applications,* Dordrecht: Reidel.

Strasnick, S. (1976), "Social choice theory and the derivation of Rawls' difference principle," *Journal of Philosophy,* 73: 85–99.

Suppes, P. (1966), "Some formal models of grading principles," *Synthese,* 6: 284–306.

Suzumura, K. (1983), *Rational choice, collective decisions and social welfare,* Cambridge: Cambridge University Press.

Tversky, A. (1975), "A critique of expected utility theory: Descriptive and normative considerations," *Erkenntnis,* 9.

Williams, B. A. O. (1973), "A critique of utilitarianism," in J. J. C. Smart and B. Williams (Eds.), *Utilitarianism: For or against,* Cambridge: Cambridge University Press.

Wilson, R. B. (1972), "Social choice theory without the Pareto principle," *Journal of Economic Theory,* 5: 478–86.

CHAPTER 3

# Utilitarian morality in a world of very half-hearted altruists

*John C. Harsanyi*

## 1 Utilitarianism and rationality

Utilitarianism is an attempt to choose our moral standards by *rational criteria* and, more specifically, by asking what moral standards would maximize expected social utility. Here the adjective "expected" is short for "the expected value of"[1] whereas social utility itself is defined either as the *sum* or as the *arithmetic mean* of all individuals' utility levels in the relevant society. (Some utilitarians prefer the first definition, others prefer the second. But, in actual fact, in analyzing specific moral problems, other than those of population policy, the total number of individuals can be regarded as *given* so that maximizing the sum of individual utilities will be mathematically equivalent to maximizing their arithmetic mean.) These definitions, of course, presuppose that individual utilities are cardinally measurable and admit of meaningful interpersonal comparisons (cf. Harsanyi 1955, 1976, Chapter 4).[2]

No doubt, nonutilitarians will deny that social utility is the right criterion for morality. But it seems to me that, even for nonutilitarian social scientists and philosophers, it should be a question of some interest what kind of social standards *would* in fact maximize social utility.

As is well known, there are two alternative interpretations of utilitarian theory. One is *act utilitarianism,* which defines a morally right action as one that would maximize expected social utility in the current situation. The other is *rule utilitarianism,* which makes the choice of a morally right action into a *two-step* procedure. The first step is to decide what

I want to thank the National Science Foundation for supporting this research through grant SES82-18938 to the Center for Research in Management, University of California, Berkeley. I also want to express my gratitude to Ken Arrow, whose student I was at Stanford University in 1956–8, for his kind help and interest over the years. I am grateful to the two referees and to one of the editors for helpful suggestions.

*moral rule* would maximize expected social utility in the current situation and in similar ones – or, preferably, to decide what *moral code* would maximize expected social utility over the range of all possible situations – were this rule or the moral code followed by all members of the society or at least by those with a serious concern for morality. The second step then is to choose a specific *action* consistent with this moral rule or with this moral code.

Actually, it seems to me that the definition relying on choice of a moral code is preferable because the social utility of a given moral rule cannot be judged in isolation since it will crucially depend on the *other* moral rules accepted by the relevant society. For instance, we cannot assess the merits of a proposed moral rule for defining the parents' moral obligations to their children without knowing what the other relatives' moral obligations are to these children in the society under consideration. Accordingly, at least in theory, the proper objects of social utility judgments are not individual moral rules but rather are entire moral codes.

## 2    Act utilitarianism versus rule utilitarianism

Is act utilitarianism or rule utilitarianism the preferable interpretation of utilitarian theory? Utilitarian theory itself provides a clear rational criterion for answering this question: That interpretation of utilitarianism must be regarded as preferable, which will yield a *higher* level of social utility.

Now it is easy to see that a rule utilitarian society would tend to enjoy a level of social utility *at least as high* as that of an act utilitarian society. Act utilitarianism itself can be regarded as one of the possible moral codes, namely, the moral code simply requiring every individual on each occasion to choose the action maximizing expected social utility under the existing conditions. Now, when a rule utilitarian society chooses its moral code, this act utilitarian moral code will obviously be one of available alternatives. Therefore, the moral code it will actually choose in the end must be one yielding a social utility level *at least as high* as the act utilitarian moral code would yield.[3]

Indeed, I will argue that a society governed by the rule-utilitarian moral code would enjoy a *much higher* level of social utility than one governed by the act utilitarian moral code would. I will show that this would be true even in a world populated by much more altruistic people than most of us are. But it is even truer and is an even more important truth in our actual world, inhabited mainly by people with very real, yet rather limited altruistic propensities.

An important advantage of rule utilitarianism over act utilitarianism is its much greater *flexiblity*. As we have seen, a rule utilitarian society can choose its moral code from a *much wider* feasible set. Moreover, it is not limited to a strictly *consequentialist* evaluation of individual actions, as is act utilitarianism. To be sure, both for rule utilitarianism and for act utilitarianism, the consequentialist criterion of social utility maximization must be the *ultimate* criterion of morality. But whereas act utilitarianism is logically committed to evaluate individual actions directly by this criterion, rule utilitarianism is logically free to adopt a moral code that evaluates individual actions by *nonconsequentialist* criteria – if such a moral code is judged to yield higher social utility. Thus, for example, the rule utilitarian moral code may make the moral value of a given action depend not only on its social utility yield but also on the social relationship between the agent and the beneficiary of the action, on procedural considerations, and so forth. This is a very valuable flexibility because use of such nonconsequentialist criteria will often make an important contribution to social utility. At the same time, by retaining the consequentialist criterion of social utility maximization, rule utilitarianism provides a clear rational criterion for identifying the socially optimal moral code.

## 3     Compliance effects and expectation effects

The primary social function of a moral code is, of course, to enjoin people to do certain things and not to do some other things. As far as people comply with these injunctions, I will call this compliant behavior and its social utility implications the *compliance effects* of this moral code. Yet, people will not only comply with the accepted moral code to a considerable degree, they will also *expect* other people to do so. People's expectations in turn will affect their *confidence* in the future and also their *incentives* to engage in various socially desirable or undesirable activities. All these I will call the *expectation effects* of the moral code in question. These expectation effects are no less important than the compliance effects are in judging the social utility of any proposed moral code. To illustrate the importance of expectation effects, consider the moral problem of *promise keeping*.

Suppose that *A* made an important promise to *B* but now finds it very inconvenient to keep it. Under what conditions will *A* be morally free to break the promise? According to commonsense morality, *A* will be permitted to do this only in rather exceptional cases, such as situations where keeping the promise would cause real hardship to him or to third parties. Rule utilitarian theory will reach much the same conclusion by analysis of the relevant expectation effects. In contrast, act utilitarianism will have to take a much more permissive position.

If *A* were permitted to break the promise, he would obtain some utility *gain* by being released from a burdensome obligation; whereas *B* would suffer some utility *loss* by losing *A*'s promised service and having his expectations disappointed. The algebraic sum of these two utilities I will call the *balance of local utilities*. Besides *A*'s and *B*'s *personal* gain and loss, we must also consider the general *social* interest in maintaining the expectation that promises will be kept. If this expectation were seriously undermined, many people would face the future with *less confidence* and would have *fewer incentives* to engage in various forms of socially useful behavior, such as, for example, performing services for other people in exchange for promised future rewards or agreeing on future joint activities with others.

The question, of course, is whether people's belief in promises would be seriously affected if *A* were permitted to break the promise in this particular case. Under the rule utilitarian assumptions, the answer would have to be in the affirmative; for a rule utilitarian could give moral approval of *A*'s breaking the promise on this *one* occasion only if he were willing to propose a moral code *generally* permitting people to break their promises on *all* similar occasions. Yet, such a moral code might easily have significant effects on people's expectations because it would tell them that even the most conscientious members of society, those fully guided by its moral code, would feel morally free to engage in the *general practice* of breaking their promises in the relevant class of situations.

Thus, from a rule utilitarian point of view, the basic theoretical problem is to find *that particular list* of exceptions to promise keeping that would yield the highest expected social utility by being the best compromise among the promisees' interests, the promisors' interests, and the general social interest in maintaining the expectation that promises will be kept, at least by conscientious people, in all but a few rather exceptional cases. More generally, rule utilitarianism seems to be the only moral theory able to provide a theoretically clear *rational criterion* (even though this is not a criterion always easy to apply in practice) for deciding *what exceptions* should be made to any specific moral rule. This criterion is, of course, that the set of morally permitted exceptions must be chosen so as to maximize expected social utility when all the relevant compliance effects and expectation effects are taken into account.

Unlike rule utilitarianism, act utilitarianism is logically prevented from considering the expectation effects (or any other social effects) of alternative *moral codes*. It can consider only the expectation effects of *individual actions.* Thus, in our example, an act utilitarian could consider only the effect that this *one* act of promise breaking by *A* is likely to have on the credibility of promises. But this one breach of promise is very likely to have a *negligible* effect. Therefore, an act utilitarian will have to conclude that, by and large, *A* will be morally free to break the promise if the resulting balance of local utilities itself is nonnegative, that is, if *A*'s interest in breaking the promise is at least as strong as *B*'s interest in having this promise kept. If an act utilitarian could extend the analysis to the expectation effects of alternative moral codes, and in particular to the very unfavorable expectation effects of his own unduly permissive act utilitarian moral code, then he would of course reach a different conclusion. But the act utilitarian's conceptual framework will prevent taking this broader view.

Yet this means that, according to act utilitarian theory, the fact that *A* made this promise to *B* will make virtually *no difference* because *A*'s moral obligations to *B* will be almost exactly the same as if he had never made a promise to *B* at all. This is, of course, another indication of how little the making of promises would mean in an act utilitarian society. It also shows how far the act utilitarian position would deviate from common sense morality.

*Note:* In defense of act utilitarianism, it might be suggested that the problem just discussed would disappear if people adopted the policy of never making a promise whose implementation would not be a social utility maximizing action at the time of its implementation. But this argument would not really help, for such a policy would be very detrimental to society because it would greatly reduce the needed flexibility in the making of promises. Moreover, such a policy would not solve the problem at all in cases where the promisor did in fact think that by implementing the promise he would maximize social utility at the relevant future time but where unexpected changes in the circumstances had the result that fulfilling the promise would in fact no longer be a social utility maximizing action. In such cases, the promisor would still be forced to choose between *fulfilling* the promise, even though doing so he would not maximize social utility, and *breaking* the promise, that is, acting in such a way as if he had never made any promise at all.

## 4    The value of free individual choice

By analysis of the relevant expectation effects, one can show that rule utilitarianism would enjoin stricter moral standards than act utilitarianism in many other social activities as well, such as telling the truth in important matters, being grateful to our benefactors, being loyal to our friends, and so on. These higher moral standards would make significant contributions to social utility. Yet, even though in many cases rule utilitarianism would propose stricter moral standards than act utilitarianism, in one important respect, it would propose *less strict* moral standards. The point is that act utilitarianism must require us at every moment to choose the action producing the *highest* expected social utility. Not even for a minute could we escape this rigid requirement of maximum performance.

In contrast, rule utilitarianism can recognize the moral value of *free individual choice* not constrained by needlessly restrictive moral obligations. Suppose I have to choose between actions $X$ and $Y$, which would produce the social utility increments $x$ and $y$, respectively, with $x > y$. Since this would make $X$ the action maximizing social utility, according to act utilitarian theory, it would be my clear moral duty to perform action $X$ rather than action $Y$. But rule utilitarian theory may assign a special *procedural utility u* to free personal choice between $X$ and $Y$. This will make it morally permissible for me to choose *either $X$ or $Y$* as long as $y + u \geq x$. Of course, $X$ will remain the *morally preferable* action because $x > y$. Yet, I would do my duty by performing either of the two actions. On the other hand, by choosing the morally superior action $X$, I would go *beyond* the call of duty and would perform a *supererogatory* action.

It seems to me that a society where people can occasionally choose to relax is a much better place to live than is a society where they are under constant moral pressure to show the highest possible level of performance. This would be true even if the lesser moral pressure in the former society gave rise to a somewhat *lower* level of economic, social, and cultural achievements – which, however, might not be the case at all.

## 5    Individual rights and special obligations

The most important advantage of rule utilitarianism over act utilitarianism lies in the fact that its moral code can establish a system of morally protected *individual rights* and *special obligations* that must normally take precedence over direct social utility maximization and that can be overridden only in exceptional cases in order to protect some fundamentally important social interests. In contrast, by its inner logic, act utilitarianism is compelled to take the position that we must always choose the action maximizing social utility – even if this action violates other people's rights or is inconsistent with our own special obligations to some other people.

The social utility of morally protected *individual rights* lies in the fact that they may greatly increase the personal freedom, independence, and security of the persons holding these rights. Some individual rights also provide important incentives to socially desirable behavior. These beneficial effects of individual rights must be weighed against the social costs they entail by restricting the freedom of action of the other members of the society. As an example of individual rights, consider an individual's private property rights over a car. By the very concept of private property, the owner of the car is morally free to use it whenever he so desires, whereas other people must not use it without the owner's consent (except perhaps in some emergency situations). According to rule utilitarian theory, such private property rights tend to have considerable social utility because they make economic relationships more secure and more predictable (confidence effects) and because they are an important incentive to hard work, saving, investment, and entrepreneurship (incentive effects). But act utilitarian theory cannot recognize such property rights because its inner logic forces it to hold that everybody is morally free to use another person's property, even without the owner's permission, as long as he thinks that a *greater* utility would be obtained by making use of it at the time in question.

On the other hand, our *special obligations* arise from the various social roles we play as parents, spouses, neighbors, members of an occupation, and so on. They are important because they establish many forms of socially very beneficial *division of labor* in the society. For example, it is desirable to have a division of labor among adults in caring for the children of the community, with each adult being in charge of no more than a rather small group of children so that he or she can easily find out each child's special needs and can develop close emotional ties with each of them. In our society, this division of labor mainly takes the form of the parents' looking after their own children. In order to protect this special relationship between parents and their children, both commonsense morality and the rule utilitarian moral code will impose special obligations on the parents toward their own children. In particular, they will require the parents to give *special priority* to their own children's needs over those of other people, whether children or adults. According to rule utilitarian theory, this arrangement has considerable social utility because it gives both parents and children a feeling of security (security effects) and gives both of them incentives to many forms of socially desirable behavior (incentive effects). But act utilitarian theory must strongly disapprove this arrangement because it must hold that the parents cannot give any special priority to their own children's needs when they might be able to produce a *greater* amount of utility by satisfying the needs of other people – whether other children or some adults.

One indication of the great social utility of morally protected individual rights and special obligations is the fact that most of us *would strongly prefer living* in a society where individual rights and special obligations were widely respected – as would be the case in a rule utilitarian society – rather than in a society where individual rights and special obligations were continually overridden by immediate social expediency considerations – as would be the case in an act utilitarian society.[4]

## 6    The difficulty of altruism

The utilitarian objective of maximizing social utility is not a *strictly* altruistic objective but is merely an *impartial* one. It does not ask me to give *more weight* to any other person's interests than to my own. It asks me only to give the *same weight* to everybody's interests, including my own. Yet, when act utilitarianism asks us to make this impartial objective of social utility maximization the direct decision rule for every action we take, it is asking us to do what would require much more altruism on our part than most of us can muster. To be sure, most people are by no means complete egoists. They may show considerable altruism toward a rather *small* group of people, such as their family members and very close friends. They may also show a rather *restricted* altruism toward people at large by a general willingness to help other people, even complete strangers – but very often only if this costs them very little in money, time, and effort.

Rule utilitarianism would make more modest moral demands on us than act utilitarianism would. It would recognize the principle that we have special obligations to our family, our friends, and other personal associates. By the same token, it would recognize the fact that, for the sake of social efficiency, each individual would be well advised to pay special attention to his or her own interests, which he or she would be likely to know best – of course, without neglecting other people's interests. Yet, even the rule utilitarian moral code would make moral demands that most of us could not satisfy without major effort. (Obviously, the effort required to comply with any given moral code must be regarded as a *social cost,* which must be taken into account in evaluating the social utility of this moral code.) But at least the rule utilitarian moral code would not be so completely unpracticable for most of us as the act utilitarian moral code would be.

## 7 The problem of economic incentives

One way the limits of human altruism become very apparent is by the well-attested need for economic incentives to motivate hard work, saving, investment, and entrepreneurial behavior. In healthy societies, many people will put forward a decent performance, even without the prospect of any reward or punishment, simply because they feel this is the right thing to do. Indeed, in social emergencies they may even go much beyond doing merely a decent job. But under normal conditions, in the absence of proper economic incentives, few people will do much more than what they feel is the minimum acceptable standard. To be sure, small communities of idealists may be able to elicit high performance by an appeal to altruistic attitudes. Even large groups of people may be induced by government propaganda to work very hard for a limited period. But as several communist countries have discovered, desirable levels of performance by the general population simply cannot be persistently maintained without adequate economic incentives.

It is important to note that the people who do not put forward very high performance levels without proper economic incentives are often very decent and perhaps even admirable people as judged by our ordinary moral standards. Even if judged by the rule utilitarian moral standards, their behavior may be perfectly unobjectionable. For, in most situations, it is, strictly speaking, presumably not our *moral duty* to reach very high levels of performance (though it is our strict moral duty to attain at least the minimum level of efficiency required by our job), and we are not necessarily acting immorally if we make our performance levels depend on the availability of proper economic incentives. Of course, it will always be morally preferable *supererogatory* behavior for us to reach high levels of performance even without any prospect of special rewards. But normally we have no strict moral obligation to do so.

On the other hand, as we saw in Section 4, act utilitarian theory does not distinguish between doing one's duty and performing supererogatory actions. In fact, the moral standards of act utilitarian theory do require everybody to reach those rather high performance levels that would maximize social utility and to do so regardless of the availability of any economic incentives. But human nature being what it is, very few people will fully comply with the act utilitarian moral standards; and we cannot really deplore this fact because, as I have argued, everything considered, compliance with the act utilitarian moral standards would often be rather harmful to society.

## 8     Morality and income redistribution

If society wants to provide economic incentives to hard work, saving, investment, and entrepreneurial behavior, then people who have earned higher incomes by these activities must be permitted to *retain* these higher incomes or at least a sizable proportion of them. This limits the extent to which *legally enforced* income redistribution by progressive taxation can go without becoming counterproductive. But it also limits the extent to which a rational moral code can make it the moral duty of the rich to transfer part of their incomes *voluntarily* to the poor – in spite of the fact that under the usual utilitarian assumptions[5] almost *any* redistribution of income in favor of people with lower incomes is likely to increase social utility. This, of course, means simply that in choosing a socially optimal moral code, we encounter the usual problem, very familiar to economists, that the two desired goals of increasing aggregate income and of improving the distribution of income often pull in opposite directions.

Note that both act utilitarianism and rule utilitarianism have the conceptual tools needed to deal with the problem of optimal taxation. But the two versions of utilitarianism would not be equally successful in dealing with the problem of voluntary income redistribution. Rule utilitarianism would have no difficulty in dealing with it. But act utilitarianism would face considerable difficulties in this regard – at least under the unavoidable realistic assumption that, even in an officially act utilitarian society, many people would *deviate* from the act utilitarian moral standards and would not put forward the socially desirable levels of performance without proper economic incentives. The point is that, without inconsistency, act utilitarianism could not avoid taking the position that rich people were always morally obliged to transfer money to the poor voluntarily (and should be placed under strong social pressure to do so in the absence of voluntary compliance) until a completely egalitarian income distribution were reached (except for higher incomes being assigned to people with special needs) – regardless of how this would affect those people's behavior who did need proper economic incentives for socially desirable levels of performance, even though this was clearly contrary to act utilitarian morality.

## 9     Conclusion

I have argued that a society governed by rule utilitarian principles would achieve a much higher level of social utility than would one governed by act utilitarian principles. One reason for this is that rule utilitarianism is a much more *flexible* theory than is act utilitarianism. Whereas act utilitarianism asks us to follow one specific moral code based on action-by-action social utility maximization, rule utilitarianism asks us to choose the socially optimal moral code from a much larger *feasible* set, that of all possible moral codes, which, of course, includes the act utilitarian moral code as a special case. One important advantage of rule utilitarianism is that it is not restricted to a purely consequentialist evaluation of individual actions, as is act utilitarianism. For instance, it can make the moral value of an action depend on the social relationship between the agent and the recipient and on procedural considerations – whenever the use of such criteria will increase social utility. At the same time, the consequentialist criterion of social utility maximization provides a clear rational standard for choosing the rule utilitarian moral code itself.

An even more fundamental advantage of rule utilitarianism is that its conceptual framework permits it to pay proper attention to the *expectation effects* (including the confidence and the incentive effects) of alternative moral codes, whereas act utilitarianism is restricted to considering the expectation effects of individual actions. As a result, it cannot take account of the very unfavorable expectation effects of the act utilitarian moral code itself. Moreover, the rule utilitarian moral code is able to provide utilitarian justification for a wide network of individual rights and special obligations, which act utilitarianism is unable to do.

Finally, because of its greater flexibility, rule utilitarianism can better adjust its moral standards to the fact that most humans are very genuine but also very *limited* altruists and that most of them need adequate economic incentives to motivate them for more than mediocre performance in a persistent manner.

### Game-theoretic appendix

The distinction between act and rule utilitarianism can be elucidated by use of game-theoretic models. Suppose that society consists of $r = n + m$ individuals, of whom $n$ individuals $i$ ($i = 1, ..., n$) are consistent *utilitarians* whereas $m$ individuals $j$ ($j = n + 1, ..., n + m$) are *nonutilitarians*. The latter may include pure egoists, followers of various nonutilitarian (or at least not consistently utilitarian) moral codes, and people mixing egoistic attitudes with various moral values.

I will use the term *strategy* in the usual game-theoretic sense. I will denote the strategy of any player $k$ ($k = 1, ..., n + m$) by $s_k$. Under a suitable interpretation of strategies, we can assume without any loss of generality that the *same* set $S$ of strategies is available to all $n + m$ players. I will write $s = (s_1, \ldots, s_n; s_{n+1}, \ldots, s_{n+m})$ to denote the *strategy combination* used by the $n + m$ players.

The *utility function* of any player $k$ will be called $U_k$. The *social utility function* will be called $\bar{U}$. As we have seen, it can be defined as

$$\bar{U} = \sum_{k=1}^{r} U_k \quad \text{or} \quad \bar{U} = \sum_{k=1}^{r} U_k / r.$$

I will consider two models. In model I, I will assume that all $n$ utilitarian players are *act utilitarians*. Thus, every utilitarian player $i$ will try to choose strategy $s_i$ so as to maximize the social utility function

$$\bar{U} = \bar{U}(s) = \bar{U}(s_1, \ldots, s_i, \ldots, s_n; s_{n+1}, \ldots, s_m), \tag{1}$$

subject to the two constraints

$$s_i \in S \tag{2}$$

and

$$s_k = \text{const.} \quad \text{for } k = 1, \ldots, i-1, i+1, \ldots, n+m. \tag{3}$$

Constraint (1) is self-explanatory, and constraint (2) expresses the fact that player $i$ will have no control over fellow players' strategies.

I will assume that the behavior of every nonutilitarian player $j$ can be interpreted likewise as maximization of some function, to be denoted by $V_j$ and to be called $j$'s *moral values function*. Function $V_j$ may be identical with $j$'s utility function $U_j$ but need not be because it may express some moral values not expressed, or insufficiently expressed, by his utility function $U_j$ measuring his personal well-being. Thus, each *nonutilitarian* player $j$ will try to choose strategy $s_j$ so as to maximize the moral values function,

$$V_j = V_j(s) = V_j(s_1, \ldots, s_n; s_{n+1}, \ldots, s_j, \ldots, s_{n+m}) \tag{4}$$

subject to two constraints similar to (2) and (3), namely, subject to

$$s_j \in S \tag{5}$$

and

$$s_k = \text{const.} \quad \text{for } k = 1, \ldots, j-1, j+1, \ldots, n+m. \tag{6}$$

If all $n + m$ players simultaneously *succeed* in choosing strategies satisfying these requirements, then the strategy combination $s$ used by them will be a *Nash equilibrium point* in the game they are playing. In fact, given the action-by-action social utility maximization requirement of act utilitarian theory, $s$ will be presumably a *subgame-perfect* or even a fully perfect equilibrium point, at least with respect to the utilitarian players' strategies. (For definitions of the two perfectness concepts, see Selten 1975.) Yet, as a practical matter, it will be extremely *hard* for the players to coordinate their strategies sufficiently for reaching an equilibrium point – and, even if they did reach one, we could hardly expect them to reach the equilibrium point yielding the highest level of social utility within the set of all equilibrium points (see Harsanyi 1977).

Next, consider model II, where I will assume that all $n$ utilitarian players are *rule utilitarians*. Suppose that the resulting game will be played in two steps, largely corresponding to the two steps used in Section 1 in defining rule utilitarian theory. At step 1, the $n$ utilitarian players will choose their moral code $M$ out of the *set* $\Omega$ of all possible moral codes; whereas at step 2, all players, both utilitarian and nonutilitarian, will choose their individual strategies. For analytical convenience, I will start my analysis with step 2, assuming that the moral code $M$ has already been selected by the utilitarian players.

The main effect of this moral code $M$ will be to restrict the utilitarian players' strategies to a *permissible set* $P(M)$ consistent with this moral code $M$. Assume that, for all $M \in \Omega$, $P(M)$ is always a *nonempty* subset of the set $S$ of physically possible strategies.

As a mathematical representation of the assumptions made in Section 4, I will postulate that each utilitarian player $i$ will try to choose a strategy $s_i$ from the permissible set $P(S)$ so as to maximize the *moral priorities function* $X_i$, expressing the relative weights he or she wants to assign to social utility maximization on the one hand and to free individual choice in accordance with personal desires on the other hand. As the reader will note, these moral priorities functions $X_i$ will resemble the moral values function $V_j$ of the nonutilitarian players in being based on a mixture of moral and nonmoral considerations; but they will differ from the latter in that the moral considerations they express will tend to be different.

Thus, given a specific moral mode $M$, each utilitarian player $i$ will try to choose strategy $s_i$ so as to maximize the moral priorities function

$$X_i = X_i(s) = X_i(s_1, \ldots, s_i, \ldots, s_n; s_{n+1}, \ldots, s_{n+m}) \tag{7}$$

subject to the constraints

$$s_i \in P(M) \tag{8}$$

and

$$s_k = \text{const.} \quad \text{for} \quad k = 1, \ldots, j-1, j+1, \ldots, n+m. \tag{9}$$

On the other hand, each nonutilitarian player will try to choose strategy $s_j$ so as to maximize the moral values function $V_j$ subject to the constraints (5) and (6) – just as he would do in the act utilitarian game.

The game just described, in which the rule utilitarian players' strategies are restricted to a permissible set $P(M)$ defined by a specific moral code $M$, will be called the *restricted game* $G(M)$ generated by this moral code $M$. If all $n+m$ players simultaneously *succeed* in choosing strategies satisfying the above requirements, then the strategy combination $s$ used by them will be a Nash equilibrium point of game $G(M)$. The set of all equilibrium points of this game will be called $E(M)$.

In case the utilitarian players are a sizable fraction of all players, then if the moral code $M$ significantly restricts the strategy choice of these players (as the social utility maximizing moral code would in fact presumably do), then it will be much *easier* for the players to reach an equilibrium point in game $G(M)$ than it would be in the act utilitarian game of model I.

Now I propose to go back to an analysis of step 1 of the rule utilitarian game at which the utilitarian players choose a social utility maximizing moral code. But first I propose to redefine the social utility function itself so as to make it dependent not only on the individual players' behavior as expressed by their strategy combination $s$ but also on the chosen moral code $M$ itself. This redefinition is needed, in accordance with our discussion in Section 4, in order to express the losses in individual utilities and the resulting loss in social utility caused by any moral code unduly restricting free individual choice. I will write the redefined social utility function as[6]

$$\bar{U} = \bar{U}(s, M) = \bar{U}(s_1, \ldots, s_n; s_{n+1}, \ldots, s_{n+m}; M). \tag{10}$$

If the utilitarian players want to maximize this social welfare function by their choice of a moral code $M$, then they must try to *predict* the strategy combination $s$ the $n+m$ players will use if any particular moral code $M$ is chosen. That is, they must select a *predictor function* $\pi$ that will always choose *one* specific equilibrium point $s = \pi[E(M)]$ from any set $E(M)$ of equilibrium points as the predicted outcome of game $G(M)$. To simplify my notation, I will denote this predicted outcome simply as $s = \pi^*(M)$.[7]

Given such a predictor function, the utilitarian players will choose their moral code $M$ so as to maximize the social utility function $\bar{U}(s, M)$, where

$$s = \pi^*(M) \tag{11}$$

and $M$ must satisfy

$$M \in \Omega. \tag{12}$$

How does this model represent what I have called the compliance effects and the expectation effects of any given moral code? Obviously, the compliance effects of a moral code will be represented by the utilitarian players' compliance with requirement (8), which restricts them to strategies consistent with this moral code. On the other hand, its expectation effects will be represented by the *reactions* of each player (including both the utilitarian and the nonutilitarian players) to *knowing* that his utilitarian fellow players' strategies are constrained by the chosen moral code but that, within these limits, these players' strategies will often be guided by their personal desires and interests in case their moral priorities function $X_i$ assigns relatively high weight to the latter. That is, these expectation effects will manifest themselves in the way this knowledge will affect each player's *best reply* in game $G(M)$ to the other $n + m - 1$ players' strategies.

As the reader will have noticed, my model of an act utilitarian society (model I) has taken the form of a *noncooperative game*. This has been the appropriate model, it seems to me, because under act utilitarian theory, each act utilitarian individual will act independently, even though all of them will have the common objective of maximizing social utility. In contrast, my model of a rule utilitarian society has made essential use of an assumption characteristic of *cooperative games* by requiring full *commitment*[8] by the utilitarian players to the rule-utilitarian moral code and by prohibiting any deviations from it even in cases where such deviations would increase social utility.[9] (For example, as we argued in Section 5, individual rights and special obligations must normally take precedence of direct social utility maximization.)

## NOTES

1  For convenience, in contexts where no ambiguity can arise, I will often omit the adjective expected from the phrase expected social utility.
2  People who reject cardinal and/or interpersonally comparable utilities but still want our moral standards and/or our public policies to be determined by maximizing some suitably chosen quantity, often prefer to call this quantity a *social welfare function* rather than *social utility*.
3  Some people will no doubt object that this argument can be *reversed*. I have argued that when a rule utilitarian society chooses its moral code, the act

utilitarian moral code will be one of the available alternatives. But, of course, it is equally true that, when in an act utilitarian society any individual chooses among alternative actions, the actions permitted (or the action prescribed) by the rule utilitarian moral code will always be among the alternative actions available. Cannot we infer from this fact that the social utility level of an act utilitarian society, resulting from all these individual actions, will be *at least as high* as that enjoyed by a rule utilitarian society? The answer is that we *cannot* make this inference. Even though the members of an act utilitarian society and those of a rule utilitarian society will have exactly the same set of possible actions available to them, the specific actions chosen by the former will often be quite *different* and will tend to yield a much *lower* level of social utility because they will be based on inferior and less informative *choice criteria*. More specifically, the members of an act utilitarian society will be forced by their act utilitarian conceptual framework to base their choices merely on the likely social effects of alternative *individual actions*. In contrast, the members of a rule utilitarian society will be in a position to consider the likely social effects of alternative *moral codes* in their entirety.

4   To be sure, this is not a rigorous argument. According to my equiprobability model of moral value judgments (Harsanyi 1953, 1955), to say that a rational person would strongly *prefer* living in society A rather than in society B is *analytically equivalent* to saying that society A must enjoy a much *higher* level of social utility than does society B. But this is true only if this person's preference for society A is an *impartial* preference (as would be the case if he formed this preference by imagining to have the *same probability* of being put in the shoes of any individual member in each society). In real life, of course, we do not know whether people's preferences between the two societies are in fact based on impartial considerations or not. Nevertheless, it seems to me that a widespread strong preference for one of the two societies is at least an important *heuristic* argument for assigning a higher social utility level to this society.

5   These assumptions are that, except for people with special needs, people's utility functions for money are fairly similar and display diminishing marginal utilities.

6   Indeed, for greater generality, we may assume that, in a predominantly (act or rule) utilitarian society, even the nonutilitarian players might be somewhat influenced by the moral code $M$ followed by the utilitarian players. To express this assumption, we may insert $M$ into each nonutilitarian player's moral values function $V_j$ and may write $V_j = V_j(s, M)$.

7   This predictor function $\pi$ could be based on the solution theory developed by Reinhard Selten and me, which always selects a *unique* equilibrium point as solution for any noncooperative game. (For a preliminary discussion of our theory, see Harsanyi 1982; a more detailed discussion is given in the forthcoming book by Harsanyi and Selten, *A general theory of equilibrium selection in games.*

8   It is a characteristic feature of many cooperative games that a player must not break any commitment he has made even if doing so could increase that player's payoff.

9   No doubt, my two models could be made more realistic, even if only at the cost of greater analytical complexity, by reinterpreting them as games with *incomplete information*. (For a discussion of such games, see Harsanyi 1967-8.)

REFERENCES

Arrow, K. J. (1978), "Extended sympathy and the possibility of social choice," *Philosophia,* 7: 223-37.
Brandt, R. B. (1979), *A theory of the good and the right,* Oxford: Oxford University Press.
Hare, R. M. (1981), *Moral thinking,* Oxford: Clarendon Press.
Harsanyi, J. C. (1953), "Cardinal utility in welfare economics and in the theory of risk taking," *Journal of Political Economy,* 61: 434-35. Reprinted in Harsanyi (1976).
Harsanyi, J. C. (1955), "Cardinal welfare, individualistic ethics, and interpersonal comparisons of utility," *Journal of Political Economy,* 63: 309-21. Reprinted in Harsanyi (1976).
Harsanyi, J. C. (1967-8), "Games with incomplete information played by Bayesian players," Parts I-III, *Management Science,* 14: 159-82, 320-34, and 486-502.
Harsanyi, J. C. (1976), *Essays on ethics, rational behavior, and scientific explanation,* Dordrecht, Holland: Reidel.
Harsanyi, J. C. (1977), "Rule utilitarianism and decision theory," *Erkenntnis,* 11: 25-53.
Harsanyi, J. C. (1980), "Rule utilitarianism, rights, obligations, and the theory of rational behavior," *Theory and Decision,* 12: 115-33.
Harsanyi, J. C. (1982), "Solutions for some bargaining games under the Harsanyi-Selten solution theory," Parts I-II, *Mathematical Social Sciences,* 3: 179-91 and 259-79.
Selten, R. (1975), "Reexamination of the perfectness concept for equilibrium points in extensive games," *International Journal of Game Theory,* 4: 25-55.
Sen, A. and B. Williams (Eds.) (1982), *Utilitarianism and beyond,* Cambridge, England: Cambridge University Press.

CHAPTER 4

# On the implementation of social choice rules in irrational societies

*Leonid Hurwicz*

## 1 Implementation for choice profiles and unordered preferences

The purpose of this essay is to show that certain concepts and results on Nash implementation of social choice rules due to Maskin and others are valid even when the underlying preferences are intransitive, cyclic, or incomplete.[1] This fact is of interest when the society whose goals are to be implemented consists of groups whose choices are defined by voting procedures. It is easy to think of examples: the United Nations Security Council (or Assembly, or any other of its voting organs), a university council whose members represent individual departments, or an association of municipalities in a metropolitan area. In what follows, we use the terms organization and group synonymously. A *group* (say a university department) consists of *individuals* (department members); the *society* (say university council) consists of groups as its *members*.

Earlier versions of this essay were presented at a conference organized by C. Plott in February 1985 at the California Institute of Technology and at the Institute for Mathematical Studies in the Social Sciences, Stanford University, Summer Seminar in July 1985. Its approach was inspired by my exposure to the ideas of three members of the Institute of Control Sciences, USSR Academy of Sciences, M. A. Aizerman, F. T. Aleskerov, and V. I. Vol'skiy who took part in the C.I.T. conference. I am grateful to the Institute for the Fairchild Scholar appointment, which provided an opportunity for these contacts, and to the Humanities and Social Sciences Division for a favorable intellectual environment. I also benefited from suggestions by J. Sobel, University of California, San Diego (see Section 5), from discussions with T. Saijo (then a graduate student at the University of Minnesota also enjoying the hospitality of C.I.T.), and from suggestions due to J. Greenberg, University of Haifa (see Section 4, especially note 13), and to S. R. Williams, Northwestern University (see especially the appendix, Remarks 2 and 3).

Since this essay was submitted for publication in the present volume, I received from R. D. McKelvey, California Institute of Technology, a most interesting paper which, using different game forms, obtains results that are, at least in some respects, of greater generality than mine.

This research was carried out with the aid from National Science Foundation Grant No. SES-8208378.

When the body consisting of such groups is to choose among alternatives, we think of each group as corresponding to an individual (agent, player, voter) in the usual voting or economic models. But it is not always natural to interpret the attitudes[2] of a group as defined by a preference relation. Rather, we may think of the attitude of the group as defined by its choice function, which specifies the subset to be chosen given the set of actually available alternatives.[3] As an example, the group's choice function may be specified by majority votes between pairs of alternatives. A social choice rule then specifies the set chosen by the "society" (i.e., the collection of groups) given the available alternatives and the profile of choice functions of the groups.

It should be noted, however, that the definitions and results in this essay are valid for any $n$-member society whose choice functions satisfy our assumptions.[4] The interpretation of each member as a group of individuals is provided to motivate the weakening of the usual postulates such as transitivity and completeness of members' preferences.

If $A$ is the set of potentially available alternatives, the $i$th group's attitudes are represented by a choice function[5] $C_i: 2^A \setminus \varnothing \to 2^A$. We shall always require that, for any $X \subseteq A$, $C_i(X) \subseteq X$, and sometimes also that $C_i(X) \neq \varnothing$. Let $N = \{1, \ldots, n\}$ be the set of groups; the $n$-tuple $\mathbf{C} = (C_1, \ldots, C_n)$ is called the choice function *profile*. Given a set $X$ of actually available alternatives (with $X \subseteq A$) and the choice profile $\mathbf{C}$, a social *goal function*[6] $F$ specifies a nonempty subset $Y \subseteq X$ to be chosen by society. That is, $F(X, C) = Y$, where $Y \subseteq X \subseteq A$.[7]

More generally, the choice of $Y$ might depend not only on the choice profile but also on status quo, the initial endowment, and so on. A general term for the argument of $F$ is *environment,* and the symbol used for the domain of $F$ is $E$ (sometimes called the *class of a priori admissible environments*). As the term indicates, a social goal function $F$ is viewed as representing societal goals, objectives, desiderata – the society's concept of optimality or, at least, acceptability. Arrow's possibility theorem and many subsequent contributions analyze the various properties of (a class of) social goal functions and, in particular, seek to determine which of their conceivable attributes are logically compatible.[8] Our interest, on the other hand, has to do with the *implementation* of societal goals, which are considered as given, rather than the formulation or merits of the goals.

The process of implementation is defined as follows: The $i$th group has a strategic domain $S_i$ from which it chooses an element $s_i$. The joint strategy space is defined as $S = S_1 \times \cdots \times S_n$. An outcome function $h: S \to A$ determines the consequences (outcome) of any profile of strategies used by the groups. The choice of strategies will depend on the environment $e = (X, \mathbf{C})$, the outcome function $h$, and the behavioral patterns of the groups. (The behavioral patterns, in turn, determine the game solution concept to be used, e.g., Nash equilibrium or maximin equilibrium.) We represent this dependence by the *equilibrium correspondence*

$$\mu_h^\beta : E \twoheadrightarrow S$$

where $\beta$ represents the behavioral patterns. More specifically, we shall think of this process as a noncooperative game in normal form, with $\beta$ chosen to be the Nash (noncooperative) equilibrium. For $\beta = \text{Nash}$, we write $\mu_h^\beta = \nu_h$. That is, for any $e$ in $E$, $\nu_h(e)$ is the set (in the joint strategy space $S$) of Nash equilibria when the environment $e$ prevails. Since Nash equilibria are usually defined in implementation theory on the assumption that each individual has a preference ordering on the set of alternatives, we shall have to provide a definition of Nash equilibria for our more general situation. In so doing, we follow in the footsteps of Shafer and Sonnenschein, who provided a generalization of the Nash equilibrium concept for a very broad class of situations.[9]

## 2      The basic framework

Although we take as a point of departure the group's choice function, we shall only use the choices from sets of at most two elements. That is, the definition of a Generalized Nash Equilibrium (GNE) as well as all other concepts used will only depend on choices from one- and two-element sets. To avoid trivialities, we shall assume that the choice from a one-element set is that element; that is,

$$C_i(\{x\}) = \{x\} \quad \text{for all } i \in N, x \in A.$$

For two-element sets, all four subsets are at this stage permitted as choices; that is, for any $i \in N$, $x, y \in A$, the set $C_i(\{x, y\})$ may be empty or $\{x\}$ or $\{y\}$ or $\{x, y\}$. In some contexts, we may wish to rule out the empty set. As for the values $C_i(X)$ for $X \subseteq A$, $\#X \geq 3$, no assumptions need to be made.

Our interpretation is as follows. The $i$th group's "attitudes" are determined by having it choose by some method of voting between any two alternatives. The outcome of the vote may be indecisive $[C_i(\{x, y\}) = \varnothing]$ or indifference $[C_i(\{x, y\}) = \{x, y\}]$ or one of the two alternatives, that is, $C_i(\{x, y\}) = \{x\}$ or $C_i(\{x, y\}) = \{y\}$.

We shall suppose that the group never votes on more than two alternatives at a time[10] and that the outcome is independent of order in which voting occurs. As a special case, it may happen that each individual in each group has a conventional (total and transitive) preference ordering, but this need not be assumed. The method of voting within the group need not be limited in any way, except that faced with a singleton to "choose" from, the group chooses that element.

Now, as in Herzberger (1973, p. 204, Definition 14) and Sen [1977, p. 64, formula (9)], given a choice function $C_i$, we define, for all $i \in N$, the corresponding binary *base relation* $R_i$ for $C_i$ by

1. for all $x \in A$, $x R_i x$ and
2. for all $x, y \in A$, $x \neq y$, $x R_i y$ if and only if $x \in C_i(\{x, y\})$.

If we identify $\{x, x\}$ with the one-element set $\{x\}$, the above can be abbreviated as: for all $x, y \in A$,

$$x R_i y \quad \text{if and only if } x \in C_i(\{x, y\}).$$

[Recall that $C_i(X) \subseteq X$ always.]

In view of 1, $R_i$ is *reflexive* for all $i$. If we were to require that $C_i(X) \neq \varnothing$ always, it would be the case that, for any $x, y \in A$ and $i \in N$, either $x R_i y$ or $y R_i x$ or both; that is, $R_i$ would be *complete* (hence *total*). But, in general, completeness is not assumed. Nor is the *transitivity* of $R_i$. We shall further define $P_i$ as the asymmetric part of $R_i$, that is, by

$$x P_i y \quad \text{if and only if } x R_i y \text{ and } \neg y R_i x,$$

where the symbol $\neg$ means "it is not the case that." It follows that $P_i$ need not be *acyclic*. For example, it may happen for some $i \in N$ and $x, y, z \in A$ that $x P_i y$, $y P_i z$, $z P_i x$. If a group's choice function has a cyclic base relation, it is not unnatural to speak of the group's "irrational preferences." Hence the title of this essay.

## 3     A comment on the results

The simple point of this essay is that the main results of implementation theory go through within the framework just described. That is, using the binary relation $R_i$ as constructed above, we can define a (generalized) Nash equilibrium as well as the properties of social choice correspondence (monotonicity, no veto power) used in Maskin-type implementation theorems. It then only remains to be verified that the proofs of such theorems are valid for any reflexive binary relation, that is, that they use neither completeness nor transitivity of the weak preference relation nor acyclicity of the strict preference relation.

The fact that strict preferences need not be acyclic is perhaps of particular interest. The well-known voting paradox can well result in a cyclic triple; hence the corresponding $P_i$ would be cyclic ($x P_i\, y P_i\, z P_i\, x$). Nevertheless, there are social choice correspondences (perhaps not very attractive) that *can* be implemented in generalized Nash equilibria under such circumstances. Examples of such correspondences are given in Section 5.

## 4      Definitions

The definitions to be used can be stated either in terms of choice profiles or base relation profiles. In some cases we do both, although it is more convenient to carry out proofs in terms of the base relation.

Let $S_i$ be the strategy domain of group $i$, $S = S_1 \times \cdots \times S_n$, and $h : S \to A$. We refer to $h$ as the *outcome function* and to $(S, h)$ as the *game form*.

A noncooperative game is defined as

$$\Gamma = (S, h; \mathbf{C}) \quad \text{or} \quad \Gamma = (S, h; \mathbf{R})$$

where $\mathbf{C} = (C_1, \ldots, C_n)$ and $\mathbf{R} = (R_1, \ldots, R_n)$. It is always understood that $x R_i\, y$ if and only if $x \in C_i(\{x, y\})$.[11] Sometimes it is helpful to use somewhat more explicit notation and write $(S, h; \mathbf{C}) = \Gamma(C)$, $(S, h; \mathbf{R}) = \Gamma(R)$.

Let $s = (s_1, \ldots, s_n) \in S$. We write $t, i/s$ to denote the element

$$(s_1, \ldots, s_{i-1}, t, s_{i+1}, \ldots, s_n)$$

of $S$.

**Definition 1.** An element $s^*$ of $S$ is a *Generalized Nash Equilibrium* (GNE) of $\Gamma$ if and only if, for all $i \in N$,

(†)        $h(s^*) \in C_i(h(s^*), h(t, i/s^*))$   for all $t \in S_i$,

or, in terms of the base relation,

(††)       $h(s^*) R_i\, h(t, i/s^*)$   for all $t \in S_i$.

In order to discuss the relationship of Definition 1 to Definition 2 given below, we speak of $\text{GNE}_1(R)$ for $\Gamma(R)$ when using relations (††) and of $\text{GNE}_1(C)$ for $\Gamma(C)$ when using relation (†).

Alternatively, in the spirit of the Shafer and Sonnenschein approach, one can define GNE in terms of irreflexive binary relations $P_i$, $i \in N$. Denoting this concept by $\text{GNE}_2(P)$, we have the following definition.

**Definition 2.** An element $s^* \in S$ is a $\text{GNE}_2(P)$ for $\Gamma(P) = (S, h; \mathbf{P})$ if and only if, for all $i \in N$ and $t \in S_i$,

$$\neg h(t, i/s^*) P_i\, h(s^*).$$

Now define the binary relation $\rho_i$ by

$$a\,\rho_i\,b \quad \text{if and only if} \quad \neg b\,P_i\,a.$$

Then $\rho_i$ is reflexive. Hence $s^*$ is a $\text{GNE}_1(\rho)$ for $\Gamma(\rho) = (S, h; \rho)$ if and only if it is a $\text{GNE}_2(P)$ for $\Gamma(P) = (S, h; \mathbf{P})$. Let other concepts used in this essay (such as monotonicity or no veto power) be interpreted in terms of the $\rho_i$. Then our results concerning GNE for $\Gamma(R) = (S, h; \mathbf{R})$, where the $R_i$ are arbitrary reflexive relations, are in particular valid for the $\rho_i$. In this manner, they can be read as valid theorems, with $\text{GNE}_2(P)$ and $\Gamma(R)$ replacing $\text{GNE}_1(R)$ and $\Gamma(R)$, respectively.

In fact, in the framework used by Kim and Richter (1985, pp. 25–6), $\rho_i$ is the *canonical conjugate* of $R_i$; in their notation, $\rho_i = R_i^*$. Our argument leading to theorems involving $\text{GNE}_2(P)$ is, in effect, an application of their canonical conjugacy metatheorem (p. 27).

In particular, $P_i$ may be interpreted as the asymmetric part of a given reflexive preference relation $R_i$, but that is not essential for the validity of the $\text{GNE}_2(P)$ counterparts of our results. [12]

It is easily seen that all of our definitions of generalized Nash equilibria specialize to the usual ones when the underlying reflexive relations ($R_i$ or $\rho_i$) are transitive and complete.

From now on, we return to the original definition, so Nash equilibrium will mean GNE in the sense of Definition 1, that is, $\text{GNE}_1(C)$ or $\text{GNE}_1(R)$ depending on the context.

We now fix the set of available alternatives so that $X = A$ and introduce $F: \mathbf{C} \mapsto Y$ or $F: \mathbf{R} \mapsto Y$ with $Y \subseteq A$. That is, $F$ is a given social choice (goal) correspondence defined either in terms of choice function profiles or base relation profiles. If $E$ is the class of a priori admissible environments (either choice function profiles or base relation profiles), we have $F: E \twoheadrightarrow A$.

A game form $(S, h)$ is said to (Nash) *implement* $F: \mathbf{C} \mapsto Y$ (or $F: \mathbf{R} \mapsto Y$) over $E$ if and only if the following two conditions are satisfied:

1.  If $\mathbf{C} \in E$ and $a \in F(\mathbf{C})$, then $\exists s^* \in S$ such that $s^*$ is a GNE for $(S, h; \mathbf{C})$ and $a = h(s^*)$.
2.  If $\mathbf{C} \in E$ and $s^*$ is a GNE for $(S, h; \mathbf{C})$, then $h(s^*) \in F(\mathbf{C})$.

Equivalently, the base relation profile $\mathbf{R}$ can be substituted for the choice function profile $C$ in the preceding definition. Naturally, a social choice (goal) correspondence $F$ is said to be *implementable* over $E$ if there exists a game form $(S, h)$ that implements $F$ over $E$.

To state the generalized Maskin theorem on implementability, we must still define two properties of social choice (goal) correspondences, mono-

tonicity and absence of veto-power (abbreviated as NVP, "no veto-power").
When interpreted in terms of base relations, all our definitions, as well
as the theorems, have wordings that are identical with Maskin's but are
valid over a broader class of profiles. In fact, when the class $E$ of a priori
admissible choice profiles is restricted to those yielding complete transitive base relations, the resulting theorems are precisely those of Maskin.
It might, therefore, seem unnecessary to write out the proofs explicitly,
but I felt that so doing may either dispel any lingering doubts or give the
readers a chance to point out any weaknesses.

A correspondence $F: \mathbf{C} \mapsto Y$, $\mathbf{C} \in E$, $Y \subseteq A$ is said to be *monotone* if the
following condition is satisfied. Let $\mathbf{C} \in E$, $\mathbf{C}' \in E$, and $a \in F(\mathbf{C})$. If it is
the case that, for all $i \in N$ and $x \in A$,[13]

$$a \in C_i(a, x) \quad \text{implies } a \in C_i'(a, x),$$

then

$$a \in F(\mathbf{C}').$$

The correspondence $F$ is said to have the *no veto-power* (NVP) property if the following condition is satisfied. If, for a subset $N^*$ of $N$ that
has either $n$ or $n-1$ members[14] and for all $i \in N^*$,

$$a \in C_i(a, x) \quad \text{for all } x \in A,$$

then

$$a \in F(\mathbf{C}).$$

Within this framework, we can now prove a generalization of Maskin's Theorem 2.

## 5  Some results

**Theorem M′2.** If the correspondence $F$ is implementable on $E$, it is monotone on $E$.

*Proof:* Let $\mathbf{C} \in E$ and $a \in F(\mathbf{C})$. Since $(S, h)$ implements $F$ on $E$, it follows from condition 1 in the definition of implementation that there exists
an $s^* \in S$ such that $s^*$ is a GNE for $(S, h; \mathbf{C})$ and

$$a = h(s^*).$$

Hence, by the definition of GNE, for all $i \in N$,

$$h(s^*) \in C_i(a, h(t, i/s^*)) \quad \text{for all } t \in S_i.$$

Now let $C'$ be such that, for all $i \in N$,

$$a \in C_i(a, x) \text{ implies } a \in C_i'(a, x) \quad \text{for all } x \in A.$$

It follows that

$$a \in C_i'(a, h(t, i/s^*)) \quad \text{for all } t \in S_i.$$

But since $a = h(s^*)$, this means that $s^*$ is a GNE for $(S, h; C')$. This, together with the hypothesis that $(S, h)$ implements $F$ over $E$, implies (by condition 2 in the definition of implementation) that $a \in F(C')$. So $F$ is monotone.    Q.E.D.

In its full generality, Maskin's main result (the sufficiency part of his Theorem 5) can be stated as follows:

**Theorem M.** Let the number of members be $n \geq 3$ and let the class of a priori admissible environments be $E = E_1 \times \cdots \times E_n$ where $E_i$ is a class of binary relations $R_i$ on the outcome set $A$, with all $R_i$ reflexive, transitive, and complete. Let goal correspondence $F: E \twoheadrightarrow A$ be monotone and have the NVP property. Then $F$ is Nash implementable over $E$.

It is our claim that this result is true without the assumption that all $R_i$ be transitive and complete. One way of showing this is to mimic a complete proof of Theorem M, such as that in Saijo (1985), originally intended for transitive complete $R_i$'s and show that these two assumptions can be dispensed with.

But there are advantages in following Maskin's original schema of proof. This schema breaks the proof of Theorem M into two stages, contained respectively in Maskin's Theorem 4 ($= $ M4) and in the construction used in the proof of his Theorem 5 ($= $ M5). Theorem M4 states that under the hypotheses of Theorem M above, the choice correspondence $F$ is Nash implementable if there exists a game form satisfying three properties (equivalent to those in Theorem M*4 below). The construction in the proof of M5 and the corresponding result in Williams (1984a, b) state circumstances under which such a form exists, although these circumstances are more restrictive than those postulated in Theorem M. However, as seen from Saijo (1985), an alternative proof establishes the validity of Theorem M without any additional restrictions.

To show that in M4 transitivity and completeness can be dispensed with, we first state and prove what we shall call Theorem M*4, using a strategy space corresponding to that of M4 but in terms of choice functions $C_i$ rather than reflexive binary relations $R_i$. Under our assumptions on the $C_i$'s, this amounts to extending M4 to relations $R_i$ that are reflexive but not necessarily transitive or complete.

But M4 (and hence also M*4) is inadequate to establish M (or its generalization) because (see Williams 1984a, b) the strategy space it uses is insufficient to yield a game form satisfying properties (i), (ii), (iii) of M*4 for all economies covered by Theorem M (or its generalization dispensing with transitivity and completeness). If we want to retain Maskin's two-stage schema, it is necessary to modify the strategy space. One such modification was suggested in an unpublished communication (November 2, 1984) by an author whose identity is not known to me.

For this modified strategy space (which is merely an expansion of that in M4 or M*4), it is possible to prove, without assuming transitivity or completeness, an analogue of Theorem M*4, with three properties that constitute only a slight modification of those in M4 or M*4. This result is given in the appendix as Lemma 1.

Furthermore, as shown in Lemma 2, the game form suggested by the unidentified author satisfies the requirements of Lemma 1. The two Lemmas together then yield a result, Theorem M′, that generalizes Theorem M to environments with "unordered preferences" (i.e., without assuming transitivity or completeness). Thus Theorem M′ may be regarded as our main result. However, we first state and prove the more limited M*4, partly to clarify the relationship of our results to those of Maskin and partly to exhibit the basic ideas of the proof in a simpler setting. Theorem M′ is stated following M*4. The two lemmas constituting the proof of M′ are found in the appendix.

To make this essay relatively self-contained, we outline a number of proofs largely due to others, since they have to be pieced together from several references not always easily accessible. Let it be acknowledged, however, that major credit is due to Maskin, Saijo, Williams, and the unidentified author, whereas the contribution of this essay is only marginal.

**Theorem M*4.** Let $n \geq 3$, and $E = E_1 \times \cdots \times E_n$, each $E_i$ consisting of choice functions [15] $C_i$ satisfying the conditions $C_i(\{x, y\}) \subseteq \{x, y\}$, and $C_i(\{x\}) = x$, and let $F$ be monotone and have the NVP property. Then $F$ is Nash implementable over $E$ if there exists a game form $(S, h)$ such that $S = S_1 \times \cdots \times S_n$, with each element $s_i$ of $S_i$ of the form $s_i = (\mathbf{C}, a)$, $\mathbf{C} = (C_1, \ldots, C_n)$, $a \in F(\mathbf{C})$, and such that the outcome function $h$ has the following three properties:

(i) *(Unanimity.)* If there is $(\mathbf{C}, a)$, $\mathbf{C} \in E$, such that $s_1 = \cdots = s_n = (\mathbf{C}, a)$, $a \in F(\mathbf{C})$, then $h(s_1, \ldots, s_n) = a$.

(ii) *(Quasi-unanimity.)* If there is $(\mathbf{C}, a)$, $\mathbf{C} \in E$, $a \in F(\mathbf{C})$, such that for $i \in N$,

$$s_j = (\mathbf{C}, a) \quad \text{for all } j \in N \setminus \{i\},$$

then[16]

$$h(S_i, s_{-i}) = \{x \in A : a \in C_i(a, x)\}.$$

(iii) If $i \in N$ is such that there does not exist $(\mathbf{C}, a)$, $\mathbf{C} \in E$, $a \in F(\mathbf{C})$, with

$$(\mathbf{C}, a) = s_1 = \cdots = s_{i-1} = s_{i+1} = \cdots = s_n,$$

then

$$h(S_i, s_{-i}) = A.$$

*Proof of Theorem M\*4.*

*Claim A:* If $a \in F(\mathbf{C})$, $\mathbf{C} \in E$, then $\exists \bar{s} \in S$ such that $\bar{s}$ is a GNE for $(S, h; \mathbf{C})$ and $a = h(\bar{s})$.

*Proof of Claim A:* Let $a \in F(\mathbf{C})$ and $\bar{s} = (\bar{s}_1, \ldots, \bar{s}_n)$, with $\bar{s}_i = (\mathbf{C}, a)$ for all $i \in N$. By property (i), $h(\bar{s}) = a$. We show that $\bar{s}$ is a GNE for $(S, h; \mathbf{C})$. It is sufficient to show that no one can benefit by defecting. Now, for any defection, property (ii) would apply. That is, for any $i \in N$,

$$h(S_i, \bar{s}_{-i}) = \{x \in A : a \in C_i(a, x)\},$$

so that

$$a \in C_i(a, x) \quad \text{for all } x \in h(S_i, \bar{s}_{-i}) \text{ and } i \in N.$$

But, since $a = h(\bar{s})$, this means that

$$h(\bar{s}) \in C_i(a, x) \quad \text{for all } x \in h(S_i, \bar{s}_{-i}) \text{ and } i \in N.$$

So $\bar{s}$ is a GNE.

*Claim B:* If $a$ is a GNE outcome for $(S, h; \mathbf{C})$, where $\mathbf{C}$ is some element of $E$, then $a \in F(\mathbf{C})$.

*Proof:* Since $a$ is a GNE outcome for $(S, h; \mathbf{C})$, there exists $\bar{s} \in \bar{S}$ such that $\bar{s}$ is a GNE for $(S, h; \mathbf{C})$ and $h(\bar{s}) = a$.

*Case B.1 (Unanimity):* Let $\bar{s}$ be unanimous. That is, there exist some $\mathbf{C}' \in E$, $a \in F(\mathbf{C}')$, such that $s_i = (\mathbf{C}', a)$ for all $i \in N$. We must show that $a \in F(\mathbf{C})$. Since $a \in F(\mathbf{C}')$, it is sufficient in view of the assumed monotonicity of $F$ to establish that, for all $i \in N$,

(\*)     $a \in C_i'(a, x) \Rightarrow a \in C_i(a, x) \quad \text{for all } x \in A.$

To prove (∗), let us suppose that $a \in C'_i(a, x)$. Since $a$ is a GNE outcome for **C**, it must be that

$$a \in C_i(a, x) \quad \text{for all } x \in h(S_i, \bar{s}_{-i}).$$

But then property (ii), applied to member $i$, yields

$$h(S_i, \bar{s}_{-i}) = \{x \in A : a \in C'_i(a, x)\}.$$

That is, $a \in C_i(a, x)$ for all $x$ such that $a \in C'_i(a, x)$, which is precisely (∗).

*Case B.2 (Absence of unanimity):* Let $\bar{s}$ be a nonunanimous GNE over $E$ for $(S, h; \mathbf{C})$. Since there is no unanimity, there exist $i$ and $j$ such that

$$\bar{s}_i \neq \bar{s}_j.$$

To simplify notation and without loss of generality, let $i = n-1$, $j = n$, so that

$$\bar{s}_{n-1} \neq \bar{s}_n. \tag{1}$$

Hence, for any $r \in \{1, \ldots, n-2\}$, the hypothesis of property (iii) is satisfied, so that

$$h(S_r, \bar{s}_{-r}) = A \quad \text{for } r \in \{1, \ldots, n-2\},$$

and so, since $a$ is a GNE outcome for **C**,

$$a \in C_r(a, x) \quad \text{for all } x \in A \text{ and } r \in \{1, \ldots, n-2\}. \tag{2}$$

Furthermore, it must be that either $\bar{s}_{n-1} \neq \bar{s}_1$ or $\bar{s}_n \neq \bar{s}_1$, since otherwise $\bar{s}_{n-1} = \bar{s}_n$, contrary to (1). Suppose, without loss of generality, that

$$\bar{s}_n \neq \bar{s}_1. \tag{3}$$

But then the hypothesis of property (iii) is satisfied for member $n-1$, since it is not the case that $\bar{s}_1 = \cdots = \bar{s}_{n-2} = \bar{s}_n$. Hence, by property (iii),

$$h(S_{n-1}, \bar{s}_{-(n-1)}) = A,$$

and, by reasoning analogous to that used above with respect to member $r$, we have

$$a \in C_{n-1}(a, x) \quad \text{for all } x \in A. \tag{4}$$

But (2) and (4) together satisfy the NVP hypothesis for $F$, since

$$\#\{1, \ldots, n-2, n-1\} = n-1.$$

Applying NVP, we then conclude that

$$a \in F(\mathbf{C}). \tag{5}$$

Q.E.D.

We now state Theorem M', which generalizes Theorem M by deleting from it the requirement that preferences be complete and transitive and introducing other minor modifications.

To relate Theorem M', as well as Lemmas 1 and 2 in the appendix, to Theorem M*4, use the base relation; that is, in M*4 replace **C** by **R**, and interpret $x \in C_i(\{x, y\})$ as $x R_i y$.

**Theorem M'.** Let the following three conditions be satisfied:[17] (1) the class of a priori admissible environments is $E = E_1 \times \cdots \times E_n$, where $E_i$ is a class of reflexive[18] binary relations $R_i$ on the outcome set $A$, and $n$ is the number of members; (2) the goal correspondence $F: E \twoheadrightarrow A$ is monotone and has the NVP property; (3) either (a) $n \geq 2$ and $F(e) = A$ for all $E$, or (b) $n \geq 3$ and $F(e') \neq A$ for some $e' \in E$. Then $F$ is Nash (GNE) implementable over $E$.

This result follows from the two lemmas stated and proved in the appendix.

## 6    Nonvacuousness of the hypotheses

In this section, we show that for environments including nontransitive and incomplete base relation profiles there exist social choice correspondences satisfying the hypotheses of the above theorems.

**Example 1.**[19] Assume that, for every $\mathbf{C} = (C_1, \ldots, C_n)$ in $E$, there are two distinct outcomes $a$ and $b$ in $A$ and a member $j$ in $N$ such that $a \in C_j(a, b)$, that is, $a R_j b$. Define the social choice rule by

$$F(\mathbf{C}) = \{x \in A : \exists i \text{ with } x \in C_i(x, y) \text{ for some } x, y \in A, x \neq y\}.$$

By hypothesis, $F(\mathbf{C})$ is nonempty for every $\mathbf{C}$ in $E$. It is obvious that $F$ satisfies the NVP property. It remains to establish monotonicity. Suppose then that $x \in F(\mathbf{C})$ for some $x \in A$ and $\mathbf{C} \in E$. Then there is $y \in A$, $y \neq x$, such that $x \in C_i(x, y)$. Now consider $\mathbf{C}'$ such that, for all $i \in N$ and $z \in A$,

$$x \in C_i(x, z) \text{ implies } x \in C_i'(x, z),$$

so that, in particular, $x \in C_i'(x, y)$.

But then, by definition of $F(\cdot)$, $x \in F(\mathbf{C}')$. So $F$ is monotone.

**Example 2.**[20] Let $A$ be finite and assume $C_i(x, y) \neq \varnothing$ for all $i \in N$ and $x, y \in A$.[21] Here, for some fixed $a \in A$,

$$F(\mathbf{C}) = \{a\} \cup \{x \in A : \exists i \text{ such that } x \in C_i(x, y) \text{ for all } y \in A\}.$$

Since $a \in F(\mathbf{C})$ for all $\mathbf{C} \in A$, $F(\mathbf{C})$ is never empty. The NVP property and monotonicity are established as in Example 1.

**Example 3.** Let $A$ be finite and $C_i(x, y) \neq \varnothing$ for all $i \in N$ and $x, y \in A$. Assume furthermore that for at least one member $i$, the base relations in $E_i$ are transitive. Define

$$F(\mathbf{C}) = \{x \in A : \exists i \text{ such that } x \in C_i(x, y) \text{ for all } y \in A\}.$$

Again we see that $F(\mathbf{C}) \neq \varnothing$ for all $C$ in $E = E_1 \times \cdots \times E_n$, and $F$ has NVP and monotonicity.

It is clear that in Example 2 $F(\mathbf{C})$ may yield outcomes that are not Pareto optimal. But this is symptomatic of a more general problem. If $E$ is broad enough to admit cyclical preferences, and $F : E \twoheadrightarrow A$ is monotone, then even weak Pareto optimality may be violated. This is seen in the next example.

**Example 4.** Let $A = \{a, b, c\}$. Using base relation notation, suppose that for some $\mathbf{C}$ and some $i$ we have a cycle

$$a P_i b P_i c P_i a.$$

Since by definition of a social choice correspondence $F(\mathbf{C}) \neq \varnothing$, we may suppose without loss of generality that $a \in F(\mathbf{C})$. Consider now $\mathbf{C}'$ in $E$ such that

$$c P_i' a P_i' b \quad \text{and} \quad c P_i' b.$$

Suppose further that for all $j \in N \setminus \{i\}$

$$C_j' = C_j.$$

Then, for all $k \in N$ and $x \in A$,

$$a \in C_k(a, x) \text{ implies } a \in C_k'(a, x).$$

Since $a \in F(\mathbf{C})$, the hypothesis in the definition of monotonicity is satisfied, and so

$$a \in F(\mathbf{C}').$$

Suppose now that for all $j \in N \setminus \{i\}$

$$b P_j a,$$

hence also

$$b P_j' a.$$

(This does involve a loss of generality.) Then $a$ is not even weakly Pareto optimal (since in $\mathbf{C}'$ everybody strictly prefers $c$ to $a$), yet $a$ is desirable according to $F$ for $\mathbf{C}$ in the sense that $a \in F(\mathbf{C}')$. So $F$ is not weak Pareto optimal over $E$ of this example.

### Appendix

The proof of Theorem M$'$ is broken up into two stages. The first is a counterpart of Maskin's Theorem 4 – Lemma 1 in this appendix;[22] it states that if there exists a game form having certain properties, one of which relates the game form to the social goal function, then this goal function is (GNE) Nash implementable. The second stage – to be called Lemma 2[23] – exhibits a game form having the properties required in Lemma 1.

**Lemma 1.** Let $E = E_1 \times \cdots \times E_n$ where each $E_i$ is a class of reflexive binary relations on $A$; let $F: E \twoheadrightarrow A$ be monotone and have the NVP property. If there exists a game form $(S, h)$, with $S$ defined in equations (6) and (7), and either (a) $n \geq 2$, $F(e) = A$ for all $e \in E$ and $h$ has Properties I and II introduced below, or (b) $n \geq 3$, $F(e') \neq A$ for some $e' \in E$, and $h$ has Properties I, II, and III, then $(S, h)$ implements $F$ in Nash (GNE) equilibria.

It is assumed that

$$S = S_1 \times \cdots \times S_n, \tag{6}$$

where, for each $i \in N$,

$$S_i = E \times A \times M, \tag{7}$$

where $M$ is an arbitrary set.

An element of $S_i$ is written

$$s_i = (e^i, a_i, m_i) = (t_i, m_i),$$

where[24] $e^i \in E$, $a \in A$, $m_i \in M$, and, by definition, $t_i = (e^i, a_i)$.[25]

*Property I.* If there exists $\bar{t} = (\bar{e}, \bar{a}) \in E \times A$ such that

$$t_i = \bar{t} \quad \text{for all } i \in N,$$

and

$$\bar{a} \in F(\bar{e}),$$

then, for $s = ((\bar{t}, m_i))_{i \in N}$,

$$h(s) = \bar{a}.$$

*Property II.* If there exists $\bar{t} = (\bar{e}, \bar{a}) \in E \times A$ such that[26]

$$t_k = \bar{t} \quad \text{for all } k \in N \setminus \{j\},$$

and

$$\bar{a} \in F(\bar{e}),$$

then, for $s_{-j} = ((\bar{t}, m_k))_{k \in N \setminus \{j\}}$,

$$h(S_j, s_{-j}) = \{x \in A : \bar{a} \, R_j(\bar{e}) \, x\}.$$

[Here $R_j(\bar{e})$ is the binary relation of member $j$ specified by $\bar{e}$; i.e., if $\bar{e} = (\bar{e}_1, \ldots, \bar{e}_n)$, $\bar{e}_k \in E_k$, we have $R_j(\bar{e}) = \bar{e}_j$.]

*Property III*

*III.1* If there exists $\bar{t} = (\bar{e}, \bar{a}) \in E \times A$ such that

$$t_i = \bar{t} \quad \text{for all } i \in N,$$

but

$$\bar{a} \notin F(\bar{e}),$$

then, for $s_{-i} = ((\bar{t}, m_k))_{k \in N \setminus \{i\}}$,

$$h(S_i, s_{-i}) = A \quad \text{for all } i \in N.$$

*III.2* If there exists $\bar{t} = (\bar{e}, \bar{a}) \in E \times A$ such that

$$t_k = \bar{t} \quad \text{for all } k \in N \setminus \{j\},$$

but

$$\bar{a} \notin F(\bar{e}),$$

then, for $s_{-j} = ((\bar{t}, m_k))_{k \in N \setminus \{j\}}$,

$$h(S_j, s_{-j}) = A.$$

*III.3* If $j \neq k \neq v \neq j$ and $t_k \neq t_v$, then

$$h(S_j, s_{-j}) = A.$$

*Proof:* We first note that Properties I and II are sufficient for the implementability of $F$ when $F(e) = A$ for all $e \in E$. Clearly, when all outcomes are in $F(e)$, every Nash outcome is in $F(e)$. On the other hand, the proof that every element of $A$ can be attained (through unanimity as to $t$'s) as a Nash outcome does not require that $n \geq 3$ and does not use Property III. This is seen from the proof of Claim A in Theorem M*4, using the base relation, that is, interpreting $x \in C_i(\{x, y\})$ as $x R_i y$.

Suppose now that $F(e') \neq A$ for some $e' \in E$. Then, by hypothesis, $h$ has Properties I, II, and III and $n \geq 3$. That every $F(e)$ outcome is attainable as a Nash outcome is proved as in Claim A of Theorem M*4, interpreting $x \in C_i(\{x, y\})$ as $x R_i y$. The proof that every Nash outcome is $F$-optimal parallels that of Claim B in Theorem M*4 except for those Nash equilibria $\bar{s}$ with unanimity (respectively, quasi-unanimity) in which $\bar{a} \notin F(e)$. But here we use Property III.1 (respectively, III.2) of $h$ and the NVP assumption on $F$ to conclude that $h(\bar{s}) \in F(e)$. For, in either case, $h(S_i, s_{-i}) = A$ and, by the NE property of $\bar{s}$, $h(\bar{s}) R_i(e_i) h(s_i, \bar{s}_{-i})$ either for all $i \in N$ (under unanimity) or for all $i \in N \setminus \{j\}$ (under quasi-unanimity) and for all $s_i \in S_i$. Hence, $h(\bar{s})$ is the top choice in $A$ for at least $n-1$ agents, which, by NVP, implies that $h(\bar{s}) \in F(e)$. This completes the argument.    Q.E.D.

*Remark 1:* It will be noted that the $m_i$ component of $s_i$ plays no role in the proof. Essentially, the $t$'s here play the role of the $s$'s in the original Maskin Theorem 4.

*Remark 2:* The proof for the case where $F(e') \neq A$ for some $e' \in E$ follows that given by Saijo for his Lemma 4.1 (1985), since his proof uses no properties of $R_i$ other than reflexivity. The fact that Properties I and II are sufficient when $\#E = 1$, say $E = \{e^*\}$, and $F(e^*) = A$ was pointed out by Williams in a private communication. He also noted that the game form of Lemma 2 need not satisfy Property III when $E = \{e^*\}$, $F(e^*) = A$, and $\#A = 2$. It is for this reason that Lemma 1 (unlike Maskin's Theorem 4 and our Theorem M*4) allows for the case where $F(e) = A$ for all $e \in E$.

**Lemma 2.** Let $E = E_1 \times \cdots \times E_n$ and let each $E_i$ be a class of reflexive binary relations on $A$. Let $S^* = E \times A \times M$, with the set $M$ given by $M = \{0, 1, \ldots, n-1\}$, and let the outcome function $h^*$ be defined by the three rules stated below. Then the game form $(S^*, h^*)$, with $S^* = S_1 \times \cdots \times S_n$ and $S_i = E \times A \times M$ for all $i \in N$, has the properties postulated for $(S, h)$ in Lemma 1.

*Rule 1:* If there exists $\bar{t} = (\bar{e}, \bar{a}) \in E \times A$ such that

$$t_i = \bar{t} \quad \text{for all } i \in N,$$

and

$$\bar{a} \in F(\bar{e}),$$

then, for $s^* = ((\bar{t}, m_i))_{i \in N}$, with the $m_i$'s arbitrary,

$$h^*(s^*) = \bar{a}.$$

*Rule 2:* If there exists $\bar{t} = (\bar{e}, \bar{a}) \in E \times A$ such that

$$t_k = \bar{t} \quad \text{for all } k \in N \setminus \{j\},$$

and

$$\bar{a} \in F(\bar{e}),$$

then, for $s_j^* = (e^j, a_j, m_j)$ and $s_{-j}^* = ((\bar{t}, m_k))_{k \in N \setminus \{j\}}$, with $m_j$ and $m_k$ arbitrary,

$$h^*(s^*) \equiv h^*(s_j^*, s_{-j}^*) = \begin{cases} a_j & \text{if } \bar{a} R_j(\bar{e}) a_j, \\ \bar{a} & \text{otherwise.} \end{cases}$$

[Here $R_j(\bar{e})$ is the binary relation of member $j$ specified by $\bar{e}$; i.e., if $\bar{e} = (\bar{e}_1, ..., \bar{e}_n)$, $\bar{e}_k \in E_k$, we have $R_j(\bar{e}) = \bar{e}_j$.][27]

*Rule 3:* Suppose that neither the hypothesis of Condition 1 nor the hypothesis of Condition 2 holds. Let $s^* = ((e^i, a_i, m_i))_{i \in N}$, and

$$r = 1 + \left( \sum_{p \in N} m_p \right)_{\mathrm{mod}\, n}.$$

Then

$$h^*(s^*) = a_r.$$

*Proof.*

**1.** Clearly, the game form $(S^*, h^*)$ has Property I of Lemma 1 since the respective hypotheses and conclusions in Property I and Rule 1 are identical.

**2.** To see that $(S^*, h^*)$ has Property II of Lemma 1, note that the hypotheses in Rule 2 [quasi-unanimity as to the $t$'s, and $\bar{a} \in F(\bar{e})$] are the same as in Property II. It suffices, therefore, to show that under these hypotheses Rule 2 implies $h^*(S_j^*, s_{-j}) = \{x \in A : \bar{a} R_j(\bar{e}) x\}$, with $s_{-j} = ((\bar{t}, m_k))_{k \in N \setminus \{j\}}$. Now if $\bar{a} R_j(\bar{e}) x$, then $x = h^*(S_j^*, s_{-j})$ for $s_j = (e^i, x, m_j)$. On the other hand, if $y \in h^*(S_j^*, s_{-j})$, one of the two alternatives in Rule 2 must be satisfied; that is, $y = h^*(s_j, s_{-j})$, $s_j = (e^i, a_j, m_j)$, and either $y = a_j$, $\bar{a} R_j(\bar{e}) a_j$, or $y = \bar{a}$. But, by reflexivity of $R_j$, we also have $\bar{a} R_j(\bar{e}) y$ in the latter case. The equality $h^*(S_j^*, s_{-j}) = \{x \in A : \bar{a} R_j(\bar{e}) x\}$ follows.

Since the argument in parts 1 and 2 of this proof do not restrict $F$ in any way, we have now established that $h^*$ satisfies the requirements of case (a) in Lemma 1.

**3.** It remains to show that $(S^*, h^*)$ satisfies Property III of Lemma 1 when $n \geq 3$ and it is not the case that $F(e) = A$ for all $e \in E$.

**3.1.** We first show that Property III.1 is satisfied. Here we have unanimity as to the $\bar{t}$'s, but $\bar{a} \notin F(\bar{e})$. We must show, for $s_{-i} = ((\bar{t}, m_k))_{k \in N \setminus \{i\}}$ and any $y \in A$, there is $s_i \in S_i^*$ such that $h^*(s_i, s_{-i}) = y$. Since $\bar{a} \notin F(\bar{e})$ implies that Rule 3 applies, this is accomplished by agent $i$ choosing $s_i = (e^i, y, m_i)$ with $m_i$ such that $1 + (m_i + \sum_{r \neq i} m_r)_{\mathrm{mod}\, n} = i$.

**3.2.** Next we show that Property III.2 is satisfied. Here we have quasi-unanimity as to the $t$'s and, again, $\bar{a} \notin F(\bar{e})$, so that Rule 3 applies. For any agent $p$, define $\hat{m}_p$ by $(1 + \hat{m}_p + \sum_{r \neq p} m_r)_{\mathrm{mod}\, n} = p$. Under the hypotheses of Property III.2, for any $y \in A$, if agent $j$ chooses $s_j = (e^j, y, \hat{m}_j)$, $e^j$ arbitrary, then Rule 3 applies and $h^*(s_j, s_{-j}) = y$. Hence $(S^*, h^*)$ satisfies III.2.

**3.3.** Finally, we must show that, when $F(e') \neq A$ for some $e' \in E$, Property III.3 is satisfied; that is, if $j \neq k \neq v \neq j$, $t_k \neq t_v$, and $y \in A$, then there is $s_j \in S_j$ such that $h^*(s_j, s_{-j}) = y$.

Suppose first that $\#E \geq 2$. If $a_v \neq a_k$, then any $a \in A$ can be attained by $j$ using Rule 3 through the choice $s_j = (e^j, y, \hat{m}_j)$, where, for $r \in \{k, v\}$, $e^j$ is chosen so that $e^j \neq e^r$ if $y = a^r$. If $a_v = a_k$, the hypothesis $t_k \neq t_v$ implies $e^k \neq e^r$. Any $y \neq a_v$ can be attained by $j$ using Rule 3 through the choice $s_j = (e^j, y, \hat{m}_j)$, where $e^j$ is arbitrary. When $y = a_v$, let $j$ choose $s_j = (e^j, a', \hat{m}_v)$, so that Rule 3 again applies but it is agent $v$'s proposal that is implemented ($e^j$ is again arbitrary). In all of these cases, $h^*(s_j, s_{-j}) = y$.

It remains to consider the case $\#E = 1$, say $E = \{e^0\}$, $n \geq 3$, and $F(e^0) \neq A$. Since the above arguments established Properties I, II, III.1, and III.2 for this case, it only remains to be shown that Property III.3 holds when $E = \{e^0\}$, $n \geq 3$, and $F(e^0) \neq A$. Here, by hypothesis, $t_k \neq t_v$, that is, $(e^k, a_k) \neq (e^v, a_v)$. Since $e^k = e^v = e^0$, it must be that $a_k \neq a_v$. We need only show that $A \subseteq h^*(S_j^*, s_{-j})$, since the reverse inclusion is obvious.

Then let $y \in A$. If $a_k \neq y \neq a_v$, let $j$ choose $s_j = (e^0, y, m_j^*)$, and Rule 3 applies since $a_k$, $a_v$, and $a_j = y$ are distinct. Hence $h^*(S_j, s_{-j}) = y$.

On the other hand, let $y = a_r$, $r \in \{k, v\}$. Then let $j$ choose

$$s_j = (e^0, a', m_r^*) \quad \text{where } a' \notin F(e^0),$$

so that Rule 3 is again applicable. [Such an $a'$ exists because $F(e^0) \neq A$.] Hence $h^*(s_j, s_{-j}) = a_r$.        Q.E.D.

*Remark 3:* The game form $(S^*, h^*)$ of Lemma 2 whose strategy domain has the additional component $M$ was originally suggested (in November 1984) in an unpublished communication by an author whose identity is not known to me, after Williams (1984a, b) pointed out the problems arising when the smaller (Maskin 1977) strategy spaces are used. In this communication, it was also asserted (but not proved) that $(S^*, h^*)$ implements a monotone NVP when $n \geq 3$. The first proof (for cases other than $n = 3$, $\#A = 2$, $\#E = 1$) was provided in Saijo (1985).

Specifically, for cases other than those with $n = 3$, $\#A = 2$, and $\#E = 1$, Theorem 4.4 in Saijo (1985) shows that the above game form has Properties I, II, and III. Saijo's proof of Theorem 4.4. uses neither completeness nor transitivity and so carries over in our Lemma 2. But Saijo's proof of implementability for the case $n = 3$, $\#A = 2$ (his Lemma 5.3) uses a different game form and makes explicit use of completeness, and hence is not suitable for our purposes. An earlier version of the present essay contained a separate argument covering the case $n = 3$, $\#A = 2$, and $\#E > 1$ without assuming completeness (transitivity is trivial when $\#A = 2$) for the game form of Lemma 2. Subsequently, a suggestion due to Williams (in a private communication) helped simplify a part of the proof showing that, except when $E = \{e^*\}$, $\#A = 2$, and $F(e^*) = A$, the above game form has Property III. With Saijo's and Williams' kind permission, their arguments are merged to yield most of the above proof of Lemma 2.

## NOTES

1  In retrospect, this seems obvious to the point of triviality. However, I am not aware of any prior contributions on this issue. Implicitly or explicitly, individuals' preferences have been assumed to be complete preorderings [often called orderings, as in Maskin (1977, p. 4)]. In Maskin (1983; 1984, pp. 4–5), individual preferences are represented by (real-valued) utility functions. Williams (1984a, pp. 3–4; 1984b, p. 3) explicitly postulates a complete preordering, hence transitivity.
2  We use the term *attitudes* to encompass preferences and choice functions.
3  This approach is used in Aizerman and Aleskerov (1985).
4  In particular, if the attitudes of group $i$ can be represented by a weak preference relation $\rho_i$ (reflexive, total, transitive) on $A$, then, for any $X \subseteq A$, $C_i(X) = \{x \in X : x \rho_i y \text{ for all } y \in X\}$.
5  Here and elsewhere $C_i$ stands for the functional relation $C_i(\cdot)$.
6  The customary terms are social choice rule or correspondence. I am using the term *goal* to emphasize the contrast with a function, say $\Psi_\pi : (X, \mathbf{C}) \mapsto Y$, called the *performance* function *of a mechanism* $\pi$. The two functions have the same respective domains and ranges, but $F$ refers to the desiderata (independent of the mechanism to be used), whereas $\Psi_\pi$ describes the workings of a particular mechanism. Using this notation, we say that $F$ is *implementable* if there is a mechanism $\pi$ such that $F = \Psi_\pi$. A set-valued function such as $F$ is, of course, a correspondence.
7  Arrow's (1951) social choice function may be viewed as a special case where the individual choice functions are defined as maximizers of individual orderings

and $F$ selects $Y$ by first choosing a social choice ordering $\rho^s = \phi(\rho)$ and then selecting $Y = \{x \in X : x \text{ maximizes } \rho^s \text{ over } X\}$. (Here $\phi$ is a social welfare function.)

8   This, in particular, is true of the Aizerman and Aleskerov study (1985).

9   Shafer and Sonnenschein (1975, p. 346) base their concept of equilibrium on that of an abstract economy $\Gamma = (X_i, A_i, P_i)_{i=1}^n$, where $X_i$ is the $i$th individual's choice set and $A_i$ as well as $P_i$ are correspondences from $X$ into $X_i$, with $X = X_1 \times \cdots \times X_n$. An *equilibrium* for $\Gamma$ is a point $\bar{x} = (\bar{x}_1, \ldots, \bar{x}_n)$ in $X$ such that, for each $i \in \{1, \ldots, n\}$, $\bar{x}_i \in A_i(\bar{x})$ and $P_i(\bar{x}) \cap A_i(\bar{x}) = \emptyset$. One of the assumptions used in their theorem [condition (c″), p. 347] implies that $x_i \notin P_i(x)$ for all $x \in X$. Subject to a reformulation that would make $P_i$ into a correspondence from $X$ into $X$, the *correspondence* $P_i$ can be interpreted as defining a strict preference *relation* on $X$, with condition (c″) implying its irreflexivity. In this essay, the strict preference relation $P_i$ is also irreflexive since it is defined as the asymmetric part of a reflexive relation $R_i$. A concept of Nash equilibrium in the spirit of the Shafer–Sonnenschein notion of equilibrium is introduced in Section 4, Definition 2. In one respect the concept of Generalized Nash Equilibrium in this essay is less general than that of Shafer and Sonnenschein [or even Debreu (1952)] because it has nothing like the correspondence $A_i(x)$, which makes a player's strategy domain dependent on the strategic choices of others.

10  So the domain of $C_i$ could be restricted to the collection of one- and two-element subsets of $A$.

11  From now on, we shall often write $C_i(x, y)$ for $C_i(\{x, y\})$.

12  Following the presentation of an earlier version of this essay at the IMSSS seminar, Joseph Greenberg (1985) suggested the following definition [here to be denoted by $GNE_2'(C)$]: An element $s^* \in S$ is a $GNE_2'(C)$ if and only if, for all $i \in N$ and $t \in S_i$, either

$$h^*(s^*) \in C_i(h(s^*), h(t, i/s^*)) \quad \text{or} \quad C_i(h(s^*), h(t, i/s^*)) = \emptyset.$$

It can be seen that $s^*$ is a $GNE_2'(C)$ for $\Gamma(C) = (S, h; \mathbf{C})$ if and only if it is a $GNE_2(P)$ for $\Gamma(P) = (S, h; \mathbf{P})$, where $P_i$ is the asymmetric part of the base relation $R_i$ for $C_i$, $i \in N$.

Greenberg also conjectured that some or all of our theorems are valid with $GNE_2'(C)$ replacing $GNE_1(R)$ and a modified concept of monotonicity. It was the stimulus of his suggestion, combined with the exposure to Kim and Richter (1985), that resulted in the above extension of our results from $GNE_1(R)$ to $GNE_1(P)$. However, the concept of monotonicity we use in this extension (substituting $\rho_i$, as defined above, for $R_i$ in our definition of monotonicity) seems somewhat different from that proposed by Greenberg.

13  Here $x$ need not be different from $a$. Recall that in this context $\{a, a\}$ is interpreted as the singleton $\{a\}$.

14  That is, either $N^* = N$ or there is a group $j$ such that $N^* = N \setminus \{j\}$.

15  Or, equivalently, of reflexive binary relations $R_i$.

16  We write $s_{-i} = (s_1, \ldots, s_{i-1}, s_{i+1}, \ldots, s_n)$, and $h(S_i, s_{-i}) = \{y \in A : y = h(t, i/s)$ for some $t \in S_i\}$.

17  Note that condition (3) does not exclude any cases satisfying (1) and (2) when $n \geq 3$, and it also covers certain (admittedly not very interesting) cases with $n < 3$. Hence Theorem M' is a generalization of Theorem M.

18  But not necessarily transitive or complete.

19  This example is due to Joel Sobel of the University of California, San Diego.

20  This example is a modification, due to Joel Sobel, of Example 3.

21  This is, the corresponding base relation $R_i$ is complete for all $i \in N$.

22  This Lemma 1 corresponds to Lemma 4.1 in Saijo (1985).

23  Corresponding roughly to Theorem 4.4 in Saijo (1985) but less general with respect to the class of strategy spaces covered.

24  Here $e^i$ can be interpreted as $i$'s "guess" as to what the environment is. For $e \in E = E_1 \times \cdots \times E_n$, we have $e^i = (e_1^i, \ldots, e_n^i)$, where $e_j^i \in E_j$ is $i$'s guess as to $j$'s characteristic.

   Unlike in Maskin (1977), but like in Maskin (1984), it is not required here that $a_i \in F(e^i)$.

25  When $M$ is a singleton, we can identify $S_i$ with $E \times A$.

26  Note that if there are two players $j'$ and $j''$ for whom the hypothesis of Rule II holds, then there is unanimity, so Rule I also applies. But there is no inconsistency.

27  If more than one player satisfies the hypothesis of Condition 2, there is unanimity, so Condition 1 also applies. But in that case, for each such $j$, $a_j = a$. So the value of $h^*(s_j^*, s_{-j}^*) = a$ according to both conditions, and there is no contradiction.

## REFERENCES

Aizerman, M. A. and F. T. Aleskerov (1985), "Voting operators in the space of choice functions," Social Sciences Working Paper 559, California Institute of Technology.

Arrow, K. J. (1951), *Social choice and individual values,* New York: Wiley; 2nd ed., 1963.

Debreu, G. (1952), "A social equilibrium existence theorem," *Proceedings of the National Academy of Sciences of the U.S.A.,* 38: 886–93.

Greenberg, J. (1985), Letter dated August 9, 1985.

Herzberger, H. G. (1973), "Ordinal preference and rational choice," *Econometrica,* 41: 187–237.

Kim, T. and M. K. Richter (1985), "Non-transitive non-total consumer theory," mimeo.

McKelvey, R. D. (1985), "Game forms for Nash implementation of general social choice correspondences," draft dated July 29, 1985.

Maskin, E. (1977), "Nash equilibrium and welfare optimality," mimeo, M.I.T.

Maskin, E. (1983/1984), "The theory of implementation in Nash equilibrium," M.I.T., Working Paper 333, revised, July 1984.

Saijo, T. (1985), "Nash implementation theory," Ph.D. Thesis, University of Minnesota.

Sen, A. (1977), "Social choice theory: A re-examination," *Econometrica,* 45: 53–89.

Shafer, W. and H. Sonnenschein (1975), "Equilibrium in abstract economies without ordered preferences," *Journal of Economic Theory,* 2: 345–8.

Williams, S. R. (1984a), "Realization and Nash implementation: Two aspects of mechanism design," Institute for Mathematics and Its Applications, University of Minnesota, preprint #69, May 1984.

Williams, S. R. (1984b), "Sufficient conditions for Nash implementation," Institute for Mathematics and Its Applications, University of Minnesota, preprint #70, May 1984.

Williams, S. R. (1985), Letter dated August 22, 1985.

CHAPTER 5

# Walrasian social choice: some simple axiomatic approaches

*Louis Gevers*

This essay attempts to connect more closely competitive analysis with axiomatic social choice theory: The latter was initiated by K. J. Arrow, who also contributed prominently to the former field of study. Our findings are directly related to results obtained earlier by Hurwicz (1979), Schmeidler (1982a), and Binmore (1980c).

We deal with social choice rules, that is, correspondences associating subsets of feasible states with utility profiles that describe consumer preferences. Various requirements may be imposed on social choice rules: These requirements reflect concepts of collective rationality, ethical considerations, and/or informational constraints.

We examine social choice rules defined on a rich domain consistent with the existence of competitive equilibria for every utility profile in a finite economy context. We require them to meet three axioms: (i) full individual rationality, (ii) monotonicity in a rather weak sense, and (iii) nondiscrimination among Pareto-indifferent allocations; for every rule under study, we observe that the set of competitive equilibria is a subset of the image associated with every profile.

The Walras correspondence meets our three axioms; therefore, it may be viewed as the most selective choice rule displaying these properties.

In this chapter, we develop alternative axiom sets leading to an analogous conclusion. The reader is invited to compare them to axiom sets

The author benefited from the hospitality of the Center for Operations Research and Econometrics, Université Catholique de Louvain, while preparing this essay, the first version of which was written at the Dalhousie Public Choice Institute, August 1984. This third revision owes much to P. Hammond's perceptive comments. I wish to thank Cl. d'Aspremont, K. Binmore, P. Champsaur, J. H. Dreze, P. Dubey, J. Greenberg, J. Ledyard, H. Moulin, D. Schmeidler, L. Shapley, W. Thomson, and J. Weymark for useful conversations. All remaining errors are mine. Financial support of the Fonds National de la Recherche Scientifique is gratefully acknowledged.

characterizing other social choice rules. Papers by Maskin (1980) and Thomson (1981) are very useful from this viewpoint.

In Section 1, we attempt to develop the model and the main results in a language that is as little technical as possible. Section 2 contains a formal summary of Section 1, proofs, and some further developments. A comparison of competitive outcomes with allocations resulting from re-distributive linear tax schemes is attempted in Section 3.

## 1     A primer

We shall consider a family of Arrow–Debreu economies that differ only as far as consumer preferences are concerned. By assumption, the econ-omy consists of one firm and a finite set of $m$ consumers. All agents are concerned with a finite set of $\ell$ private commodities. Each consumer's activity is described by a consumption plan, that is, an ordered list of $\ell$ numbers, each positive number denoting the agent's consumption of a particular good and each negative entry designating the reduction of leisure time due to a specific type of work. Each individual's consump-tion plan has to belong to a given set, called consumption set, which is not related to any budgetary constraint but takes into account the indi-vidual's physical and physiological limitations. When we refer to the firm, we also describe its activities by means of an ordered sequence of $\ell$ num-bers, hereafter called production plan. Every such plan has to belong to a given set, called production set, that describes the firm's technological capabilities. An allocation or state of the economy, hereafter denoted $v$, is a complete list made up of one production plan and $m$ consumption plans: thus, it contains a description of all activities deemed relevant in our analysis. Assuming that the initial resources of the economy are fixed, the set of allocations that can be obtained with the amount of resources available is supposed to be nonempty. We call it the set of feasible allo-cations and denote it $V$.

We also assume that every individual $i$ is endowed with a binary prefer-ence relation, which can be represented by a utility function $u_i$, a member of a given set of individual utility functions defined on $i$'s consumption set. Such feelings as pity or envy are thus ruled out by assumption. To complete the description of any particular economy, we select a specific profile $u = (u_i)_{i \in M}$, where $M$ stands for the set of consumers.

Having in mind a purpose that may be either predictive or prescrip-tive, one will want, for each particular economy, to eliminate those states that are in some sense considered unreasonable for the utility profile at hand. In this fashion, one is led to the definition of a social choice rule, that is, a correspondence $f$ that maps every profile $u$ in a given domain onto the nonempty subset of feasible allocations that have not been rejected. Many examples of social choice rules come at once to mind. We proceed by discussing a few of them. We also examine some axioms one might want to impose on them.

Consider, for instance, the rule associating with every profile the corresponding set of Pareto-efficient states, that is, states such that there does not exist other feasible allocations for which at least one consumer is better off and the rest of consumers are not worse off. This Pareto set is usually very large. It is therefore common to require $f$ to be *Pareto efficient,* that is, to select a subset of the Pareto set. However, if information concerning preferences, consumption sets, endowments, and/or participation in production is private, Pareto efficiency may be attainable only at the cost of excessive inequality. It is, of course, possible to treat informational constraints as feasibility constraints and to apply the Pareto criterion in a second-best sense, as we do in Section 3.

At this stage, we introduce private property rights. Each consumer $i$ owns by assumption a fixed initial endowment of goods $w_i$ and a fixed share $\vartheta_i \geq 0$ in the unique firm making up the productive sector so that individual $i$ contributes a fraction $\vartheta_i$ of all inputs and gets a fraction $\vartheta_i$ of all outputs.

Let us consider first the polar case of complete information. Whenever all information about the economy is public knowledge, we can meaningfully introduce another well-known example of social choice rule, namely, the core correspondence, provided we assume that the production set is convex and displays constant returns to scale.

In order to define the core of an economy, we shall introduce some preliminary notions. A coalition is any nonempty subset of $M$. A coalition can always sever its links with the rest of the economy and form a subeconomy so that goods are produced and exchanged by its members in autarky. If a coalition does so or threatens to do so in the face of a proposed allocation, and if some of its members can obtain a utility gain while the others retain their utility level, then we shall say that the coalition can improve upon the proposed allocation.

The core of an economy consists of the subset of feasible allocations that cannot be improved upon by any coalition. If we maintain the assumption of complete information, the core correspondence looks like a forceful implication of the three notions of individual property rights, decentralization, and collective rationality. Thus, if these notions are taken seriously, and if the core correspondence is sufficiently selective, we might stop our investigations. In large economies, where each consumer is insignificant, the core coincides with the set of competitive equilibria, as Debreu and Scarf (1963) showed. This may look quite selective, but this property does not hold in general in the case of finite economies, with which we are concerned.

In conclusion, we may want to retain as an axiom the *core consistency* property: If the core is nonempty for some profile $u$, then $f(u)$ is a subset of the core.

On the other hand, it is desirable to have a social choice rule the use of which does not depend exclusively on a specific cooperative mode of behavior. For this purpose, it is useful to consider a game in strategic form. Each consumer has access to a strategy set $S_i$ defined by the game designer or center. Before the game is played, the latter also informs consumers about the trades associated with every conceivable array of individual strategies. The game is well defined if a feasible allocation $v \in V$ is associated by the rule of the game $g$ with every $m$-tuple of strategies in the set $\prod_i S_i$. Because competitive equilibria are so often referred to in economic theory, it may be worthwhile to point out that competitive budget sets do not fit the strategy set definition even when they are consistent with equilibrium prices; indeed, starting from an equilibrium position with every price positive, the only thing a consumer can do unilaterally is to reduce consumption. Large economies with insignificant consumers do not share this worrying feature.

If we reject the trivial game assigning consumers the no-trade allocation in every case, feasibility raises a serious problem to the game designer in a finite economy whenever the shape of consumption sets and/or the size of individual endowments and/or the extent of their participation to production are private information. This point has been examined by Hurwicz, Maskin, and Postlewaite (1982) and by Maskin (1980). See also the survey papers by Schmeidler (1982b) and by Groves and Ledyard (1984). Suppose, for instance, that the shape of consumption sets is public knowledge, in contrast with endowments and involvement in production. Individual strategies might, for instance, consist of announced trade proposals, or else of announced demand and supply schedules. In a disequilibrium situation, nothing prevents an individual from bluffing by proposing an individually infeasible trade.

Then the center would be well inspired to require consumers to file reports disclosing their endowment and participation in production. This element would thus become integrated in the description of every $S_i$.

Some useful information could then be secured by the center; indeed, exaggerated reports could easily be detected: It is natural to rule them out. Underreporting is thornier to handle: If neither private consumption nor endowments nor productive involvement can be monitored by the center, we call this a situation of imperfect monitoring. In this case, as Maskin (1980) points out, the center will have to allow consumers a no-trade option, since they can report that circumstances have located them on the boundary of their consumption set so that nothing can be taken away from them.

In conclusion, whatever esteem one may have for private rights, prohibitive monitoring costs may justify the *weak individual rationality axiom:* Any $v \in f(u)$ must assign to each $i$ a consumption plan at least as good as a plan resulting from the addition of $i$'s participation in production to his or her initial endowment. If, moreover, the production plan is to be selected so as to maximize $i$'s welfare, we shall say that $f$ is *fully individually rational.*

The last clause is not too generous for $i$ when returns to scale are constant and the production set is convex. Indeed, feasible production plans may then be added or divided arbitrarily. Under these two assumptions, even the last axiom is of course much weaker than the core consistency axiom.

Returning to the rule of the game or game form $g: \prod_i S_i \to V$, we can introduce an equilibrium behavior assumption $e$. This amounts to eliminating systematically all strategy $m$-tuples that fail to display a specific property. Given a particular profile $u$, we can study the corresponding set of equilibrium allocations $g(s_e(u))$.

When individual preferences are private information, the game designer has to choose a constant game form for a whole set of profiles, and we are interested in the equilibrium correspondence $g \circ s_e$. If $f = g \circ s_e$, we say that $f$ is implemented by $g$ in $e$.

The Nash noncooperative equilibrium concept is the best known and simplest one: A strategy $m$-tuple fits this definition if no player can gain by moving away from it unilaterally. Thus, our last axiom may be interpreted as a necessary condition for implementability of $f$ in Nash equilibrium under imperfect monitoring.

Whatever the monitoring constraints may be, implementability of $f$ in Nash equilibrium requires it to display yet another property, namely, *Maskin monotonicity* [see Maskin (1977)]. This is an interprofile property. Take any two profiles $u^0, u^1$ in the domain of $f$. Suppose $v^1 \in f(u^0)$. Consider profile $u^0$ and the subset of $V$ consisting of elements that are not better than $v^1$ from individual $i$'s viewpoint. Suppose it is a subset of the corresponding set for profile $u^1$, and suppose this holds true for every $i$. Then, Maskin monotonicity requires $v^1 \in f(u^1)$.

This property is related to, but stronger than, Arrow's (1951) axiom of positive responsiveness, which is based on $v^1$ getting a higher rank in every $i$'s preference preordering under $u^1$ than under $u^0$, whereas all other alternatives do not change in relation with each other. Arrow's specification is, of course, ill-adapted in the context of continuous preferences.

As Roberts (1979) noted, Maskin monotonicity is required for implementation both in Nash equilibrium, a result stated by Maskin (1977), and in every form of conjectural variation equilibrium. Conjectural variations are the anticipated moves of a player's opponents that are associated to the player's strategy changes. Given a complete description of the players' conjectures, a strategy $m$-tuple is an equilibrium if no player believes he or she can gain by initiating a strategy change.

A Nash equilibrium is one form of conjectural variation equilibrium, where every player believes that other players are not going to change strategy even though he or she does. When we speak of implementability without further qualification, we have in mind implementability for every possible form of conjectural variation equilibrium.

In what follows we shall rely on a property that we call *monotonicity* for short and that looks close to Maskin monotonicity. We obtain it by replacing $V$ with $X_i$ in Maskin's definition. The condition requiring that $v^1$ be still in the choice set for $u^1$ is thus more demanding; and this seemingly slight change is fatal to implementability. To conclude, every implementable choice rule is Maskin monotonic and, thus, also monotonic according to our definition. Similarly, implementability requires full individual rationality under imperfect monitoring.

Evaluating allocations through their consequences insofar as they affect individual welfare is a time-honored tradition in economics. To reflect this viewpoint, at least to a certain extent, we introduce an axiom of *nondiscrimination between Pareto-indifferent allocations:* For every $v^0, v^1 \in V$, for every $u$ in the domain of $f$, $v^0 \in f(u)$ implies $v^1 \in f(u)$ if $v^0$ and $v^1$ are Pareto indifferent, that is, if all consumers consider $v^0$ and $v^1$ as equally good.

For the sake of completion, let us also recall the definition of a competitive allocation associated with a given profile $u$. This is an allocation $v$ in $V$ to which we can associate a price vector $p > 0$ such that $v$ combined with $p$ displays the following features: Profit, that is, the net value of the production plan at $p$, is maximized over the entire production set, whereas each individual chooses a consumption plan maximizing his or her utility, subject to a budgetary constraint, where the value of wealth consists of the value of initial endowments at $p$ to which the individual's profit share has been added; moreover, the price of any good is zero if the amount supplied exceeds the quantity demanded.

The Walrasian choice rule, or Walras correspondence, associates with every profile in a given domain the set of corresponding competitive allocations.

Armed with the above axioms and definitions, we can now state several results relying on a common assumption: That is, the domain of $f$ contains the set of all utility profiles having the same flat indifference surfaces (with nonnegative marginal utilities). Any such domain is called rich in the sequel.

Our first result says that every competitive allocation is picked by every social choice rule displaying the three properties we described above.

**Theorem 1.1.** Let $f$ be any monotonic and fully individually rational social choice rule that does not discriminate among Pareto-indifferent allocations. Then if the domain $U$ of $f$ is rich, $\forall u \in U, \forall v \in V, v \in f(u)$ whenever $v$ is a competitive allocation with respect to $u$.

*Remark 1:* It should be clear that the three properties imposed on social choice rules in Theorem 1.1 are logically independent of each other. On the other hand, monotonicity and/or full individual rationality may be replaced with stronger properties. For instance, implementability may replace monotonicity, and if the production set is convex and displays constant returns to scale, implementability under imperfect monitoring may replace both properties. In contrast, in Section 2 we replace monotonicity with a weaker condition related to the Nash axiom of independence of irrelevant alternatives.

*Remark 2:* Theorem 1.1 does not rely on Pareto efficiency. In particular, it applies when indifference curves are thick so that competitive allocations may fail to be Pareto efficient.

If we are ready to work with a slightly less general family of economies, we can weaken our individual rationality axiom and rephrase Theorem 1.1 at the cost of requiring $f$ to be Pareto efficient.

In what follows, we call a weakly nonsatiable profile a vector of nondecreasing utility functions that are strictly increasing in at least one argument.

**Theorem 1.2.** Let $f$ be any monotonic, Pareto-efficient, and weakly individually rational social choice rule that does not discriminate among Pareto-indifferent allocations. Then if $U$ is a rich domain of weakly nonsatiable profiles, $\forall u \in U, \forall v \in V, v \in f(u)$ whenever $v$ is a competitive allocation with respect to $u$.

Hurwicz (1979) offers an analogous theorem: To reach much the same conclusion, he requires $f$ to be Pareto efficient, individually rational (in a slightly different sense), and implementable in Nash equilibrium with an upper semicontinuous equilibrium correspondence. Hurwicz (1979) and Schmeidler (1982) also offer conditions under which interior Nash equilibrium allocations are competitive. The interpretation of these conditions seems to be mostly of technical interest.

Instead of looking for a converse or a complete characterization of the Walrasian choice rule, we shall content ourselves with a couple of observations designed to sharpen the edges.

**Theorem 1.3.** For every rich domain $U$ of weakly nonsatiable profiles on which it is well defined, the Walras correspondence is a Pareto-efficient (P) and monotonic (M) social choice rule that does not discriminate among Pareto-indifferent allocations (ND); moreover, it is both weakly and fully individually rational (WIR and FIR). Furthermore, it is the most selective member in the class of rules meeting requirements M, ND, and FIR. It is also the most selective member in the class of rules meeting requirements M, ND, WIR, and P. Indeed, for every profile in $U$, the set of competitive allocations associated with it is in either case the intersection of the corresponding images for all the rules in the class.

The first part of Theorem 1.3 would perhaps look more interesting if the word *monotonic* could be replaced by *implementable in Nash equilibrium*. However, this cannot be done because we rely on a definition of monotonicity that is weaker than Maskin's. In fact, in the context of pure exchange economies, Hurwicz, Maskin, and Postlewaite (1982) show that noncompetitive allocations are also typically picked by any Nash equilibrium correspondence containing the Walras choice rule as a subcorrespondence. These allocations are however efficient, and they would be competitive if, through a contraction of consumption sets, every agent's demands were constrained to make sure they do not exceed the economy's resources. It is easy to see that the constrained Walrasian choice rule that is so defined is the most selective of the rules meeting ND, WIR, and P.

The second part of Theorem 1.3 would be more appealing if any of our axioms could be weakened so that the Walras choice rule might be considered as the intersection of an even larger set of rules. We attempt to do so in Section 2.

## 2    And now something not much different

In this section, we give a brief formal treatment of the model presented above. We also introduce and discuss an axiom weaker than the monotonicity axiom that is related to the Nash axiom of independence of irrelevant alternatives. Finally, we prove statements of the same nature as the previous theorems.

The economy we deal with consists of one firm and a set $M$ of consumers, all of which are concerned with a set $L$ of private goods. Both $M$ and $L$ are finite. Their cardinals are respectively denoted by $m$ and $\ell$. A production plan is denoted by $y \in \mathbb{R}^{\ell}$. Plans that are feasible for the firm make up a given set $Y$, called the production set. Similarly, a consumption plan of consumer $i$ $(i = 1, \ldots, m)$ is denoted $x_i \in \mathbb{R}^{\ell}$. Plans that are feasible for $i$, independently of any specific exchange institutions, make up a given set $X_i$, called $i$'s consumption set. By assumption, $\forall i \in M$, $X_i$ is closed and bounded below. Consumer $i$'s initial endowment of goods is denoted $w_i \in \mathbb{R}^{\ell}$. His or her share in the firm is denoted $\vartheta_i \geq 0$. By assumption $\sum_i \vartheta_i = 1$.

An allocation $v$ is defined as $v = (y, (x_i)_{i \in M})$. We shall say that $v \in V$, the set of feasible allocations, if three conditions are met:

(i)   $y \in Y$;
(ii)  $\forall i \in M$, $x_i \in X_i$; and
(iii) $\forall h \in L$, $\sum_i x_{ih} \leq y_h + \sum_i w_{ih}$.

By assumption, $V$ is nonempty.

A utility profile $u$ is an $m$-tuple of utility functions $u = (u_i)_{i \in M}$, where, $\forall i \in M$, $u_i$ is a numerical function defined on $X_i$.

Sets of profiles we deal with are rich. This means that they contain as a subset the set $U^{\star}$, which consists of every profile of the form $\forall i \in M$, $\forall x_i \in X_i$, $u_i(x_i) = G_i(px_i)$, where $p$ can be any nonnegative $\ell$-vector such that $\sum p_h = 1$ and $G_i$ can be any strictly increasing and continuous numerical function defined on the real line.

We also define a rich set of strictly nonsatiable profiles as one containing all those members of $U^{\star}$ having $p_h > 0$, $\forall h \in L$, whereas the remaining profiles are made up of utility functions that are strictly increasing in every argument and continuous.

Given a set of profiles $U$, we can now define a social choice rule as any nonempty-valued correspondence $f : U \rightrightarrows V$.

A classical example is provided by the Walras correspondence or choice rule, which is denoted $f_w$ and associates with every profile $u$ the set of competitive allocations for $u$. A competitive (equilibrium) allocation $v^0$ for profile $u^0$ is defined in turn as follows: $v^0 \in V$ and there exists a price vector $p \in \mathbb{R}^{\ell}_+$, $\Sigma_h \, p_h = 1$, such that $y^0$ is a maximizer of $py$ over $Y$, whereas $\forall i \in M$, $x_i^0$ is a maximizer of $u_i(x_i)$ under the constraints $x_i \in X_i$ and $px_i \le pw_i + \vartheta_i \max_{y \in Y} py$; moreover, $\forall h \in L$, $\Sigma_i \, x_{ih}^0 < y_h^0 + \Sigma_i \, w_{ih}$ implies $p_h = 0$.

Next we introduce formally the five axioms used in Theorems 1.1–1.3.

1.  *Nondiscrimination of Pareto-indifferent allocations:* $\forall u \in U$, $\forall v^0, v^1 \in V$, $v^0 \in f(u)$ implies $v^1 \in f(u)$ if, $\forall i \in M$, $u_i(x_i^0) = u_i(x_i^1)$.
2.  *Full individual rationality:* $\forall u \in U$, $\forall v^0 \in f(u)$, $\forall i \in M$,

$$u_i(x_i^0) \ge \max_{y \in Y}\{u_i(w_i + \vartheta_i \, y)\}.$$

3.  *Weak individual rationality:* $\forall u \in U$, $\forall v \in f(u)$, $\forall i \in M$,

$$u_i(x_i) \ge u_i(w_i + \vartheta_i \, y).$$

4.  *Pareto efficiency:* $\forall u \in U$, $\forall v^0 \in f(u)$, $v^1 \notin V$ if $\forall i \in M$, $u_i(x_i^1) \ge u_i(x_i^0)$ with at least one strict inequality.
5.  *Monotonicity:* $\forall u^0, u^1 \in U$, $\forall v^1 \in V$ such that, $\forall i \in M$, $\forall x_i \in X_i$, $u_i^0(x_i^1) \ge u_i^0(x_i)$ implies $u_i^1(x_i^1) \ge u_i^1(x_i)$, $v^1 \in f(u^0)$ implies $v^1 \in f(u^1)$.

The stage is now set for proving our theorems. Prior to doing this, we consider some implications of the first four axioms whenever all consumer preference relations are the same, with flat indifference surfaces.

**Lemma 1.** For every $v \in V$, $\forall p \in \mathbb{R}^{\ell}_+$, $\Sigma_h \, p_h = 1$, if,

$$\forall i \in M, \ px_i \ge pw_i + \vartheta_i \, py, \quad \text{then} \quad \forall i \in M, \ px_i = pw_i + \vartheta_i \, py.$$

*Proof:* Suppose not: then, $\Sigma_i \, px_i > \Sigma_i \, pw_i + py$. Now, for feasibility, $\forall h \in L$, $p_h \Sigma_i \, x_{ih} \le p_h \Sigma_i \, w_{ih} + p_h y_h$. Summing over $h$, we get $\Sigma_i \, px_i \le \Sigma_i \, pw_i + py$, which contradicts our first inequality. ∎

**Lemma 2.** For every $v^0, v^1 \in V$, $\forall p \in \mathbb{R}^{\ell}_+$, $\Sigma \, p_h = 1$, if $py^0 > py^1$ and $\forall k \in \{0, 1\}$, $\forall i \in M$, $px_i^k \ge pw_i + \vartheta_i \, py^k$, then, $\forall i \in M$, $px_i^0 \ge px_i^1$ with at least one strict inequality.

*Proof:* By assumption, $\forall i$, $\vartheta_i \ge 0$ and $\Sigma_i \, \vartheta_i = 1$. In view of this, Lemma 2 is directly implied by Lemma 1. ∎

**Lemma 3.** For every $p \in \mathbb{R}_+^\ell$, $\Sigma\, p_h = 1$, $\forall y^0 \in Y$ such that $py^0$ maximizes $py$ over $Y$, if the subset $V^0 = \{v \in V,\ \forall i \in M,\ px_i \geq pw_i + \vartheta_i\, py^0\} \neq \varnothing$ and if $\forall i \in M$, $u_i^0(x_i) = px_i$, then $V^0 = f(u^0)$ whenever $f$ does not discriminate among Pareto-indifferent allocations, is weakly individually rational, and, moreover, is either Pareto efficient or fully individually rational.

*Proof:* Suppose $f$ is fully individually rational. Then, by definition,

$$f(u^0) \subseteq V^0.$$

Suppose, alternatively, that $f$ is weakly individually rational and Pareto efficient. Then, by Lemma 2, $f(u^0) \subseteq V^0$. In either case, all allocations of $V^0$ are Pareto indifferent by Lemma 1. Hence, since $f$ is nonempty, $f(u^0) = V^0$. ∎

*Remark:* Lemma 3 generalizes in a straightforward way to the case in which, $\forall i \in M$, $u_i^0(x_i) = G_i(px_i)$, where $G_i$ is a continuous strictly increasing numerical function defined on the real line.

*Proof of Theorem 1.1:* Consider any $u^1 \in U$ and any competitive allocation $v^1 \in f_w(u^1)$; then, as a consequence of our equilibrium definition, $\forall i \in M$, $px_i^1 = pw_i + \vartheta_i \max_{y \in Y} py$, where $p$ is an equilibrium price vector associated with $v^1$, $p \in \mathbb{R}_+^\ell$, $\Sigma_h\, p_h = 1$. Moreover, by definition, $\forall i \in M$, $\forall x_i \in X_i$, $px_i^1 \geq px_i$ implies $u_i^1(x_i^1) \geq u_i^1(x_i)$. We define next, $\forall i \in M$, $\forall x_i \in X_i$, $u_i^0(x_i) = px_i$. Thus, by monotonicity, $v^1 \in f(u^1)$ if $v^1 \in f(u^0)$. But this is directly implied by Lemma 3; indeed, by definition, $v^1 \in V^0$. ∎

The proof of Theorem 1.2 is just the same.

We turn next to the proof of Theorem 1.3. The second part of the theorem is a direct corollary of the first part combined with Theorems 1.1 and 1.2. As to the first part, it is almost self-evident that $f_w$ is Pareto efficient, monotonic, and fully individually rational. We content ourselves with a proof of the following statement: $\forall v^0, v^1 \in V$, for every weakly nonsatiable profile $u$ such that $\forall i \in M$, $u_i(x_i^0) = u_i(x_i^1)$, $v^0 \in f_w(u)$ implies $v^1 \in f_w(u)$.

Indeed, let $p$ be the price vector associated with $v^0$. By nonsatiation, $\forall i \in M$, $px_i^1 \geq px_i^0 = pw_i + \vartheta_i\, py^0$. Moreover, for feasibility,

$$py^1 + p \sum_i w_i \geq p \sum_i x_i^1.$$

Summing the first inequalities over $i$ and combining, we get

$$py^1 + p \sum_i w_i \geq p \sum_i x_i^1 \geq p \sum_i x_i^0 = p \sum_i w_i + py^0.$$

It follows that $py^1 = py^0 = \max_{y \in Y} py$ and that, $\forall i \in M$, $px_i^1 = px_i^0$. Hence $p$ is a price vector such that $v^1 \in f_w(u)$.

In the remaining part of this section, we discuss a possible weakening of the monotonicity axiom, and, on this basis, we relate the competitive model with some alternative models of cooperative bargaining.

It should be noted that the monotonicity axiom may be reexpressed as follows:

$\forall u^0, u^1 \in U$, $\forall v^1 \in V$ such that, $\forall i \in M$, $\forall x_i \in X_i$, $u_i^1(x_i) > u_i^1(x_i')$ implies $u_i^0(x_i) > u_i^0(x_i')$, $v^1 \in f(u^0)$ implies $v^1 \in f(u^1)$.

Indeed, if $u_i^1(x_i) > u_i^1(x_i')$ goes together with $u_i^0(x_i') \geq u_i^0(x_i)$, whereas the latter inequality implies $u_i^1(x_i') \geq u_i^1(x_i)$, we clearly get a contradiction. Similarly, if $u_i^0(x_i') \geq u_i^0(x_i)$ goes together with $u_i^1(x_i) > u_i^1(x_i')$, whereas the latter inequality implies $u_i^0(x_i) > u_i^0(x_i')$, we get another contradiction.

A natural weakening of the axiom would be obtained by narrowing down the set of pairs of profiles $u^0$ and $u^1$ for which $v^1 \in f(u^0)$ implies $v^1 \in f(u^1)$.

Shifting to a cardinalist spirit, we could, for instance, weaken the axiom by strengthening our two-sided inequalities as follows:

$\forall u^0, u^1 \in U$, $\forall v^1 \in V$ such that, $\forall i \in M$, $\forall x_i \in X_i$, $u_i^0(x_i') \geq u_i^0(x_i)$ implies $u_i^1(x_i') - u_i^1(x_i) \geq u_i^0(x_i') - u_i^0(x_i)$ and $u_i^1(x_i) > u_i^1(x_i')$ implies $u_i^0(x_i) - u_i^0(x_i') \geq u_i^1(x_i) - u_i^1(x_i')$, $v^1 \in f(u^0)$ implies $v^1 \in f(u^1)$.

We can, of course, further weaken the axiom by requiring that $u^0$ and $u^1$ also be such that $u_i^0(x_i') = u_i^1(x_i')$ for every $i \in M$. If we do so, we get a new axiom, which we call the *strong cardinalist nonnegative responsiveness (SCNR) property*:

$\forall u^0, u^1 \in U$, $\forall v^1 \in V$ such that, $\forall i \in M$, $\forall x_i \in X$, $u_i^0(x_i) \geq u_i^1(x_i)$ and $u_i^0(x_i') = u_i^1(x_i')$, $v^1 \in f(u^0)$ implies $v^1 \in f(u^1)$.

It is fairly easy to see that the two formulations are equivalent. If we denote by $u_i^{\star}$ the common utility value $u_i^0(x_i') = u_i^1(x_i')$, we can rewrite the former condition as $u_i^{\star} \geq u_i^0(x_i)$ implies $u_i^0(x_i) \geq u_i^1(x_i)$ whereas $u_i^1(x_i) > u_i^{\star}$ implies $u_i^0(x_i) \geq u_i^1(x_i)$. Observe that the cases that are not explicitly covered are such that $u_i^0(x_i) > u_i^{\star} \geq u_i^1(x_i)$, so that $u_i^0(x_i) \geq u_i^1(x_i)$. The reverse statement is even easier to prove.

The SCNR axiom is easy to interpret: It says that a contraction of the image of $V$ in the utility space that leaves unchanged the image of an allocation picked initially should not prevent it from being picked after the profile alteration provided the new profile may be derived from the former through a generalized deflation of individual utilities, the utility level of the allocation picked at the beginning remaining constant.

If we drop the last proviso, we get close to an axiom used by Chernoff (1954). The Nash axiom of independence of irrelevant alternatives is weaker than the Chernoff axiom, as it requires the image in the utility space of the no-trade point to be the same for either profiles under consideration, whereas the SCNR axiom requires it to be equally or less advantageous for every player after the profile alteration.

Having shown that the set of social rules meeting the SCNR axiom contains as a subset the set of monotonic rules, we proceed by paraphrasing the theorems stated in Section 1.

**Theorem 2.1.** Let $f$ be any fully individually rational social choice rule that does not discriminate among Pareto-indifferent allocations and displays the SCNR property. Then if $U$ is a rich domain of strictly nonsatiable profiles, $\forall u \in U$, $\forall v \in V$, $v \in f(u)$ whenever $v$ is a competitive allocation with respect to $u$.

*Proof:* By assumption, $v^1 \in V$ is a competitive allocation for some $u^1 \in U$. Then, by definition, for some $p \in \mathbb{R}_+^\ell$, such that $\sum_h p_h = 1$, we get $\forall i \in M$, $\forall x_i \in X_i$ such that $px_i \le pw_i + \vartheta_i \max_{y \in Y} py$, $u_i^1(x_i) \le u_i^1(x_i^1)$. By nonsatiation, we get, $\forall i \in M$, $px_i^1 = pw_i + \vartheta_i \max_{y \in Y} py$. Moreover, $\forall h \in L$, $p_h > 0$. For each $i \in M$, $\forall x_i \in X_i$, let us further define

$$B(px_i) = \{z \in X_i, \ pz \le px_i\},$$

and

$$u_i^0(x_i) = \max_{z \in B(px_i)} u_i^1(z).$$

This can be done because $u_i^1$ is continuous and $B(px_i)$ is a compact set. Observe that, by definition, $\forall x_i \in X_i$, $u_i^0(x_i) \ge u_i^1(x_i)$, since $x_i \in B(px_i)$. Moreover, as we remarked initially, $\forall x_i \in X_i$, $u_i^1(x_i) \le u_i^1(x_i^1)$ if $px_i \le px_i^1$. Therefore, $u_i^0(x_i^1) = u_i^1(x_i^1)$. These inequalities hold for every $i$, and hence we are in position to invoke the SCNR property, that is, $v^1 \in f(u^1)$ if $v^1 \in f(u^0)$. We proceed to show that $v^1 \in f(u^0)$. By definition, $u_i^0$ may be rewritten, $\forall x_i \in X_i$, as $u_i^0(x_i) = G_i(px_i)$. Indeed, $\forall x_i, x_i^\star \in X_i$, $px_i = px_i^\star$ implies $B(px_i) = B(px_i^\star)$, and hence $u_i^0(x_i) \equiv u_i^0(x_i^\star)$. Because $u_i^1$ is continuous and strictly increasing, so is $G_i$. In view of the remark following Lemma 3, $v^1 \in f(u^0)$ because $v^1 \in V^0$ by definition. ∎

Observant readers will have noticed that strict nonsatiation and the fact that every $X_i$ is closed and bounded below are used in the proof to establish that $u_i^0(x_i)$ is well defined. These assumptions can be dispensed with if we adopt the monotonicity axiom, as in Theorem 1.1.

The proof of our next theorem is left as an easy exercise for the reader.

**Theorem 2.2.** For every rich domain $U$ of strictly nonsatiable profiles on which it is well defined, the Walras correspondence $f_w$ is a fully individually rational social choice rule that does not discriminate among Pareto-indifferent allocations and displays the SCNR property; moreover, it is the most selective member in the class of rules meeting these requirements; indeed, $\forall u \in U$, $f_w(u)$ is the intersection of the corresponding images for all rules in the class.

As in Theorems 1.2 and 1.3, Pareto efficiency and weak individual rationality may be used as joint substitutes for full individual rationality in presence of the SCNR property.

In view of Theorem 2.2, competitive theory may appear to offer an appropriate solution concept for bargaining problems in the context of an Arrow–Debreu economy, even though $m$ may be small. This point has been carefully argued by Binmore (1980c). If $m = 2$, the Nash (1950) bargaining theory seems to be one of the major contenders in the fields. For recent reformulations, see Roth (1979), Thomson (1981), and Binmore (1980a, b, c), who offers a beautiful noncooperative model implementing the Nash solution. We proceed by sketching a comparison of the two theories. Let us first recall that, considered as a social choice rule, the Nash solution associates with every profile $u$ in the relevant domain the set of allocations that maximize over $V$ the Nash product $\prod_i q_i$, where $q_i = u_i(x_i) - \max_{y \in Y} u_i(w_i + \vartheta_i y)$, under the constraints $\forall i \in M$, $q_i \geq 0$. Here again we assume that $Y$ is convex and displays constant returns to scale.

Nash's bargaining theory is best expressed in the space of utilities: His symmetry axiom implies that players receive equal utility treatment if the image of $V$ is symmetric in the utility space. This is not consistent with the Walras choice rule; in the Edgeworth box case, we get symmetric treatment if the consumers' indifference curves are symmetric with respect to the competitive price line. Comparing the Nash axiom of independence of irrelevant alternatives with the SCNR property indicated also that the latter is sensitive to changes affecting qualitatively every individual utility in the same direction, whereas the former is only concerned with a contraction of $V$ in the utility space, which can occur if one individual gains in utility terms and the other loses enough to outweigh his opponent's gain.

Being more abstract than competitive theory, the Nash bargaining theory applies potentially to a much wider universe, although it is meant to be relevant only when the image of $V$ in utility space is convex. Other bargaining theories, such as the Kalai–Smorodinsky (1975) theory do not suffer from this limitation.

However, all two-person bargaining theories developed in the utility space share a basic weakness; as Shapley (1969) has shown, they cannot be based on an ordinalist utility theory. Cardinality without interpersonal comparability seems to be a natural invariance property to require in this context.

In contrast, the fact that competitive theory can be established on purely ordinal comparisons may appear as a decisive advantage in its favor. It is paradoxical indeed that, among the lists of axioms designed to justify the Walras choice rule, the least demanding one relies on the strong cardinalist nonnegative responsiveness property, which is cardinalist in spirit. Let us, however, hasten to point out that the Shapley impossibility result we just mentioned does not hold for $m \geq 3$, as he himself recently proved. An axiomatic approach of the new bargaining solution concept he proposed in Shubik's (1982, p. 95) book for $m \geq 3$ would be well worth developing, as it is based on ordinalist utility theory.

## 3    Linear tax schemes and the Ramsey choice rule

In this section, we introduce linear taxation as a means of redistributing income uniformly among agents. We adapt our axiomatic approach to capture the set of allocations that can be reached with this form of taxation and that are Pareto efficient in a second-best sense. For this purpose, we enlarge the family of economies we work with. Indeed, we consider as alternative production sets nonempty subsets of our original set $Y$. Accordingly, we generalize our definition of a social choice rule, and we specify a conservative internal consistency condition one might want them to satisfy. Moreover, we adapt our weak individual rationality axiom. These are virtually the only changes required to reach our goal.

Given any subset $Y_s \subset Y$, we define a corresponding set of feasible allocations $V(Y_s) = \{v \in V, y \in Y_s\}$. We are, of course, only interested in closed subsets $Y_s$ of $Y$ for which $V(Y_s)$ is nonempty. Their complete collection is denoted by $Q(Y)$ in the sequel.

For any given set of utility profiles $U$, we define $f: U \times Q(Y) \rightrightarrows V$. We call $f$ a social choice rule if and only if it is nonempty valued and, $\forall u \in U$, $\forall Y_s \in Q(Y)$, $f(u, Y_s) \subset V(Y_s)$.

Next, we fit linear taxation in a competitive setup: our model is inspired by the work of Ramsey (1927) and the papers by Diamond and Mirrlees (1971). Instead of being based on a single price vector, decentralization relies on two generally distinct sets of prices; as a rule, consumers face a price system that is not the same as the one used to guide the production sector. The difference is accounted for by taxes levied on the trading of goods and services between the consumption sector and the production sector and also by a profit tax. To simplify, we assume a 100% profit tax in the sequel. Under this assumption, consumer prices are disconnected from producer prices and we can forget the latter. Moreover, we assume that every consumer receives from government a uniform lump-sum transfer $(qy/m)$, where $q$ stands for the consumer price vector.

More formally, for every profile $u$ in a given domain $U$ and for every $Y_s \in Q(Y)$, we call a sustainable linear tax scheme an allocation $v^0 \in V(Y_s)$ together with a price vector $q \in \mathbb{R}_+^\ell$, $\Sigma_h q_h = 1$, such that $\forall i \in M$, $x_i^0$ is a maximizer of $u_i(x_i)$ subject to $x_i \in X_i$ and $qx_i \leq qw_i + (1/m)qy^0$.

Given any sustainable linear tax scheme $(v^0, q^0)$ defined as above, we write $v^0 \in f_R(u, Y_s)$ if and only if there does not exist any other sustainable tax scheme $(v^1, q^1)$ for $u$ and $Y_s$ such that $v^1$ is Pareto preferred to $v^0$.

The correspondence we just defined is called the *Ramsey choice rule* hereafter.

The notion of Pareto efficiency that applies here is clearly invoked in a second-best sense. In the same spirit, for every $u \in U$, and for every $W \subset V$, we define $P(W)$ as the set of allocations $v^0 \in W$ such that there does not exist $v^1 \in W$ that is Pareto preferred to $v^0$.

We are now ready to introduce two new axioms. First, we require $f$ to satisfy a highly conservative internal consistency property, which we call the *Pareto-inclusive property*. According to this, given a profile $u$, the image by $f$ of the union of any family of subsets of $Y$ must include the Pareto set for the union of images corresponding to each subset:

$$\forall u \in U, \ \forall (Y_s)_{s \in S} \subset Q(Y), \quad v \in P\left(\bigcup_{s \in S} f(u, Y_s)\right) \text{ implies } v \in f\left(u, \bigcup_{s \in S} Y_s\right).$$

Our other axiom expresses a *weak egalitarian individual rationality* property:

$$\forall u \in U, \ \forall Y_s \in Q(Y), \quad v \in f(u, Y_s) \text{ implies } \forall i \in M, \ u_i(x_i) \geq u_i(w_i + y/m).$$

Translating the other axioms used in Theorem 1.3 raises no problem. We realize at once that, suitably transposed, Theorem 1.3 provides an axiomatic approach of the Ramsey choice rule restricted to production sets that are singletons. Making use of the Pareto-inclusive property, we can write the following theorem.

**Theorem 3.1.** For every rich domain of weakly nonsatiable profile on which it is well defined, the Ramsey choice rule is the most selective member in the class of monotonic Pareto-inclusive choice rules that do not discriminate among Pareto-indifferent allocations and display the weak egalitarian individual rationality property.

Thus, two main features distinguish the Ramsey choice rule from the Walras correspondence. On the one hand, the Ramsey rule is based on a more egalitarian individual rationality requirement. On the other hand, it relies on the Pareto criterion only in a subordinate manner whereas Walrasian allocations are always Pareto efficient. There is, of course, nothing novel in pointing out that the two distinguishing features we just mentioned are implied by the choice rules under study. We are facing here an abstract version of the equity efficiency trade-off so often met in the taxation literature.

Our results have added a new emphasis on this pair of contrasting features: Indeed, by combining them with two common requirements, namely, monotonicity and nondiscrimination of Pareto-indifferent allocations, we have come to realize that the families of choice rules meeting jointly the corresponding sets of four axioms have as respective intersections the Walras correspondence and the Ramsey choice rule. As we emphasized in Section 2, however, the latter is too little selective to be really useful. Further research is required to replace our Pareto-inclusive property with more discriminating axioms, in line, for instance, with recent work done by Moulin (1984) in theoretical political economy.

REFERENCES

Arrow, K. J. (1951), *Social choice and individual values,* New York: Wiley (2nd ed., 1963).

Binmore, K. (1980a, b, c), "Nash bargaining theory I, II, III," ICERD papers 09, 14 and 15, mimeo.

Chernoff, H. (1954), "Rational selection of decision functions," *Econometrica,* 22: 423–43.

Debreu, G. and H. Scarf (1963), "A limit theorem on the core of an economy," *International Economic Review,* 4: 235–46.

Diamond, P. and J. Mirrlees (1971), "Optimal taxation and public production I: production efficiency and II: tax rules," *American Economic Review,* 61: 8–27, 261–278.

Groves, T. and J. Ledyard (1984), "Incentive compatibility ten years later," mimeo.

Hurwicz, L. (1979), "On allocations attainable through Nash equilibria," *Journal of Economic Theory* 21: 140–65.

Hurwicz, L., E. Maskin and A. Postlewaite (1982), "Feasible implementation of social choice correspondence by Nash equilibria," mimeo.

Kalai, E. and M. Smorodinsky (1975), "Other solutions to Nash's bargaining problem," *Econometrica,* 43: 513–18.

Maskin, E. (1977), "Nash equilibrium and welfare optimality," mimeo.

Maskin, E. (1980), "On first-best taxation," in *Income distribution: the limits to redistribution,* D. Collard, et al. (Eds.), Bristol, Scientechnica.

Moulin, H. (1984), "Choosing from a tournament," mimeo.

Nash, J. (1950), "The bargaining problem," *Econometrica,* 18: 155–62.

Ramsey, F. P. (1927), "A contribution to the theory of taxation," *Economic Journal,* 37: 47–61.

Roberts, K. (1979), "The characterisation of implementable choice rules," in *Aggregation and revelation of preferences,* J. J. Laffont (Ed.), Amsterdam: North-Holland.

Roth, A. (1979), *Axiomatic models of bargaining,* Berlin: Springer-Verlag.

Schmeidler, D. (1982a), "A condition guaranteeing that the Nash allocation is Walrasian," *Journal of Economic Theory,* 28: 376–78.

Schmeidler, D. (1982b), "Economic analysis via strategic outcome functions: A survey of recent results," in *Games, economic dynamics, and time series analysis,* Wien: Physica-Verlag.

Shapley, (L.) (1969), "Utility comparison and the theory of games," in *La décision: agrégation et dynamique des ordres de préférence,* Paris: Editions du CNRS.

Shubik, M. (1982), *Game theory in the social sciences,* Cambridge, Mass.: MIT Press.

Thomson, W. (1981), "Nash's bargaining solution and utilitarian choice rules," *Econometrica,* 49: 535–38.

# PART II

# Decision making in the public sector

The study of "market failure" had a long history before Arrow. Most of this work involved identifying areas in which decentralized markets would not reach the first best (monopolies, public goods, externalities) and discussing appropriate modifications for those situations. For example, Lindahl shares could be used to allocate public goods, and Pigovian taxes could be used to correct for externality. Subsequently, Arrow was a significant contributor to this literature; he developed a general model that showed that virtually every type of nonmarket interaction could be corrected in principle through the use of appropriate "extended" markets. However, he pointed out very clearly the limitations of this approach, arguing that the information requirements and/or monopoly incentives inherent in extended markets would render them unworkable in many circumstances.

If we concede the impossibility of first-best pseudomarket procedures, then public sector planning must move in one of two directions. On the one hand, we can back away from "markets" and think about planning problems in an institution-free setting. Arrow contributed to this approach in a series of papers and a book (coauthored with M. Kurz) analyzing intertemporal consumption and public investment problems. Two chapters in this section deal with this approach. Scarf looks at planning problems in the presence of indivisibilities, which render market approaches unworkable. He discusses computational procedures that will "solve" a restricted class of such problems. Intriligator and Sheshinski consider problems of planning in an intertemporal context with uncertainty. They focus on simple planning rules that can be implemented with limited information and discuss ways of choosing among them in various contexts.

The second approach involves studying a "mixed" economy in which a large market sector operates as a backdrop to nonmarket public activity. Arrow anticipated the formal development of this model with several early examples. Among the better known of these pieces were his study of the economics of medical care and the allocation of resources to invention. The context that emerged was one of "second best": It was argued that we would generally find markets operating in situations where they will not necessarily be "first best"; and it followed that one could not always rely on market prices as guides to scarcity. Other measures of benefit were needed in order to correctly evaluate policy.

It would be overstating the case to say that Arrow is the father of modern applied welfare economics, as this subject has many distinguished parents. However, his work on the social rate of discount (together with the aforementioned pieces) went a long way toward suggesting subsequent formalizations. The rate of discount would appear as a market price in a first-best setting. Arrow asked how it should be evaluated in a number of second-best settings and showed how some general principles could be applied to determine correct "shadow prices" in situations involving second best.

One important lesson from the new framework is that shadow prices can be evaluated only relative to some well-specified second-best context. Starrett adopts some recent models of "incomplete markets" and reexamines the social rate of discount. He finds parallels between correct shadow prices and corresponding asset pricing formulas. Further, he explores ways in which the public tax system can affect risk sharing and looks at consequent implications for government risk discounting.

Much recent literature has focused on the distortion caused by taxation of saving and its implications for second-best welfare economics. Bradford examines the conditions under which this distortion exists in the context of a dividend tax and suggests ways of removing the distortion through policy. Lind suggests that the distortion is much larger than might be expected. His argument relies on the fact that any distortion will compound over time (just as interest does) and implies that the so-called excess burden attributable to government spending will be quite sensitive to underlying supply and demand elasticities.

# CHAPTER 6

# Testing for optimality in the absence of convexity

*Herbert E. Scarf*

## 1 The fundamental theorems of welfare economics

The modern treatment of the fundamental theorems of welfare economics was developed by two of the masters of our trade: Kenneth J. Arrow (1951) and Gerard Debreu (1951). The contrast between their presentation and that offered by a distinguished predecessor – Abba Lerner – is a striking illustration of the emergence of a new line of argumentation in economic theory. The index to Lerner's book, *The economics of control* (1944), contains not a single reference to convex sets nor to the separating hyperplane theorem: The basic mathematical tools used by Arrow and Debreu to demonstrate the relationship between prices and Pareto optimality.

The first major theorem of welfare economics states that a competitive equilibrium is a Pareto-optimal production and distribution plan. The proof offered by Arrow is astonishingly brief; a line or two of mathematical argument replaces the tedious evaluation of vast arrays of marginal productivities and marginal rates of substitution. Moreover, convexity assumptions are required neither on the consumption nor production sides of the economy, though, of course, in the absence of such assumptions, the theorem is, in general, vacuous. The second major theorem – that a Pareto-optimal production and distribution plan can be supported by competitive prices – does require that consumer preferences satisfy a convexity assumption and that production sets be convex. Its proof is then a simple exercise in the application of Minkowski's separating hyperplane theorem.

The separating hyperplane theorem was in the air during the late 1940s. It had been used to provide an elementary proof of von Neumann's minimax theorem for two-person zero-sum games; and as Arrow remarks in his collected papers (1983), he had been present at a lecture given by Albert Tucker in which a variant of the separating hyperplane theorem was used to demonstrate the existence of supporting prices for the general convex programming problem. The Kuhn–Tucker theorem can, of course, be viewed as a special case of the second welfare theorem in which there is a single consumer with a utility function depending only on the good whose output is being maximized. A further specialization to the linear activity analysis model of production leads directly to the economically significant aspect of the duality theorem for linear programming: the existence of prices that yield a zero profit for those activities in use at the optimum and a nonpositive profit for the remaining activities.

The general convex programming problem can be put in the form

$$\max f_0(x_1, \dots, x_n)$$
$$\text{subject to } f_1(x_1, \dots, x_n) \leq b_1,$$
$$\vdots$$
$$f_m(x_1, \dots, x_n) \leq b_m,$$
$$x \geq 0,$$

and the appropriate convexity requirement is embodied in the assumption that $f_0$ is a concave function and that $f_1, \dots, f_m$ are convex functions of their arguments. Assuming that the constraints are consistent, that the problem has a finite maximum at $x^*$, and that a mild regularity condition known as the constraint qualification holds, the second welfare theorem asserts the existence of nonnegative prices $\pi_1^*, \dots, \pi_m^*$ with the property that

$$f_0(x^*) - \sum_1^m \pi_i^* b_i \geq f_0(x) - \sum_1^m \pi_i^* f_i(x) \quad \text{for all } x \geq 0.$$

The first welfare theorem may be interpreted in this context by saying that a feasible vector of activity levels $x^*$ is the constrained maximum if there exists a nonnegative vector of prices $\pi^*$, one for each constraint, such that profits are maximized at $x^*$. A test based on prices is sufficient to verify that a proposed feasible solution is optimal, and under the assumption of convexity, such a pricing test is always available.

With the additional assumption that $f_0(x)$ is *strictly* concave, and that each $f_i(x)$, for $i = 1, \dots, m$, is *strictly* convex, a numerical algorithm based on the Walrasian *tâtonnement,* may be shown to converge globally to the correct vector of prices $\pi^*$. Let $\pi$ be an arbitrary nonnegative price vector, and let $x(\pi)$ maximize

$$f_0(x) - \sum_1^m \pi_i f_i(x) \quad \text{for all } x \geq 0.$$

The excess demand for the $i$th factor of production is then

$$f_i(x(\pi)) - b_i.$$

Our economic intuition that the price of a factor in excess demand will rise, and that the price of a factor whose demand is less than its supply will fall, may be captured by the system of nonlinear differential equations

$$d\pi_i/dt = f_i(x(\pi)) - b_i.$$

Given an arbitrary initial price vector $\pi$, the system of differential equations will typically have a solution $\pi_i(t)$ with $\pi_i(0) = \pi_i$. In the interest of simplicity, let us assume that $\pi_i(t) > 0$ for all $t$ and that $\pi_i^* > 0$; otherwise, the differential equations must be modified so as to ensure that none of the prices become negative.

This system of differential equations is formally identical to the system introduced by Samuelson (1941–2) and studied extensively by Arrow and Hurwicz (1958) and Arrow, Block, and Hurwicz (1959) in the more general context in which consumers are explicitly incorporated in the model. I was first made aware of the problem of global stability of the price adjustment mechanism by Arrow himself during the close personal and professional association that I was privileged to enjoy in the late 1950s at Stanford.

With the considerable hindsight offered by several decades of continued research we now know that the Walrasian *tâtonnement* need not be globally stable; a model of exchange may easily be constructed so that the solution to the system of differential equations traces out any path on the nonnegative part of the unit sphere. But these complexities are related to the presence of consumers in the model; in the special case of convex programming, the price adjustment mechanism may be shown to be globally stable by verifying that $\sum_i (\pi_i(t) - \pi_i^*)^2$ decreases to zero along the solution path.

The pricing test for optimality is also available for the general linear programming problem:

$$\begin{aligned}
\max\; & a_{01}x_1 + \cdots + a_{0n}x_n, \\
& a_{11}x_1 + \cdots + a_{1n}x_n \geq b_1, \\
& \qquad\qquad \vdots \\
& a_{m1}x_1 + \cdots + a_{mn}x_n \geq b_m, \\
& \qquad x \geq 0.
\end{aligned}$$

A feasible solution to the system of inequalities is optimal if a vector of prices can be found such that each activity in use makes a profit of zero and the remaining activities make a nonpositive profit. And in a spirit that is similar to the Walrasian price adjustment mechanism, the search for economically significant prices is at the heart of that workhorse of linear programming: the simplex method. In the simplex method, a feasible solution to the system of linear inequalities is proposed, and prices are found so as to yield a profit of zero for those activities being used. The feasible solution is optimal if none of the remaining activities make a positive profit; otherwise, we select one of the profitable activities and use it at a positive level, making compensating changes in the activity levels previously specified. When one of those activity levels drops to zero, the pricing test is repeated, and optimality is reached in a finite number of iterations.

The convexity assumption is the mortar that binds together this remarkable edifice of existence theorems and computational algorithms. Unfortunately, convexity of the production set is not a strikingly realistic description of economic reality. Convexity requires that the production possibility set exhibit constant or decreasing returns to scale: That you or I can manufacture automobiles in our own backyards with the same degree of efficiency as that achieved by the Ford Motor Co. Economies of scale based on large indivisible pieces of machinery or forms of productive organization such as the assembly line, which are not economically merited at small scales of operation, are a major ingredient of the industrial revolution of the last 100 years. And their workings cannot be captured, either theoretically or computationally, by the competitive paradigm.

The following quotation shows most clearly Lerner's appreciation of the incompatibility between indivisibilities and competitive markets: "We see then that indivisibility leads to an expansion in the output of the firm, and this either makes the output big enough to render the indivisibility insignificant, or it destroys the perfection of competition. Significant indivisibility destroys perfect competition" (Lerner 1944, p. 176).

## 2    Neighborhood systems for production sets with indivisibilities

The most extreme example of a production possibility set involving indivisibilities is that described by an activity analysis model in which the activity levels are required to assume integral values. The mathematical programming problems that then arise by specifying a particular factor endowment are known as *integer programming problems* and have the form

$$\max a_{01}h_1 + \cdots + a_{0n}h_n,$$
$$a_{11}h_1 + \cdots + a_{1n}h_n \geq b_1,$$
$$\vdots$$
$$a_{m1}h_1 + \cdots + a_{mn}h_n \geq b_m,$$
and $h_1, \ldots, h_n$ integral.

In contrast to linear programming, the optimal solution to an integer programming problem need not be supported by competitive prices. Consider, for example, the integer program

$$\max -4h_1 - 3h_2,$$
$$2h_1 + h_2 \geq 3,$$
$$h_1 \geq 0,$$
$$h_2 \geq 0,$$

and $h_1, h_2$ integral. The constraint set is drawn in Figure 1, with the objective function indicated by a dashed line.

When the integrality assumption is relaxed, the optimal solution to the corresponding linear program is to use only the first activity at the level of $\frac{3}{2}$. If the prices associated with the objective function and the first constraint are in a 1:2 ratio, the first activity will make a profit of zero and the second activity a negative profit. A decentralized profit maximizing response will lead to the selection of activities that are consistent with the optimal solution to the programming problem. On the other hand, when the variables are required to be integral, the optimal solution is at the point $(1, 1)$. Both activities are used at the optimal solution, and there is no price ratio yielding a zero profit for the two activities simultaneously.

The phenomenon illustrated by this example is a general one: Indivisibilities in production are incompatible with competitive factor markets. Prices are not available to verify that a feasible solution to an integer programming problem is actually optimal, and no computational algorithm based on prices can be successful in general. Of course, the subject of integer programming is not a new one, and there are many algorithms that perform quite well in practice, but I am unaware of any computational procedure the steps of whose execution are capable of the most rudimentary economic interpretation in terms of prices.

What I have proposed in a series of publications (Scarf 1981; in press) is the replacement of the neoclassical pricing test for optimality by a quantity test; more specifically, by a search through neighbors of a proposed feasible solution to see whether a nearby vector of activity levels is also

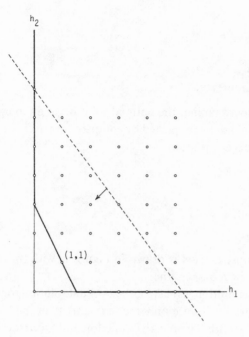

Figure 1. An example.

feasible and yields an improvement in the objective function. Consider the general integer program with $n$ variables, ranging over all lattice points in $n$-dimensional Euclidean space. By a *neighborhood system,* I mean the association with each lattice point $h$ of a *finite* set of neighbors $N(h)$; the association is arbitrary aside from the following two requirements:

1. if $k \in N(h)$, then $h \in N(k)$ and
2. $N(h) = h + N(0)$.

The first assumption states that the neighborhood relation is a symmetric one and the second that the neighbors of any two lattice points are translates of each other.

Given an integer program described by the technology matrix

$$
A = \begin{bmatrix}
a_{00} & a_{01} & \cdots & a_{0n} \\
a_{10} & a_{11} & \cdots & a_{1n} \\
\vdots & \vdots & \ddots & \vdots \\
a_{m1} & a_{m2} & & a_{mn}
\end{bmatrix}
$$

and a specification of the right-hand side $b = (b_1, b_2, ..., b_m)$, an arbitrary neighborhood system can be used to define the concept of a *local maximum:* a feasible vector of activity levels $h$ all of whose neighbors $k \in N(h)$ are either infeasible or yield an inferior value of the objective function.

In general, a local maximum with respect to a particular neighborhood system need not be a global maximum to the programming problem; a particular neighborhood of a feasible point may simply omit some vector of activity levels that is also feasible and that improves the objective function. Moreover, such an improvement need not take place at a lattice point that is close to the original feasible vector in the sense of Euclidean distance. To see this, we merely remark that integer programs based on the technology matrices $A$ and $AU$, with $U$ a *unimodular* matrix (a nonsingular matrix with integer entries and a determinant of $\pm 1$) are equivalent: If $h$ is the optimal solution to an integer program with technology matrix $A$, then $h' = U^{-1}h$ is the optimal solution to the corresponding problem with matrix $AU$. But unimodular transformations do not preserve Euclidean distance, and nearby points may be mapped into points that are quite far apart.

The following theorem may be demonstrated quite easily (Scarf, 1984).

**Theorem 2.1.** Under mild regularity assumptions on the technology matrix $A$, there exists a *unique, minimal* neighborhood system such that a local maximum is global for all integer programs based on $A$. This neighborhood system depends on the technology matrix alone and not on the specification of the particular factor endowment.

The regularity assumptions referred to in the statement of Theorem 2.1 may be stated as follows:

**Assumption 2.2.** For each $b = (b_0, b_1, ..., b_m)$, the set of integral vectors $h$ such that $Ah \geq b$ is finite. Moreover, the entries in each row of $A$ are independent over the integers in the sense that $\sum_j a_{ij} h_j = 0$ for *any* $i$ implies that $h = 0$.

To demonstrate Theorem 2.1, we argue that two lattice points $h$ and $h'$ must be neighbors – in any neighborhood system for which a local maximum is global – if there is some vector $b = (b_0, b_1, ..., b_m)$ such that the only lattice points satisfying $Ah \geq b$ are $h$ and $h'$ themselves. For let $b$ be such a vector and assume that $\sum_j a_{0j} h'_j > \sum_j a_{0j} h_j$. It follows that $h$ is a feasible solution to the integer program

$$\max a_{01}h_1 + \cdots + a_{0n}h_n,$$
$$a_{11}h_1 + \cdots + a_{1n}h_n \geq b_1,$$
$$\vdots$$
$$a_{m1}h_1 + \cdots + a_{mn}h_n \geq b_m,$$
$$h \text{ integral},$$

and that $h'$ is the only other feasible solution yielding a higher value of the objective function. If $h'$ were not a neighbor of $h$, then $h$ would – incorrectly – be chosen as the optimal solution for this particular problem.

The set

$$S = \left\{ x \,\middle|\, \sum_j a_{ij}x_j \geq \min\left( \sum_j a_{ij}h_j, \sum_j a_{ij}h'_j \right), \text{ for } i = 0, 1, \ldots, m \right\}$$

is the smallest convex body containing the two lattice points $h$ and $h'$ obtained by varying the right-hand side $b$. If this set contains some additional lattice points, then $h$ and $h'$ need not be selected as neighbors in the minimal neighborhood system. For if this were so, then in any particular problem for which $h$ is feasible, the test for optimality need not involve $h'$; the other lattice points in $S$ will do just as well.

Invariance under translation implies that a complete description of the minimal neighborhood system is given by the set of neighbors of the origin. A formal proof of Theorem 2.1 is then obtained by defining, for each lattice point $k$, the set

$$S_k = \left\{ x \,\middle|\, \sum_j a_{ij}x_j \geq \min\left( 0, \sum_j a_{ij}k_j \right), \text{ for } i = 0, 1, \ldots, m \right\},$$

and a partial ordering among nonzero lattice points by $k \precsim k'$ if and only if $S_k \subseteq S_{k'}$. From Assumption 2.2, each lattice point is preceded by a finite number of other lattice points in this ordering, and there are no pairs for which $k \precsim k'$ and $k' \precsim k$. The minimal points in this ordering constitute the minimal neighborhood system for which a local maximum is global.

The minimal neighborhood system is robust under small changes in the technology matrix $A$ as long as Assumption 2.2 is maintained. There may be a sudden discontinuity in the neighborhood system when we pass through a position in which a nonzero lattice point happens to lie on one of the hyperplanes $\sum_j a_{ij}x_j = 0$. Moreover, as Figure 2 illustrates, there may be a certain ambiguity at such a position in the definition of the minimal neighborhood system itself. The ambiguity, though not the discontinuity, may be resolved by adopting a lexicographic tie-breaking rule for coordinates of the vectors $y = Ah$.

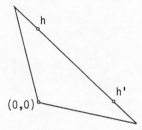

Figure 2. Degeneracy.

## 3     Complexity of the neighborhood system

Given a description of the minimal neighborhood system, the most immediate algorithm for the solution of integer programming problems is a repeated neighborhood search: A specific feasible solution is proposed and all of its neighbors are examined to see whether one of them is also feasible and yields a higher value of the objective function. If there is such a neighbor, we move to it and iterate; if not, the original feasible vector is optimal.

The amount of computational work associated with this algorithm depends at first glance on the cardinality of the set of neighbors. It is elementary to show that for a technology matrix with three rows and two columns, the minimal neighborhood system will consist of precisely six points. But, aside from this special case, the cardinality of the set of neighbors is not bounded by any function of the number of rows and columns of $A$ and may become arbitrarily large for problems in which $m$ and $n$ are fixed.

The cardinality of the set of neighbors is, however, a crude estimate of the work required by a neighborhood test for optimality. The set of neighbors of the origin may display sufficient structure so that each neighbor need not be examined individually. The minimal neighborhood of the origin may, for example, be the disjoint union of a small number of integral linear segments, as illustrated in Figure 3. Since deciding whether some neighbor in a linear set yields a feasible improvement can be carried out by a small number of divisions, structural regularities in the minimal neighborhood system may lead to a considerable reduction in computational work.

The language of the theory of computational complexity may be used to formulate a general conjecture about minimal neighborhood systems that,

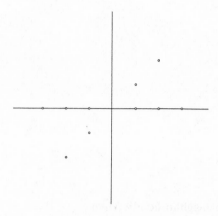

Figure 3. Neighbors of the origin.

if correct, would convert repeated neighborhood searches into an efficient algorithm for integer programming problems. In this theory, the size or complexity of the technology matrix $A$ is defined to be the number of binary bits required to store the entries of $A$ in a digital computer. The number of binary bits required to store an integer $a$ is given by $1 + \lceil \log_2(|a| + 1) \rceil$, with $\lceil x \rceil$ the smallest integer greater than or equal to $x$ (the additional 1 preceding the logarithm is used to store the sign of $a$). If the entries in the technology matrix are integers, its size is therefore given by

$$S = \sum_{i=0}^{m} \sum_{j=1}^{n} (1 + \lceil \log_2(|a_{ij}| + 1) \rceil).$$

An algorithm for the solution of integer programming problems is said to be *polynomial* if the number of steps required for the algorithm to execute successfully is bounded from above by a polynomial function of the size of the problem. Integer programming problems are known to be NP complete, a class of difficult problems for which a polynomial algorithm is extremely unlikely to exist. When the number of variables, or for that matter the number of constraints, is fixed in advance, the class of problems is no longer NP complete and Lenstra (1983) has provided a remarkable algorithm that is indeed polynomial in the size as the remainiong parameters of the technology matrix vary. To the best of my knowledge, however, Lenstra's algorithm has not been tested on a variety of problems, and it may be similar to Katchian's algorithm for linear programming – polynomial in theory, but computationally inefficient.

In a previous publication, I have determined the minimal neighborhood system for a small class of integer programming problems including the transportation problem and the knapsack problem with two activities. In each of these problems, the neighborhood system displays sufficient structure so that a repeated neighborhood search may be accelerated so as to yield a polynomial algorithm. Based on these examples and Lenstra's conclusion, I conjecture that the minimal neighborhood system has a structural description that is polynomial in the data of the problem whenever the number of variables is fixed in advance. Such a description, if possible, may also be capable of economic interpretation in terms of the internal organizational structure of a large economic enterprise whose production possibility set is dominated by significant indivisibilities.

## 4 Example

In this section, I shall describe a class of technology matrices whose minimal neighborhood systems can be determined by means of a relatively simple algorithm. I do not know, however, whether these neighborhood systems are capable of being described in a polynomial fashion, though I suspect rather strongly that such is the case. The examples show, in a striking fashion, the subtle number-theoretic considerations involved in verifying the general conjecture concerning a polynomial description of the minimal neighborhood system and certainly warrant continued investigation.

One of the basic problems in integer programming is the following: Given a finite set of lattice points in $R^n$, is there an additional lattice point in their convex hull? I shall consider a specialization that is by no means devoid of interest. The finite set will consist of $n+1$ lattice points, the first $n$ of which are the unit vectors, and the $(n+1)$st point a general integer vector $a = (a_1, a_2, ..., a_n)$ all of whose coordinates are strictly positive.

Mathematically, we are concerned with finding an integer vector $(h_1, h_2, ..., h_n)$ such that

$$\begin{pmatrix} h_1 \\ \vdots \\ h_n \end{pmatrix} = \begin{bmatrix} a_1 & 1 & \cdots & 0 \\ \vdots & \vdots & \ddots & \vdots \\ a_n & 0 & & 1 \end{bmatrix} \begin{pmatrix} \alpha_0 \\ \vdots \\ \alpha_n \end{pmatrix},$$

with $1 > \alpha_j \geq 0$, and $\alpha_0 + \cdots + \alpha_n = 1$. There is a simple algorithm that permits us to determine such a vector if it exists. Adding the $n$ equations, we obtain

$$(h_1 + \cdots + h_n) = \alpha_0(a_1 + \cdots + a_n) + \alpha_1 + \cdots + \alpha_n$$

$$= \alpha_0(a_1 + \cdots + a_n) + 1 - \alpha_0,$$

so that $\alpha_0 = h/D$ with $h = h_1 + \cdots + h_n - 1$ and $D = a_1 + \cdots + a_n - 1$. But then $h_j = \alpha_j + h \cdot a_j / D$, so that $h_j = \lceil ha_j / D \rceil$. If we define, for integer $h$ between 1 and $D - 1$, the function

$$f(h) = \sum_{j=1}^{n} \lceil ha_j / D \rceil,$$

we see that a necessary and sufficient condition for the existence of an additional lattice point in the convex hull is that

$$f(h) = h + 1,$$

for some $h = 1, 2, \ldots, D - 1$. The lattice point will be strictly interior to the convex hull if $\alpha_j > 0$ for $j = 1, 2, \ldots, n$, or if $ha_j / D$ is not integral. It will simplify our subsequent analysis if we impose the following condition, which implies that all such lattice points are strictly interior.

**Assumption 4.1.** For each $j$, $a_j$ and $D$ are relatively prime.

For example, let $n = 3$, and $(a_1, a_2, a_3) = (3, 4, 5)$, so that $D = 11$. The function $f(h)$ is then

| $h$ | 1 | 2 | 3 | 4 | 5 | 6 | 7 | 8 | 9 | 10 |
|---|---|---|---|---|---|---|---|---|---|---|
| $f(h)$ | 3 | 3 | 5 | 6 | 7 | 8 | 9 | 10 | 12 | 12 |

The fact that $f(2) = 3$ implies that

$$(1, 1, 1) = \lceil 3 \cdot 2/11 \rceil, \lceil 4 \cdot 2/11 \rceil, \lceil 5 \cdot 2/11 \rceil$$

is the convex hull of the three unit vectors and $(3, 4, 5)$.

The problem has an analytical answer only when $n = 2$ or 3. For $n = 2$, a necessary and sufficient condition that the triangle with vertices $(1, 0)$, $(0, 1)$, and $(a_1, a_2)$, with $a_1, a_2$ positive integers, be free of additional lattice points is simply that $(a_1, a_2) = (1, 1)$. (See Fig. 4.)

The solution for $n = 3$ provided by Roger Howe a number of years ago is striking. [Proofs of Howe's theorem may be found in Scarf (1985) and Resnick (in press).] A necessary and sufficient condition that the tetrahedron with vertices $(1, 0, 0)$, $(0, 1, 0)$, $(0, 0, 1)$, and $(a_1, a_2, a_3)$, with $a_j$ positive integers, be free of additional lattice points is that *one* of the

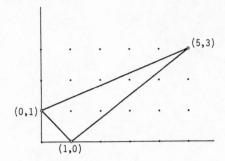

Figure 4. The case $n = 2$.

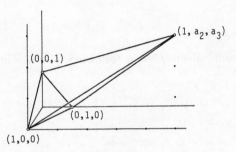

Figure 5. The case $n = 3$.

three integers $a_1, a_2, a_3$ be *unity* and the other two relatively prime. (See Fig. 5.)

When $n > 3$, no characterization is presently known for those positive integral vectors $(a_1, \ldots, a_n)$ that, in conjunction with the $n$ unit vectors, give rise to a convex body free of additional lattice points; it seems highly unlikely that there is a simple characterization. The algorithm based on the function $f(h)$ is available for any such vector $(a_1, a_2, \ldots, a_n)$, but it requires $D = -1 + \sum a_j$ steps, a quantity that is not polynomial in the size of the problem: $\sum_j (1 + \lceil \log_2(a_j + 1) \rceil)$. It will be instructive to pose the problem as an integer program and to determine its minimal neighborhood system.

The convex hull of our set of $n+1$ lattice points is the intersection of $n+1$ half-spaces, each generated by a hyperplane of dimension $n-1$. The hyperplane passing through the $n$ unit vectors is $x_1 + \cdots + x_n = 1$; the

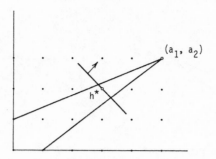

Figure 6. A pair of neighbors.

hyperplane passing through $(a_1, a_2, ..., a_n)$ and all of the unit vectors other than the $j$th unit vector is

$$Dx_j - a_j(x_1 + \cdots + x_n) = -a_j.$$

It follows that the convex hull is defined by the following system of linear inequalities:

$$\begin{bmatrix} 1 & 1 & \cdots & 1 \\ D-a_1 & -a_1 & \cdots & -a_1 \\ -a_2 & D-a_2 & \cdots & -a_2 \\ \vdots & \vdots & \ddots & \vdots \\ -a_n & -a_n & & D-a_n \end{bmatrix} x \geq \begin{pmatrix} 1 \\ -a_1 \\ -a_2 \\ \vdots \\ -a_n \end{pmatrix}.$$

The matrix of coefficients will be denoted by $A$.

The solution to the integer program

$$
\begin{aligned}
\max \quad & h_1 + & h_2 + \cdots + & h_n, \\
& (D-a_1)h_1 - & a_1 h_2 - \cdots - & a_1 h_n \geq -a_1, \\
& -a_2 h_1 + (D-a_2)h_2 - \cdots - & a_2 h_n \geq -a_2, \\
& \quad \vdots & \\
& -a_n h_1 - & a_n h_2 - \cdots + (D-a_n)h_n \geq -a_n, \\
& h \text{ integral,}
\end{aligned}
$$

is $(a_1, a_2, ..., a_n)$. If the convex hull contains an additional lattice point (let $h^*$ be one that maximizes $h_1 + \cdots + h_n$), then $h^*$ and $(a_1, a_2, ..., a_n)$ will be neighbors of each other. (See Fig. 6.)

The entries in the technology matrix $A$ are integers and therefore violate the second part of the nondegeneracy Assumption 2.2. In order to resolve the resulting ambiguity in the definition of the minimal neighborhood system, we adopt the following lexicographic tie-breaking rule:

**Lexicographic rule 4.2.** Let $y = Ah$ and $y' = Ah'$. For any particular coordinate $i$, we say that $y'_i >_i y_i$ if the vector $(y'_i, y'_{i+1}, ..., y'_0, ..., y'_{i-1})$ is lexicographically larger than $(y_i, y_{i+1}, ..., y_0, ..., y_{i-1})$.

The vector $y = Ah$ will then be a neighbor of the origin if there is no other vector $y' = Ah'$ with

$$y'_0 > \min(y_0, 0),$$
$$y'_1 > \min(y_1, 0),$$
$$\vdots$$
$$y'_n > \min(y_n, 0),$$

all of the inequalities being interpreted in this lexicographic sense.

As the following theorem indicates, the neighbors of the origin for the technology matrix $A$ bear an intimate relationship with our algorithm for deciding whether there exists an additional lattice point in the convex hull.

**Theorem 4.3.** Let $(h_1, h_2, ..., h_n)$ be a neighbor of the origin with $h = \sum_1^n h_j > 0$. Then, for each $j = 1, 2, ..., n$,

$$h_j = \lceil a_j h/D \rceil \quad \text{or} \quad \lceil a_j h/D \rceil - 1.$$

We begin the proof of Theorem 4.3 by showing that $-D \le y_i \le D$ for $i = 0, 1, ..., n$, for any neighbor of the origin. Assume, to be specific, that $y_2 > D$. Then

$$A \begin{bmatrix} h_1 + 1 \\ h_2 - 1 \\ \vdots \\ h_n \end{bmatrix} = \begin{bmatrix} y_0 \\ y_1 + D \\ y_2 - D \\ \vdots \\ y_n \end{bmatrix} > \begin{bmatrix} \min(y_0, 0) \\ \min(y_1, 0) \\ \min(y_2, 0) \\ \vdots \\ \min(y_n, 0) \end{bmatrix},$$

since each coordinate of $(y_0, y_1 + D, y_2 - D, ..., y_n)$, other than the second, is lexicographically greater than the corresponding coordinate of $(y_0, y_1, y_2, ..., y_n)$, and $y_2 - D > 0$. Moreover, since $y_2 > D$, $(h_1 + 1, h_2 - 1, 0, ..., 0)$ is not equal to 0 and is therefore a third vector in the smallest convex set obtained by parallel movements of the inequalities containing $h$ and 0. A similar argument shows that $y_i \le D$ for every $i$; the inequality

$-D \le y_i$ follows from the fact that the negative of a neighbor of the origin is also a neighbor of the origin.

The inequalities $-D \le y_i \le D$ may be rewritten as

$$-D \le Dh_i - a_i \sum_1^n h_j \le D \quad \text{or} \quad -1 + \frac{a_i h}{D} \le h_i \le 1 + \frac{a_i h}{D},$$

and unless $a_i h/D$ is an integer, it follows that

$$h_i = \lceil a_i h/D \rceil \quad \text{or} \quad \lceil a_i h/D \rceil - 1.$$

Theorem 4.3 tells us that the neighbors of the origin with $\sum h_j \ge 1$ are contained in the set of points obtained by rounding up or down the coordinates of $(a_1, a_2, ..., a_n)h/D$, with $h = 1, 2, ..., D$. Not all of these points are neighbors of the origin, however. If we write $h_i = \lceil a_i h/D \rceil - \delta_i$ with $\delta_i = 0, 1$, then since $\sum h_i = h$, we must have $\sum_i \delta_i = f(h) - h$. Moreover, if $a_i h = k_i D + r_i$ with $0 < r_i < D$ ($r_i \ne 0$ since $a_i$ and $D$ are relatively prime), then $\lceil a_i h/D \rceil = k_i + 1$, and the vector

$$y = (y_0, y_1, y_2, ..., y_n) = (h, (1-\delta_1)D - r_1, (1-\delta_2)D - r_2, ..., (1-\delta_n)D - r_n).$$

It follows that

$$\min(0, y_i) = \begin{cases} 0 & \text{if } \delta_i = 0, \\ -r_i & \text{if } \delta_i = 1, \end{cases}$$

for $i = 1, 2, ..., n$. The neighbors of the origin with $h \ge 1$ are then obtained by constructing the list of vectors $\min(0, y)$ and eliminating those that are dominated. When this exercise is carried out for our previous example in which $(a_1, a_2, a_3) = (3, 4, 5)$, we obtain the following set of neighbors:

| | | |
|---|---|---|
| $(0, 1, 0)$ | $(1, 1, 0)$ | $(1, 2, 2)$ |
| $(0, 0, 1)$ | $(1, 1, 1)$ | $(2, 2, 3)$ |
| $(0, 1, 1)$ | $(1, 2, 1)$ | $(2, 3, 3)$ |
| $(1, 0, 1)$ | $(1, 1, 2)$ | $(2, 3, 4).$ |

This calculation can be performed quite easily on a computer, but it is, unfortunately, not polynomial in the data of the problem.

A neighbor of the origin with $h = \sum k_j = 0$ will also satisfy $-D \le y_i \le D$. Since $y_i = h_i D - a_i h$ for $i = 1, 2, ..., n$, we see that such a neighbor will have $h_i = -1, 0$, or $1$, and $y_i = -D, 0$, or $D$. This observation permits us to characterize – in terms of the minimal neighborhood system – those vectors $(a_1, a_2, ..., a_n)$ that, in conjunction with the $n$ unit vectors, generate a convex body free of additional lattice points.

**Theorem 4.4.** Assume that $a_i$ and $D$ are relatively prime for each $i$. The convex hull of $(a_1, \ldots, a_n)$ and the $n$ unit vectors will contain no other lattice points if and only if the minimal neighborhood of the origin associated with the matrix $A$ contains some vectors $(h_1, h_2, \ldots, h_n)$ with $\sum h_j = 0$.

The proof of Theorem 4.4 proceeds as follows: If the convex hull contains an additional lattice point, then $f(\hat{h}) = \hat{h} + 1$ for some $\hat{h}$. Any neighbor of the origin with $\sum h_j = 0$ will have $y_{i^*} = -D$ for some $i^*$. If we then define $\hat{h}_i = \lceil a_i \hat{h}/D \rceil - \delta_i$ with $\delta_i = 1$ for $i = i^*$ and $\delta_i = 0$ otherwise, the vector $\hat{y} = A\hat{h}$ will have the form

$$(\hat{h}, D - r_1, D - r_2, \ldots, -r_{i^*}, \ldots, D - r_n)$$

and will be strictly larger, in all coordinates, than $\min(0, y)$. It follows that there are no neighbors of the orgin with $\sum h_j = 0$.

On the other hand, if the convex hull of $(a_1, a_2, \ldots, a_n)$ and the $n$ unit vectors contains no other lattice points, it will be true that $f(h) \geq h + 2$ for all $h$. From Theorem 4.3, we see that any neighbor of the origin $\xi = (\xi_0, \xi_1, \ldots, \xi_n)$, with $\xi_0 \geq 1$, will have at least *two* coordinates $\xi_i$ and $\xi_j$ that are strictly negative. But if $h = (1, -1, 0, \ldots, 0)$, then

$$y = Ah = (0, D, -D, 0, \ldots, 0);$$

$\min(0, y)$ cannot be dominated by any neighbor of the origin, and $y$ must therefore be a neighbor of the origin itself. This demonstrates Theorem 4.4.

REFERENCES

Arrow, K. J. (1951), "An extension of the basic theorems of classical welfare economies," in J. Neyman (Ed.), *Proceedings of the second Berkeley symposium on mathematical statistics and probability,* Berkeley and Los Angeles: University of California Press, pp. 507-32.

Arrow, K. J. (1983), *Collected papers: General equilibrium,* Cambridge, Mass.: Harvard University Press.

Arrow, K. J. and L. Hurwicz (1958), "On the stability of the competitive equilibrium, pt. 1," *Econometrica,* 26: 522-52.

Arrow, K. J., H. D. Block, and L. Hurwicz (1959), "On the stability of the competitive equilibrium, pt. 2," *Econometrica,* 27: 82-109.

Debreu, G. (1951), "The coefficient of resource utilization," *Econometrica,* 19: 273-92.

Lenstra, H. W., Jr. (1983), "Integer programming with a fixed number of variables," *Mathematics of Operations Research,* 8: 538-48.

Lerner, A. (1944), *The economics of control,* New York: Macmillan.

Resnick, B. (in press), "Lattice point simplices," *Discrete Mathematics*.

Samuelson, P. A. (1941–42), "The stability of equilibrium," *Econometrica,* 9: 97–120; 10: 1–25.

Scarf, H. E. (1981), "Production sets with indivisibilities," *Econometrica,* 49: 1–32; 395–423.

Scarf, H. E. (1985), "Integral polyhedra in three space," *Mathematics of Operations Research,* 10(3): 403–38.

Scarf, H. E. (in press), "Neighborhood systems for production sets with indivisibilities," *Econometrica*.

CHAPTER 7

# Toward a theory of planning

*Michael D. Intriligator and Eytan Sheshinski*

## 1    Introduction

*Planning* refers to the elaboration of an explicit set of decisions concerning the present and future values of certain choice variables by a decision maker (planner) in order to achieve certain goals. Planning, therefore, involves the determination of a strategy that, in turn, involves decisions on both actions and their timing or pattern of implementation.[1] Planning in this sense is pervasive in the economy, and it is exemplified by national economic planning, corporate capital planning, inventory planning, household expenditure planning, investor portfolio planning, and planning in many other areas, for example, defense planning, development planning, environmental planning, energy planning, and educational planning. Most previous studies have treated the problem of planning in such a particular institutional or sectoral context. The purpose of this chapter is to contribute a general theory of planning that treats certain common features of all these particular forms of planning. These features involve certain basic choices concerning timing and implementation and typically must be chosen in advance of any specific plan. First is the choice of a *horizon,* that is, the time interval covered by the plan. Second is the choice of a *period,* that is, the time interval during which the plan remains in effect before it is revised. There is also a choice between *time planning,* in which the horizon and period are fixed time intervals, and *event planning*, in which the period may be influenced by the state of the system, with particular events triggering a revision of the plan.

Section 2 presents the basic concepts of horizon and period, and Section 3 develops the distinction between time planning and event planning.

We would like to acknowledge the useful comments and suggestions made by D. L. Brito, William Brock, David Cass, Sergiu Hart, Mordecai Kurz, Michael McGill, Lionel McKenzie, Semyon Meerkov, William Oakland, Bojan Popovic, David Starrett, and Robert Wilson.

Section 4 presents a formal framework for the analysis of these choices. This framework leads in Section 5 to five theorems on planning. The theory is illustrated in Section 6 by the problem of a monopolistic firm adjusting prices in a situation of inflation. Conclusions are summarized in Section 7.

Before turning to the specific aspects of planning, it is important to consider both the nature of planning in several different organizations and its usefulness.

In many organizations, both public and private, planning is embodied in a budget or, more typically, in an interrelated set of budgets. There are often many overlapping plans at various levels, such as the operating and capital budgets in a corporation. There can be severe problems in obtaining consistency between these plans and in integrating short- and long-term plans, for example, annual budgets and five-year plans.

In other institutional settings, planning can take other forms. An example is household expenditure planning, which can involve purchases at fixed times (e.g., buy groceries on Monday), purchases when certain levels of goods fall below predetermined critical levels (e.g., purchase gasoline when the tank is one-quarter full), or purchases at random times (e.g., impulse purchases). A related example is inventory planning. Yet another example is the problem of a monopolistic firm revising its prices in a period of inflation (as discussed in Section 6) where there are costs associated with this action (e.g., printing new catalogs); the firm must determine both when to revise prices and what the new prices will be. Another example is a change in government, involving political rather than economic decisions. One alternative is the presidential system, in which a new administration is elected every certain number of years (e.g., four years in the United States and six years in Mexico). An alternative is the parliamentary system, such as that found in Western Europe and Canada, in which a new government is elected when there is a vote of no confidence. A third alternative is the quasipermanent system, such as that found in Eastern Europe and in most developing nations, in which a government lasts until a leader dies or the next coup replaces it. On the basis of these examples, it is clear that planning includes many different situations and a great variety of institutional contexts.

## 2     Horizon and period

Two fundamental decisions that must be made in advance of any specific plan and in any specific institutional setting concern the horizon and the period of the plan. The horizon of the plan is the time period covered by the plan, whereas the period of the plan is the time period during which the plan remains in effect. These decisions are often made on the basis of traditional choices or rules of thumb rather than on the basis of conscious choices. Perhaps the most widely used rule of thumb is the annual budget, for which a plan covering one year (the horizon) is revised annually (the period). These traditional choices of horizon and period are based on seasonal factors, especially the harvest in agricultural planning. In other settings, they have been replaced by more deliberately chosen alternatives that are more appropriate to the particular set of decisions to be made. For example, many major corporations use capital budgets that extend over three years and are revised every six months, involving a three-year horizon and a half-year period. Another example is a consumer who plans purchases over horizons longer than one year, as recognized in the permanent income hypothesis, but who may revise plans more frequently than once a year, for example, a four-year horizon and a four-month period.

In most traditional approaches to planning, the horizon decision is linked to the period decision by the requirement that the time interval covered by the plan be the same as the interval between successive plans, so that the horizon and the period are equal. This requirement is clearly not necessary. It is possible (and generally desirable) to have plans overlap by choosing a horizon that is longer than the period. Such a choice implies that the decisions can be made over a long enough horizon to take account of their long-range impacts, although at the same time these decisions can be revised in the light of new information. In practice, this process of having a horizon longer than the period is frequently achieved by having both short- and long-term plans, the former referring to the period of the plan and the latter referring to the horizon of the plan.

The choice of a particular horizon and period depends on the degree of uncertainty concerning the decisions to be made.[2] Substantial uncertainty, particularly over the very long term, would imply that there is little value in planning over a very long horizon. An example is the use of relatively short horizons in the development of high-technology projects, such as advanced energy and weapons systems, because of their high degree of uncertainty. In such projects, short horizons of sequential decisions and prototypes result in more informed decisions than does integrated development, since each stage in the sequence can use information obtained during a previous stage.

However, whereas an infinite horizon is generally not optimal because of substantial uncertainty, a zero horizon is also generally not optimal since there is usually some information about the near future, and decisions as to this near future are closely interrelated to those pertaining to the present. Thus, as stated in Theorem 1 (see Sec. 5), a positive but finite horizon is generally optimal.

Cost factors, in particular the costs of planning and of processing new information, are also important considerations in the choice of a particular horizon and period. Theorem 3 (see Sec. 5) states that if there were no costs of planning, then it would be desirable to plan over the indefinite future and to revise plans each instant, thus resulting in a *rolling plan* with a zero period and an infinite horizon.[3] All planning entails some costs, however, so it is generally desirable to choose a finite horizon and a nonzero period for a plan.

Political, social, legal, and other constraints often set limits on the horizon and period of a plan. For example, the requirement that Congress must approve the U.S. federal budget implies that the period cannot exceed two years. In general, the horizon and period for many organizations, particularly for governments, are closely related to the decision makers' length of tenure.

## 3     Time planning and event planning

Decisions concerning the period of the plan can be made in several different ways. The traditional approach is time planning, in which the plan is revised after a fixed time interval has elapsed. Examples include the one-year period for annual budgets, the six-month period frequently used for corporate capital budgets, and the four-year U.S. presidential term. An alternative approach is event planning, in which the plan is revised after a certain event or set of events occurs. The event that triggers the drawing up of a new plan is usually closely related to the goals of the decision maker. Frequently, it is defined as the time that one or a set of the state variables describing the system under consideration reaches a particular value or values.

An example of event planning is a portfolio manager who reviews the portfolio when certain market measures reach predetermined values (e.g., the Dow Jones average passes above a particular ceiling or below a particular floor). By contrast, the portfolio manager who reviews the portfolio at fixed dates (e.g., the first of each month) would be an example of time planning. A second example of event planning is national economic planning in which a new fiscal plan is drawn up in the event of war or if inflation or unemployment rises above particular critical levels. A similar example is household expenditure planning in which the plan is revised in the event of a major illness or a loss of a job. A fourth example is inventory planning in which a reorder decision may be triggered when inventory falls below a certain level. A specific illustration of this last example of event planning is the $(s, S)$ inventory policy in which new inventory is ordered when the level of inventory falls below $s$ and enough is ordered to bring the level up to $S$.[4] This inventory policy may be contrasted to the $(t, T)$ policy of time planning in which new inventory is ordered at fixed times $t$, with enough ordered to carry (expected) positive levels of inventory up to time $T$.[5] This optimality of the $(s, S)$ policy is an example of the general optimality of event planning in situations of uncertainty, formalized below as Theorem 5. A fifth example is investment for capacity expansion, where the time phasing of new investment depends on a projection of future demand.[6]

*Hybrid planning* represents a combination of time planning and event planning. In this case, either time or some event(s) can trigger a new plan being developed. Typically, a new plan is formulated if either a particular event occurs or a certain time interval has passed since the last plan revision. An example is the formulation of a new fiscal plan if either one year has elapsed since the last plan or if the inflation or unemployment rate exceeds 10 percent. Another example is a parliamentary system in which a new government is elected if there is a vote of no confidence or if five years has elapsed since the last election. This approach to planning has the desirable properties of both pure types of planning. It recognizes the existence of uncertainty by allowing events to trigger action. At the same time, it recognizes that a particular event or small set of events cannot embody all relevant information concerning a system.

Theorem 5 states that in any system involving uncertainty, revising plans on the basis of events is preferable to revising plans only on the basis of time. Thus, if the results of the plan or the state of the world are uncertain, then events should influence the period of the plan. A major problem of event (or hybrid) planning, however, is identifying the particular event(s) that would trigger the new plan. The event(s) should summarize relevant information available concerning the state of the system, involving certain significant changes in some fundamental variables of the system. Given a relevant index or set of indexes, the particular level(s) that would trigger a new plan would generally depend on the cost of planning and the opportunity cost of not revising the plan.[7]

## 4 A formal framework for the analysis of planning decisions

The concepts introduced so far, those of horizon, period, and time versus event planning, can be defined and analyzed in a formal framework.

This framework is introduced and used here to characterize optimal choices of horizon and period and in the next section to develop five theorems on planning. The development of the formal framework proceeds in four steps: from the overall planner to a sequence of subproblems to the individual subproblem planner to the overall results.

### 4.1     Overall planner

In the first step, the overall planner must select a trajectory over the entire time interval from time $t_0$ for a set of control variables. Letting $\alpha(t)$ be the vector of control variables at time $t$, the overall planner, starting at time $t_0$, solves the problem of maximizing expected net benefit

$$\max_{\{\alpha(t)\}} V_0 = E\left\{\int_{t_0}^{\infty} B(x(t),\alpha(t))e^{-rt}\,dt - Ce^{-rt_0}\right\}. \tag{1}$$

Here $\{\alpha(t)\}$ refers to the entire trajectory for $\alpha(t)$ from $t_0$ to $\infty$; $V_0$ is expected net benefit, to be maximized by the choice of trajectories for the control variables; $B(x(t),\alpha(t))$ is the benefit derived from the vector of state variables $x(t)$ and the vector of control variables $\alpha(t)$, discounted at the rate $r$, which is assumed given; and $C$ is the cost of planning the trajectory $\{\alpha(t)\}$, which is incurred at time $t_0$. Benefits are discounted continuously, and the costs of planning are discounted from the beginning of the period when they are incurred.

The system dynamics are given by the equations of motion

$$\dot{x}(t) = f(x(t),\alpha(t),u(t),t), \tag{2}$$

$$x(t_0) = x_0, \tag{3}$$

where $f(x(t),\alpha(t),u(t),t)$ gives the time rate of change of each of the state variables in $x$ as functions of their levels $x(t)$; the control variables $\alpha(t)$; a stochastic disturbance term $u(t)$, which provides the underlying uncertainty in the problem and is assumed independent of $x(t)$ and $\alpha(t)$; and possibly time itself.[8] The initial state of the system $x_0$ and initial time $t_0$ are given in (3).

### 4.2     Sequence of subproblems

In the second step, the overall planner is assumed to treat this problem by breaking it into a sequence of subproblems due to the complexity of formulating a trajectory over the entire interval $[t_0, \infty)$. The overall planner chooses a sequence of decisions times $t_0, t_1, t_2, ..., t_\tau, t_{\tau+1}, ...$ and delegates the problem of choosing the trajectory to a sequence of planners. The zeroth planner is responsible for the interval $[t_0, t_1)$, the first planner is responsible for the interval $[t_1, t_2), \ldots,$ and the $t$th planner is responsible for the interval $[t_\tau, t_{\tau+1})$. Each planner is replaced by the next planner at the end of the interval, with the $\tau$th planner replaced at time $t_{\tau+1}$ by the $(\tau+1)$st planner. The $\tau th\ plan$ is the trajectory $\{\alpha_\tau(t)\}$ for $\alpha(t)$ over the period from $t_\tau$ to $t_{\tau+1}$, representing a set of decisions concerning present and future values of certain choice variables.[9] The period of the plan is then simply the time interval between successive decisions times, period $\tau$ being

$$P_\tau = t_{\tau+1} - t_\tau.$$

The overall planner chooses the decision times $t_\tau$ as the solution to the problem

$$\max_{\{t_\tau\}} V = E\left\{ \sum_{\tau=0}^{\infty} \int_{t_\tau}^{t_{\tau+1}} B(\hat{x}(t), \hat{\alpha}(t)) e^{-rt}\, dt - C_\tau e^{-rt_\tau} \right\}, \qquad (4)$$

where $\{t_\tau\}$ is the sequence of decision times.[10] Here $V$ is the expected net benefit, the expectation of a sum, the sum covering all plans, indexed by $\tau$ and ranging from the initial plan at $t_0$, corresponding to $\tau = 0$, through all future plans, and $C_\tau$ is the cost at time $t_\tau$ of planning for period $\tau$. As before, benefits are discounted continuously, and the costs of planning are discounted from the beginning of each period, when they are incurred. To solve (4), the control variables are set at expected values $\hat{\alpha}(t)$, which may, for example, reflect past trends or extrapolations. The state variables are also set at expected values $\hat{x}(t)$, which satisfy the equations of motion for expected values,

$$\dot{\hat{x}}(t) = f(\hat{x}(t), \hat{\alpha}(t), \hat{u}(t), t), \qquad (5)$$

$$\hat{x}(t_0) = x_0, \qquad (6)$$

where $\hat{u}(t)$ is the expected stochastic disturbance at time $t$. It is assumed that the sequence $\{t_\tau\}$ solves (4) subject to (5) and (6) for given expected values of control and state variables.

### 4.3    Individual subproblem planner

In the third step the $\tau$th individual subproblem planner is assumed to solve a subproblem involving not just the interval from $t_\tau$ to $t_{\tau+1}$ but beyond this time to $t_\tau + H_\tau$, where $H_\tau$ is the horizon chosen by the $\tau$th planner. The horizon is chosen subject to the condition that it be at least as long as the period

$$H_\tau \geq t_{\tau+1} - t_\tau = P_\tau \tag{7}$$

so that there are not "gaps," that is, times for which decisions regarding actions to be taken have not been made. It is advantageous for the $\tau$th planner to formulate plans over the interval $[t_\tau, t_\tau + H_\tau)$, even though only the portion from $t_\tau$ to $t_{\tau+1}$ is put into effect since considering the state and controls beyond $t_{\tau+1}$ can possibly improve decisions made for the interval up to $t_{\tau+1}$.[11] To the extent that the horizon exceeds the period, there is an interval in which actions planned at a particular time are superceded by actions planned at the next decision time, that is, by the $(\tau+1)$st planner.

The $\tau$th planner solves

$$\max_{\{\alpha_\tau(t)\}, H_\tau} V_\tau = E\left\{ \int_{t_\tau}^{t_\tau + H_\tau} B(x(t), \alpha(t)) e^{-rt} \, dt - C_\tau(H_\tau) e^{-rt_\tau} \right\} \tag{8}$$

subject to (2) and (3). The $\tau$th planner chooses the trajectory $\{\alpha_\tau(t)\}$ for $\alpha(t)$ over the interval up to the horizon, from $t_\tau$ to $t_\tau + H_\tau$, where the horizon $H_\tau$ is also chosen by this planner subject to (7). Note that the integral ranges from $t_\tau$ to $t_\tau + H_\tau$ and that $H_\tau$ influences the cost of planning since planning over a longer horizon generally entails higher costs of planning. In general, the $\tau$th planner first chooses an optimal horizon $H_\tau$ and then chooses an optimal trajectory for the control variables $\{\alpha_\tau(t)\}$ within an admissible class of such trajectories $A_\tau$, where $\{\alpha_\tau(t)\} \in A_\tau$ summarizes all actions at time $t$ for $t_\tau \leq t < t_\tau + H_\tau$. The admissible class $A_\tau$ is chosen by the overall planner, and it embodies all of the technical constraints of the problem.

The equations of motion are given for the $\tau$th planner by

$$\dot{x}(t) = f(x(t), \alpha_\tau(t), u(t), t) \quad \text{for } t \in [t_\tau, t_\tau + H_\tau),$$

$$x(t_\tau) = \lim_{t \uparrow t_\tau} x(t),$$

where $x(t_\tau)$ is determined, in part, on the basis of actions taken by past planners.

Figure 1 illustrates this formulation of horizon and period for the case of a single control variable $\alpha$ in which the admissible set $A_\tau$ is the real line, shown as the vertical axis. The decision times $t_\tau$ appear on the time axis, the horizon $H_\tau$ gives the span over which actions are planned, and the period $P_\tau$ gives the time until the plan is revised. Any one curve is a plan $\alpha_\tau(t)$ chosen at time $t_\tau$. Overlapping curves indicate plans that are superceded by later plans. In such cases, the horizon exceeds the period, so the time interval from $t_{\tau+1}$ to $H_\tau$ is one in which the initial plans are

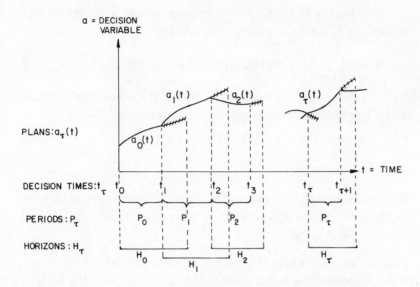

Figure 1. Plan $\alpha_\tau(t)$, extending from $t_\tau$ to $t_\tau + H_\tau$, is put into effect at decision time $t_\tau$, where the horizon is $H_\tau$ and the period is $P_\tau = t_{\tau+1} - t_\tau$.

revised and replaced by new plans. These portions of the plans are shown as the shaded segments of Figure 1. They can be interpreted as decisions concerning the future levels of the control variable that are superceded on the basis of information available at a later point in time. Consider, for example, the case of corporate capital budgeting introduced in Section 2, for which the horizon is three years and the period is six months. In this case, the last two and one-half years of plans are superceded and can be revised. In such a case, it is desirable to plan over a three-year period, but it is also desirable to reconsider and revise the plan every six months on the basis of the most recently available information. As another example, a U.S. president might commit his or her administration to a series of decisions extending over perhaps ten to fifteen years or even longer, but the latter portion of such a plan can possibly be revised by a new administration.

### 4.4     Overall results

The fourth and last step is that of overall results for the overall planner choosing decision times $\{t_\tau\}$ and delegating the problem of planning to a sequence of planners, planner $\tau$ choosing horizon $H_\tau$ and the trajectory

$\{\alpha_\tau(t)\}$ over $[t_\tau, t_\tau + H_\tau)$ and being replaced at the end of the period $t_{\tau+1}$ by planner $\tau + 1$. The resulting expected net benefit is

$$V = E\left\{ \sum_{\tau=0}^{\infty} \int_{t_\tau}^{t_{\tau+1}} B(x(t), \alpha_\tau(t)) e^{-rt}\, dt - C_\tau(H_\tau) e^{-rt_\tau} \right\}, \tag{9}$$

where $\alpha_\tau(t)$ depends on the horizon $H_\tau$. Note that $V$ is not the sum of the $V_\tau$ in (8). The system dynamics are then summarized by

$$\dot{x}(t) = f(x(t), \alpha_\tau(t), u(t), t) \quad \text{for } t \in [t_\tau, t_{\tau+1}), \tag{10}$$

$$x(t_\tau) = \lim_{t \uparrow t_\tau} x(t). \tag{11}$$

*Traditional* approaches to planning utilize a fixed time interval for both the horizon and period and set them equal to one another

$$H_\tau = H = P = P_\tau,$$

as in annual budgets, where $H = P = 1$ year. More generally, *autonomous* approaches to planning utilize fixed time intervals for both the horizon and period, which need not be equal,

$$H_\tau = H \geq P = P_\tau, \tag{12}$$

such as the corporate capital budgets that cover three years and are revised every six months, where $H = 3$ years $> P = \frac{1}{2}$ year. In *general* approaches to planning, only condition (7) is imposed, allowing both the horizon and the period to change over time and also allowing for the period to be determined possibly by events as well as by the time interval, as in the $(s, S)$ inventory policy, parliamentary systems of government, and investment for capacity expansion. Thus, the autonomous approach is a special case of the general approach, whereas the traditional approach is a special case of the autonomous approach. When $u(t)$ is a stationary stochastic process, the solutions for the horizon and period involve the autonomous approach. If $u(t)$ is a nonstationary stochastic process, however, the optimal horizons and periods are generally not autonomous.

The formal framework thus far has involved time planning, in which the decision times $t_\tau$ are determined in (4) as certain specific times. In event planning, the overall planner determines not the specific $t_\tau$ but a decision rule under which the plan is revised when the state variables attain certain values in a given *revision manifold R* in $E^{n+1}$ as

$$t_\tau \quad \text{defined by } (x(t_\tau), t_\tau) \in R \tag{13}$$

The overall planner solves (4) for $R$ rather than for $t_\tau$. An example is the $(s, S)$ inventory plan where the manifold is defined by the two parameters $s$ and $S$.

## 5          Five theorems on planning

The optimal planning framework introduced in the last section leads to five theorems on planning.

**Theorem 1.** In general, a positive horizon is better than a zero horizon.

Here, a zero horizon refers to the extreme case, in which decisions are made at each instant with no account taken of future decisions over later periods. This extreme case generally leads to a lower value of the expected net benefit of the plan than the case of an optimal horizon, which is generally not zero and, at time $t$, is generally determined from the first-order condition for problem (7):

$$E[B(x(t_\tau + H_\tau), \alpha_\tau(t_\tau + H_\tau)]e^{-(r(t_\tau + H_\tau)} - \frac{\partial C}{\partial H_\tau}e^{-rt_\tau} = 0. \qquad (14)$$

The theorem holds other than in certain extreme cases, where the difference in (14) is negative when computed at $H_\tau = 0$. In such cases, $H_\tau^* = 0$ is optimal. For example, if the discount rate is infinite, $r = \infty$, so that no account is taken of the future, then the optimal horizon is zero. Another extreme case is one in which the cost function is discontinuous in $H_\tau$, rising from a small (e.g., zero) value to a large (e.g., infinite) value in moving from $H_\tau = 0$ to $H_\tau > 0$. In this case, it is not worthwhile to take account of the future due to the extreme cost of doing so. In such extreme cases with $H_\tau^* = 0$, the expected net benefit function reduces to the discounted sum of benefits less costs, as in benefit–cost analysis, where $\alpha_\tau(t)$ summarizes the decisions made at time $t_\tau$. Leaving aside such extreme cases, however, this type of analysis, in which no account is taken of the future values of the state variables, in particular, the effects of current choices on future states, is, by the theorem, generally worse than an analysis in which such effects are taken specifically into account. For example, weapons systems planning that takes into account only the first year's cost, as was done by the Department of Defense in the 1950s, is inferior to planning that takes into account the later years' costs as well, for example, planning over five years or over the lifetime of the weapons system.

**Theorem 2.** A permanent plan is optimal when there are no costs of planning and there is no uncertainty.

Here, a permanent plan is one with an infinite period, for which $P_0^* = \infty$, so $H_0^* = \infty$. In this case, all decisions are made at the outset, at $\tau = 0$, covering all decisions to be made in the infinite future. Once this plan is put into effect, there is no revision of the plan. Furthermore, the horizon is infinite, since it must cover all future time. In this case, the expected net benefit function in (9) reduces to

$$V = \int_{t_0}^{\infty} B(x_t, \alpha_0(t))e^{-rt} \, dt - C_0 e^{-rt_0}, \tag{15}$$

as in the usual *optimal control problem* where $\alpha_0(t)$ represents the time paths of the control variables chosen at $t_0$ and covering all future time.

To demonstrate this theorem, note that since there is no uncertainty, the equations of motion (10) can be integrated forward from the given $x_0, t_0$ values to yield values of the state variables at any time as functions of the present and all past (optimal) plans,

$$x(t) = F_t[\alpha_\tau(t), \alpha_{t-1}(t), ..., \alpha_0(t)] \quad \text{for } t \in [t_\tau, t_{\tau+1}). \tag{16}$$

Thus, the expected net benefit in (9) can be expressed in this case as

$$\max V = \sum_{\tau=0}^{\infty} \int_{t_\tau}^{t_{\tau+1}} B(F_t[\alpha_\tau(t), \alpha_{t-1}(t), ..., \alpha_0(t)], \alpha_\tau(t))e^{-rt} \, dt, \tag{17}$$

the expectation sign being dropped because of the fact that there is no uncertainty and the cost function being dropped because of the assumption of no costs of planning. Consider an increase in $P_0 = t_1 - t_0$, or, equivalently, an increase in $t_1$ since $t_0$ is fixed. All of the later periods $P_\tau$ can be adjusted in such a way that there is no change in each of the integrals in (7) starting from $\tau = 1$. Thus, the effect of the increase in $t_1$, which would reduce the second integral from $t_1$ to $t_2$, can be offset entirely by an increase in $t_2$. The effect of the increase in $t_2$ can, in turn, be offset by an increase in $t_3$, and so on. Then the effect of an increase in $t_1$ is

$$\frac{\partial V}{\partial t_1} = B(F_{t_1}[\alpha_0(t)], \alpha_0(t))e^{-rt_1} = \frac{\partial V}{\partial P_0} > 0.$$

Since this partial is positive for all $t_1$, the optimal $t_1$ is infinite, so $P_0^* = \infty$, involving a permanent plan. Since $H_0 \geq P_0$, it follows that $H_0^* = \infty$. Thus, in this case, a permanent plan, with $P_0^* = H_0^* = \infty$, is optimal.

**Theorem 3.** A rolling plan with an infinite horizon is optimal when there are no costs of planning and there is uncertainty.

Here a rolling plan is one with a zero period, $P_\tau^* = 0$, so decisions are being continuously revised in the light of new information. In this case,

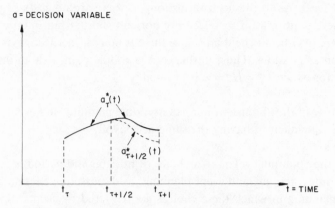

Figure 2. The plan $\alpha_\tau^*(t)$ is optimal conditional on information available up to $t_\tau$, specifically all $x_t$ for $t \le t_\tau$. The plan $\alpha_{\tau+1/2}^*(t)$ is optimal conditional up to $t_{\tau+1/2}$.

the benefit and cost functions take explicit account of the effects of current decisions on all future values of the state variables.

This theorem can be illustrated using a geometric argument. Consider the optimal plan $\alpha_\tau^*(t)$ at time $t_\tau$ conditional on information available up to time $t_\tau$, specifically the set of all $x_t$ for $t \le t_\tau$. In the case of a single decision variable, this optimal plan is shown as the solid curve in Figure 2, and it remains in effect from $t_\tau$ to $t_{\tau+1}$. Consider now dividing the interval in half, at $t_{\tau+1/2}$, allowing for a revision of the plan at this halfway point. The plan $\alpha_\tau^*(t)$ is now in effect from $t_\tau$ to $t_{\tau+1/2}$. A new plan $\alpha_{\tau+1/2}^*(t)$ starts at $t_{\tau+1/2}$, shown as the dotted curve Figure 2. This new plan, which remains in effect from $t_{\tau+1/2}$ to $t_{\tau+1}$, uses information available from $t_\tau$ to $t_{\tau+1/2}$, specifically the values assumed by $x_t$ for $t_\tau < t < t_{\tau+1/2}$. This information was not available at time $t_\tau$ since $x_t$ is affected by the stochastic term $u_t$. This added information may be of use in planning over the period from $t_{\tau+1/2}$ to $t_{\tau+1}$. Thus, the value of the expected net benefit function must be greater or at least no worse for the shorter interval between planning times. The same division-in-half argument can then apply for $t_{\tau+1/4}$. The argument can continue to be applied for any finite interval between successive plans so long as the two assumptions – that $x_t$ is affected by the stochastic term (so there is a value in using the information in the later part of the interval between plans) – and that there is no cost of planning (so there is no cost in using a shorter interval between plans) are maintained. The result of this process is an optimal period $P_\tau^* = 0$. As to the horizon, as long as there are no costs of planning, there is no reason to select any horizon short of an infinite one, since there may be a benefit and since there is no cost in selecting as long a horizon as possible. Thus, in this case, a rolling plan with an infinite horizon for which $P_\tau^* = H_\tau^* = \infty$ is optimal.

**Theorem 4.** In the absence of uncertainty, time planning and event planning are equivalent in having the same net payoff.

Here time planning refers to a choice of horizon and period based on specific time intervals, and event planning, as discussed in Section 3, refers to planning in which these choices are triggered by events. Specifically, in event planning, the plan is revised when the state variables attain values in a given revision manifold $R$ as in (13).[12] Time planning, then, is the special case for which the revision manifold does not depend on $x(t_\tau)$, with it depending only on the $t_\tau$. In the case of certainty, where the future of the system can be determined solely on the basis of decisions made by the planner, events can be predicted exactly, so there is no difference between time planning and event planning.

To demonstrate this theorem, note that here, as in Theorem 2, no uncertainty makes it possible to integrate the equations of motion forward to obtain the values of the state variables as functions of all past plans, as in (16). Time planning and event planning are then equivalent. Knowing the times $t_\tau^*$ at which plans are optimally revised, it is possible to define the revision manifold in terms of these $t_\tau^*$, independent of $x(t_\tau)$. Conversely, given the optimal revision manifold $R^*$, knowledge of the time paths of the state variables implies that it is possible to determine explicitly those times $t_\tau^*$ such that $(x(t_\tau^*), t_\tau^*) \in R^*$.

**Theorem 5.** In the presence of uncertainty, event planning has a higher expected net payoff than time planning.

With uncertainty, events cannot be predicted exactly, so taking account of new information conveyed by the state of the system, which responds to uncertain "outside" influences as well as to the decisions of the planner, can improve performance as measured by the expected net benefit. An exceptional case is that for which $P_\tau^* = 0$, as in this continuous revision case there can be no difference between time planning and event planning.

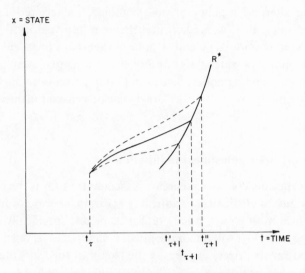

Figure 3. The anticipated optimal path for the state variable is the solid curve. Alternative possible paths are dotted. With event planning using the revision manifold $R^*$, the plan is revised at $t'_{\tau+1}$, $t_{\tau+1}$, or $t''_{\tau+1}$, depending on which path is taken by the state variable.

This theorem can be illustrated using a geometric argument, as in Theorem 3. Figure 3 shows, in the case of a single state variable, its anticipated optimal path from $t_\tau$ to $t_{\tau+1}$ as the solid curve. The plan is revised at time $t_{\tau+1}$. Because of the uncertainty that is present, however, the state variable may take a different path, and two alternative paths are shown as dotted lines. The revision manifold is given as $R^*$. Under time planning, the plan is revised at time $t_{\tau+1}$ (which can be considered the special case of a vertical revision manifold at $t_{\tau+1}$). Under event planning, the plan is revised at time $t_{\tau+1}$ if the actual path is the same as the anticipated optimal path or at time $t'_{\tau+1}$ or $t''_{\tau+1}$ if the actual path veers away from the anticipated optimal path. The decision to revise the plan is thus based on information on the state, which can increase the value of the expected net benefit of the plan.

An example of Theorem 5 on the optimality of event planning is the optimality of the $(s, S)$ inventory policy. The $(s, S)$ policy is one of reordering at times when the inventory level falls below a certain critical level $s$, which is precisely event planning, decisions being determined not a priori but in response to the (uncertain) evolution of the system. This policy is superior to the alternative policy of time planning, namely reordering at certain fixed intervals.[13] A fundamental theorem in inventory theory states that $(s, S)$ is an optimal inventory policy. Theorem 5 broadens and extends this theorem to a wider class of problems, stating that event planning is an optimal planning policy. The next section presents an application of event planning to yet another area, that of price adjustment in inflation.

## 6     Example: price adjustment in inflation

An example of the concepts and theorems presented thus far is the planning used by a monopolistic firm in adjusting prices in a period of inflation.[14] Such a firm must choose a horizon for its prices, specifically over how long a time interval it will honor the prices it announces. It must also choose a period for its prices, specifically the length of the time interval before it establishes new prices, and this time interval could be determined via time or event planning. A traditional plan would, for example, be an annual catalog, where the published prices are honored for a year and where at the end of the year a new catalog is published, entailing both a one-year horizon and a one-year period. A less traditional plan would, by contrast, involve a catalog published every six months where the published prices are honored for a year, entailing a one-year horizon and a six-month period. Such a firm must also choose between time planning, as in these examples, or event planning, where the decision to revise prices is influenced by the state of the system, such as the level of the aggregate price level. For example, in event planning, prices might be revised if the aggregate price level has risen by more than 50 percent.

All five theorems discussed earlier are relevant to this example. As in Theorem 1, a positive horizon is better (i.e., more profitable to the firm) than a zero horizon, with the firm honoring price commitments over the positive horizon. As in Theorem 2, a permanent plan is optimal if there are no costs of planning and there is no uncertainty. In this case, the firm might, for example, simply announce once and for all the rate at which its prices are rising. This fixed rate might be related (e.g., equal to) the (known) inflation rate. As in Theorem 3, if there are no costs of planning (i.e., costs of revising prices) and uncertainty, then a rolling plan is optimal. In this case, the firm continually revises its prices, based on the realized aggregate rate of inflation. As in Theorem 4, if there is no uncertainty (i.e., inflation is perfectly anticipated), then time planning and event planning are equivalent. Both will lead to the same level of profits, and the firm could revise its plan at either fixed intervals or in response to a particular realized level of inflation. Finally, as in Theorem 5, event planning is superior to time planning in the case of uncertainty. In this case, where the inflation rate is not known or fully anticipated, the firm that revises its prices based on the realized rate of inflation will have a higher expected profit than an identical firm that revises its prices at fixed time intervals. The remainder of this section will summarize some results concerning the last two cases, involving the firm adjusting prices both where inflation occurs at a known constant rate and where inflation occurs at an uncertain rate.

The case of inflation at a known constant rate illustrates Theorem 4 on the optimality of time planning in the absence of uncertainty. Letting $p(t)$ be the nominal price charged by the firm at time $t$, if the general price level $\bar{p}(t)$ is rising exponentially at the known constant rate of inflation $g$, then the real price charged by the firm is

$$z(t) = p(t)/\bar{p}(t) = p(t)e^{-gt},$$

where, by normalization, $\bar{p}(0) = 1$. The firm revises its nominal prices at the times $t_\tau$, starting from $t_0 = 0$, so that over the period from $t_\tau$ to $t_{\tau+1}$, the real price is given as

$$z_\tau(t) = p_\tau e^{-gt}, \qquad t \in [t_\tau, t_{\tau+1}), \tag{18}$$

where $p_\tau$ is the fixed nominal price during the period $[t_\tau, t_{\tau-1})$. The firm chooses a set of decision times $t_\tau$ and a set of nominal prices $p_\tau$ so as to maximize the total discounted profits, given, as in (9), as

$$V_0 = \sum_{\tau=0}^{\infty} \int_{t_\tau}^{t_{\tau+1}} F(z_\tau(t))e^{-rt} \, dt - \beta e^{-rt_{\tau+1}}.$$

Here, $F(z_\tau(t))$ is the real profit function of the firm, which depends on the real price level in (18) and is comparable to the benefit function $B(\cdot)$ in (9), and $\beta$ is the real cost of nominal price adjustment assumed to be incurred at the end of the period, $t_{\tau+1}$. In this case of no uncertainty, the firm can, according to Theorem 4, optimally use time planning, and Sheshinski and Weiss (1977) proved that such planning is indeed optimal. In particular, they showed that the optimal policy is one in which the periods $P_\tau = t_{\tau+1} - t_\tau$ are all equal,

$$P_\tau = \epsilon, \quad \text{for all } \tau, \quad \text{i.e.,} \quad t_{\tau+1} = t_\tau + \epsilon, \quad \text{for all } \tau, \tag{19}$$

and the nominal prices are chosen so that the real prices are the same at the beginning of each period

$$z_\tau(t_\tau) = S, \quad \text{for all } \tau,$$

$$\text{i.e., } \quad z_\tau(t) = Se^{-g(t-t_\tau)}, \qquad t \in [t_\tau, t_{\tau+1}). \tag{20}$$

Since the periods are all the same, the real prices are the same at the beginning of each period, and since inflation occurs at a constant rate, the real prices are also the same at the end of each period

$$z_\tau(t_{\tau+1}) = s, \quad \text{for all } \tau \quad \text{where } s = Se^{-g\epsilon}.$$

The real price thus moves between $S$ and $s$ in each period, declining, given the constant nominal price, at the inflation rate $g$. The firm thus starts at time $t_0 = 0$ by setting a nominal price $P_0 = S$, and it retains this nominal price up to time $t_1 = \epsilon$, at which time it revises the nominal price $p_1 = Se^{g\epsilon}$, so the real price is $S$. It retains this new nominal price up to time $t_2 = 2\epsilon$, at which time it revises the nominal price to $p_2 = Se^{2g\epsilon}$, and so on.

The interval between decision times is constant ($\epsilon$), and the real price at each of the decision times is also constant ($S$). These two constants, determined on the basis of the rate of inflation ($g$), the cost of price adjustment ($\beta$), and the parameters characterizing the net revenue function ($F(\cdot)$), completely characterize the optimal pricing plan of the monopolistic firm in a situation of inflation in which there is no uncertainty. This solution is one of time planning, as in Theorem 4.

The case of inflation at an unknown and stochastically determined rate illustrates Theorem 5 on the optimality of event planning in the presence of uncertainty.[15] In this case, if the general price level $\bar{p}(t)$ responds to random shocks instead of rising exponentially, then, at time $t$,

$$\log \bar{p}(t) = \sum_{i=1}^{N_t} y_i. \tag{21}$$

Here the $y_i$ are assumed independently and are identically distributed as $h(y)$, and the number of random shocks influencing the system at time $t$, given as $N_t$ in (21), is determined by the Poisson process, where

$$\text{Prob}\{N_t = n\} = e^{-\lambda t} \frac{(\lambda t)^n}{n!}$$

so that

$$E(\log \bar{p}(t)) = \lambda t E(y).$$

Under these assumptions, Sheshinski and Weiss (1983) proved the optimality of event planning, where the firm always sets a nominal price $p_\tau$ at the decision times $t_\tau$ so that the real price is always $S$ at these times, as in the case of a certain inflation rate (20). By contrast to the certainty case, however, in this case of uncertainty, the periods are not constant. Rather, the real price floats down, depending on the random shocks in (21), and the optimal policy is one of event planning where the next decision time is determined as that time when the real price assumes the value $s$, as in $(s, S)$ inventory planning. Because of the uncertainty in the system, the lengths of the periods are not constant, in contrast to (19), and they are not predictable a priori. This type of event planning, where the period is determined endogenously by the evolution of the uncertain system, yields a higher value for expected profits than does time planning, where the period is determined as a fixed time interval. It thus illustrates Theorem 5.

An extension of this case of price adjustment by a monopolistic firm in the case of stochastic inflation would treat the case in which the general price level is not known but must be determined, where its determination entails certain costs. For example, the general price level relevant to a particular firm may be obtained only via subscribing to trade journals or by sampling prices of firms in related markets. In such a situation, the optimal policy is one in which the firm determines the general price level at certain fixed time intervals but then adjusts its own price relative to the general price level as determined at these fixed times, according to event planning, as described above. Thus, at the time the general price level is determined, the nominal price would be left unchanged or revised upward according to whether the real price is above or below $s$. This case of stochastic inflation (in which the price level must be determined) therefore leads to hybrid planning, combining time planning for the determination of the general price level with event planning for the revision of the firm's nominal price.

This example of price adjustment in inflation illustrates the nature of time and event planning, the theorem on event planning, and also the nature of hybrid planning. It is, in fact, one of two problems discussed in the literature where the concepts of planning (as developed here) have been treated, the other being inventory planning, particularly the $(s, S)$ inventory policy. An important implication of this chapter is that these concepts apply not just to these problems but, in fact, to a much wider range of planning problems for not only firms but also for all planners, whether firms, individuals, government agencies, or nations.

## 7 Conclusions

This chapter has identified two decisions that are part of any planning process, namely the horizon of the plan and the period of the plan. A for-

Table 1. *Optimal planning depends on whether or not there are costs of planning and whether or not there is uncertainty*

| Cost of planning | Uncertainty | |
| --- | --- | --- |
| | No uncertainty | Uncertainty |
| No cost of planning | *Permanent plan:* an initial plan covering all future time adopted at $t_0$ and never revised ($P_0^* = \infty$, $H_0^* = \infty$) (Theorem 2) | *Rolling plan with an infinite horizon:* continuous revision of the plan at each point in time, with planning over all future time ($P_\tau^* = 0$, $H_\tau^* = \infty$) (Theorem 3) |
| Costs of planning | *Time planning or event planning:* period chosen either as a specific time interval or dependent on certain events ($P_\tau^*$ and $H_\tau^*$ can be chosen independently of the state of the system) (Theorem 4) | *Event planning:* period dependent on events, with the revision of the plan possibly triggered by events rather than time ($P_\tau^*$ determined as $t_{\tau+1}^* - t_\tau^*$, where $(x(t_\tau^*), t_\tau^*) \in R_\tau^*$, a revision manifold at time $t_\tau$) (Theorem 5) |

mal framework for planning has been introduced in which the first stage is that of choosing the horizon and period, and the second stage is that of choosing a specific plan. This framework has led to five theorems on planning, of which the first states that a positive horizon is generally preferable to a zero horizon. The other four theorems are summarized in Table 1, showing the optimality of different types of planning in different situations, depending on the presence or absence both of costs of planning and of uncertainty. The problem of price adjustment in inflation illustrates the nature of these theorems. This problem and that of inventory planning by the firm (in particular, the $(s, S)$ policy) are the two cases in which the issues treated here – in particular the concepts of horizon and period and the contrast between time planning and event planning – have been discussed in the literature. A principal conclusion of this chapter is that these concepts can be applied to a much wider class of planning problems.

It is hoped that this chapter will contribute toward more deliberately set and more informed choices about planning, which can significantly improve performance in a wide variety of settings. It is also hoped that models of specific planning processes, such as capacity expansion and portfolio selection, will be expanded to include specific consideration of the choices of horizon and period and to allow for the possibility of event as well as time planning. Finally, it is hoped that this essay will stimulate the further development of a pure theory of planning.

NOTES

1  For discussions of planning and its different aspects, typically in the context of national economic policy, see Tinbergen (1952, 1954, 1956, 1964), Theil (1961, 1964), Hickman (1965), Kornai (1967), Hansen (1967), Chakravarty (1969), Lange (1971), Heal (1973), Czerwinski and Porwit (1977), Deleau and Malgrange (1977), and Intriligator (1978).
2  Using a numerical linear-quadratic formulation that allows for both the cost of uncertainty and progressively acquired information on uncontrolled factors, Deleau and Malgrange (1974) found that for a five-year horizon, revision near the end of the period (years 3, 4, and 5) is favored. Their numerical results in fact suggest that a four-year period is optimal, with the plan being revised in the fourth year. See Intriligator (1971) for a discussion of linear-quadratic control problems.
3  For a discussion of a rolling plan in the context of an optimal growth model, see Goldman (1968). For a discussion of a shifting finite time horizon, see Inagaki (1970).
4  For a discussion of the $(s, S)$ inventory policy, see Scarf (1960).
5  For a discussion of the $(t, S)$ policy and its relation to the $(s, S)$ policy, see Naddor (1962).
6  See Srinivasan (1967) and Manne (1967). For related models dealing with the timing of investments, see Flemming (1969), Weitzman (1970), and Dixit, Mirrlees, and Stern (1975).
7  If there are several indicators of the state of the system, then the event triggering the need for a new plan should be based on all these indicators. Radner (1964) investigated this issue with reference to command and control decisions. He considered the case of two sensors, such as lights on a panel, that, when lit indicate the need for action; when not lit, involve no need for action; and which could be accidentally turned on, involving a known probability distribution. He showed that a desirable rule for action in such a case is the likelihood ratio rule of acting if $w_1 > \bar{w}_1$ or $w_2 > \bar{w}_2$ or $\min(w_1, w_2) > \bar{w}$, where $w_i$ is the length of elapsed time during which the $i$th sensor is turned on $(i = 1, 2,)$ and $\bar{w}_1$, $\bar{w}_2$, and $\bar{w}$ are parameters obtained from the probability distribution and the disutility for a type I error (do not act when should act) as compared to that for a type II error (act when should not act). The examination of this rule and its comparison to other rival rules is instructive, but the major problem is probably that of identifying and obtaining the sensors in the first place or recognizing critical events, rather than in adjudicating between them.

8  As formulated here, the stochastic disturbance term applies only to the equations of motion (2). More generally, the benefit–cost functions in (1) can also be influenced, in part, by stochastic disturbance terms.

9  Note that a *plan* is a set of decisions concerning present and future values of certain choice variables. In particular, it is not the same as a *strategy*, which relates the choice variables to the state variables of the system.

10  For a similar formulation of a criterion function for a related problem, see Sheshinski and Weiss (1977, 1978). See also Chakravarty (1969) for a related approach.

11  As an example, weapons procurement decisions that treat only costs of the first few years can lead to commitments with ballooning costs in later years – the "camel's nose under the tent" approach, avoided by using longer horizons.

12  The state variables may cross these values several times. To determine at which of these times the plan should be revised, it is necessary to discriminate among these several crossings. One such way is to introduce as added state variables the first, second, and higher time derivatives of the original state variables and to discriminate on the basis of these higher derivatives.

13  For the optimality of the $(s, S)$ policy in inventory planning, see Scarf (1960). For the result that states that in the case of a separable cost function, the $(s, S)$ policy of reordering at times when the level of inventory falls below a certain critical level (event planning) is superior to the $(t, S)$ policy of reordering at fixed time intervals (time planning), see Naddor (1962).

14  See Sheshinski and Weiss (1977, 1978) for a treatment of price adjustment in the presence of a perfectly anticipated aggregate rate of inflation. For extensions to the case in which the aggregate rate of inflation is stochastic, see Padon (1981), Sheshinski and Weiss (1983), and Danziger (1984). For an empirical analysis of price adjustment in inflation, see Sheshinski, Tishler, and Weiss (1981). For related work on price adjustment by a monopolist firm, see Arrow (1962) and Barro (1972).

15  The developments reported here are based on Sheshinski and Weiss (1983), who developed event planning for the case of uncertain inflation. Danziger (1984) also treated uncertain inflation but developed only time planning for this case.

## REFERENCES

Arrow, K. J. (1962), "Toward a theory of price adjustment," in M. Abramowitz et al. (Eds.), *The allocation of economic resources,* Stanford: Stanford University Press.

Barro, R. J. (1972), "A theory of monopolistic price adjustment," *Review of Economic Studies,* 39: 17–26.

Chakravarty, S. (1969), *Capital and development planning,* Cambridge, Mass.: MIT Press.

Czerwinski, Z. and K. Porwit (1977), "The role of quantitative methods in central planning in Poland," in M. D. Intriligator (Ed.), *Frontiers of quantitative economics,* Vol. III, Amsterdam: North-Holland.

Danziger, L. (1984), "Stochastic inflation and the optimal policy of price adjustment," *Economic Inquiry,* 22: 98–108.

Deleau, M. and P. Malgrange (1974), "Information and contrastochastic dynamic economic policies," *European Economic Review,* 5: 159–75.

Deleau, M. and P. Malgrange (1977), "Recent trends in French planning," in M. D. Intriligator (Ed.), *Frontiers of quantitative economics,* Vol. III, Amsterdam: North-Holland.

Dixit, A., J. Mirrlees, and N. Stern (1975), "Optimum savings with economies of scale," *Review of Economic Studies,* 42: 303–25.

Flemming, J. S. (1969), "The utility of wealth and the utility of windfalls," *Review of Economic Studies,* 36: 55–66.

Goldman, S. M. (1968), "Optimal growth and continual planning revision," *Review of Economic Studies,* 35: 145–54.

Hansen, B. (1967), *Long and short term planning in underdeveloped countries,* Amsterdam: North-Holland.

Heal, G. M. (1973), *The theory of economic planning,* Amsterdam: North-Holland.

Hickman, B. (Ed.) (1965), *Quantitative planning of economic policy,* Washington, D.C.: Brookings Institution.

Inagaki, M. (1970), *Optimal economic growth,* Amsterdam: North-Holland.

Intriligator, M. D. (1971), *Mathematical optimization and economic theory,* Englewood Cliffs, N.J.: Prentice-Hall.

Intriligator, M. D. (1978), *Econometric models, techniques and applications,* Englewood Cliffs, N.J.: Prentice-Hall.

Kornai, J. (1967), *Mathematical planning of structural decisions,* Amsterdam: North-Holland.

Lange, O. (1971), *Optimal decisions: Principles of programming,* Oxford: Pergamon Press.

Manne, A. S. (Ed.) (1967), *Investments for capacity expansion: Size, location, and time phasing,* Cambridge, Mass.: MIT Press.

Naddor, E. (1962), "A comparison of $(t, S)$ and $(s, S)$ policies," *Operations Research,* 10: 401–03.

Padon, O. (1981), "Optimal price adjustments under stochastic inflation," Ph.D. Dissertation, The Hebrew University, Jerusalem.

Radner, R. (1964), "Command control based on time to failure," SDC, SP-1530/000/000.

Scarf, H. (1960), "The optimality of $(S, s)$ policies in the dynamic inventory problem," in K. J. Arrow, S. Karlin, and P. Suppes (Eds.), *Mathematical methods in the social sciences, 1959,* Stanford: Stanford University Press.

Sheshinski, E. and Y. Weiss (1977), "Inflation and costs of price adjustment," *Review of Economic Studies,* 44: 287–303.

Sheshinski, E. and Y. Weiss (1978), "Demand for fixed factors, inflation, and adjustment costs," *Review of Economic Studies,* 45: 31–45.

Sheshinski, E. and Y. Weiss (1983), "Optimal pricing policy under stochastic inflation," *Review of Economic Studies,* 50: 513–29.

Sheshinski, E., A. Tishler, and Y. Weiss (1981), "Inflation costs of adjustment, and the amplitude of real price changes," in M. J. Flanders and A. Razin (Eds.), *Development in an inflationary world,* New York: Academic Press.

Srinivasan, T. N. (1967), "Geometric growth of reward," in A. S. Manne (Ed.), *Investment for capacity expansion: Size, location, and time-phasing,* Cambridge: MIT Press.

Theil, H. (1961), *Economic forecasts and policy,* 2nd ed., Amsterdam: North-Holland.

Theil, H. (1964), *Optimal decision rules for government and industry,* Chicago: Rand-McNally and Amsterdam: North-Holland.

Tinbergen, J. (1952), *On the theory of economic policy,* Amsterdam: North-Holland.

Tinbergen, J. (1954), *Centralization and decentralization in economic policy,* Amsterdam: North-Holland.

Tinbergen, J. (1956), *Economic policy: Principles and design,* Amsterdam: North-Holland.

Tinbergen, J. (1964), *Central planning,* New Haven: Yale University Press.

Weitzman, M. L. (1970), "Optimum growth with scale economies in the creation of overhead capital," *Review of Economic Studies,* 37: 555-70.

CHAPTER 8

# On the social risk premium

*David A. Starrett*

Kenneth Arrow (1966, 1971; Arrow and Lind 1970) pioneered much of what we know about individual risk aversion and the social rate of discount. He couched most of his analysis in the context of partial equilibrium models or the Arrow–Debreu complete market structure. Since that time, much work has been done to develop useful models of incomplete market structure. I have in mind especially the Diamond–Dreze model for studying the stock market (Diamond 1967; Dreze 1974) and the capital asset pricing (CAP) model introduced by Lintner (1965) and Sharpe (1964). The purpose of this chapter is to reexamine some of Arrow's early contributions in the context of these structures. First, we develop measures of the social risk premium in the context of the Diamond–Dreze model. These measures turn out to involve the degree of individual risk aversion [as captured in the measures developed by Arrow (1965) and Pratt (1964)], as we should expect. But, in addition, they incorporate project betas, which reflect the degree of correlation between project risk and the underlying uncertainty. These project betas play much the same role as asset betas in the CAP model.

Having developed the appropriate corrections for risk, we ask whether the public sector should behave any differently from the private sector in risk discounting. Aside from differences in betas, we find no compelling reasons for unequal treatment when comparing small projects. However, with respect to large projects, we argue that the government may well be justified in discounting less for risk than the private sector.

## 1    The Diamond–Dreze model

We start with the two-period model of Diamond and Dreze. In this model, the spot markets are ignored (or at least suppressed) by assuming that consumption at each date is represented by a market aggregate. This framework nests itself naturally in a more general model under the additional assumption that spot prices are unaffected by social decisions (so that we can think in terms of a Hicksian aggregate).

Since there is nothing left to decide in the second (last) period, all decisions are made ex ante in the first period, when the household splits its resources between consumption now and a set of assets that allow for a limited degree of risk sharing across states of the world ex post in the second period. These assets may be offered through the market (in which case they are best thought of as equity or bonds in private or public firms) or directly by the government through tax/subsidy arrangements. Given our present aggregation, there is no useful way to discuss indirect taxation, so we will assume for now that any taxes or subsidies are lump sum. To emphasize the connections between direct and market risk sharing, we will give payments a positive (subsidy) orientation and label them $s$. Finally, we asume away any other sources of lump-sum income. Aside from its historical interest, this model enables us to isolate issues involving uncertainty from those involving other elements that are second best in an intertemporal environment. We will comment briefly later on the implications these other elements may have for optimal social discounting. [A more complete discussion of these issues is presented in Starrett (forthcoming, Chapter 12).]

A typical market asset $(k)$ pays off in a specific configuration of returns over states of the world $[d_2^k(\omega)]$ per unit held. Let asset $k$ sell at price $e_k$. As an example, it is useful to think of a "safe" government bond (if one exists, we will think of it as the zero*th* asset). Then, $d_2^0(\omega)$ is a constant and $e_0/d_2^0$ would be the safe discount factor (cost today of getting a sure dollar tomorrow). When it exists, we label the safe discount factor $\rho$.

Our typical household now faces a portfolio problem of the form:

$$\max_{c_1, a} E_\omega[U^h(c_1, d_2(\omega)a + s_2^h(\omega))] \tag{1.1}$$

subject to

$$c_1 + e(a - \bar{a}^h) = s_1^h,$$

where $a$ stands for the vector of final asset holdings, $\bar{a}^h$, for initial holdings and $c$ is net consumption purchases (consumption minus resource holding). [Prices (and shadow prices) generally will be represented as row vectors, and quantities are treated as column vectors. The $d$ act like prices in this regard and so become row vectors.] We will let $V^h(s_1, e, d_2[\cdot], s_2[\cdot])$

stand for the associated indirect utility function. Note that we impose no inequality constraints on $a$ so there are no retrictions on short sales.

We exhibit, for future reference, the first-order optimality conditions [we use the gradient symbol $(\nabla_x)$ to indicate partial derivatives with respect to a vector $x$ and retain this notation (as, e.g., here) even when $x$ happens to be a scalar]:

$$E_\omega[\nabla_{c1}U^h] = \lambda^h, \tag{1.2}$$

and

$$E_\omega[\nabla_{c2}U^h(\omega)d_2(\omega)] = \lambda^h e. \tag{1.3}$$

In these expressions, $\lambda^h$ is the budget constraint multiplier and represents the marginal utility of an ex ante dollar to consumer $h$.

The scope of government projects is limited here to making changes in $d$ or $s$. When $d$ is involved, we can think of the planners as either *changing* the return structure on their own bonds or *regulating* the behavior of private firms. Welfare is measured according to a standard aggregator function $W(V^1, \ldots, V^n)$.

We restrict ourselves, in this section, to projects which are *first order,* meaning that their contribution to welfare can be measured using a first-order Taylor expansion. Thus, we will evaluate welfare change using expressions of the form

$$\delta W = \sum_h \frac{\partial W}{\partial V^h}\delta V^h = \sum_h \beta^h \frac{\delta V^h}{\lambda^h}, \tag{1.4}$$

where $\beta^h$ stands for the marginal welfare of a dollar given to consumer $h$. For simplicity, we will assume that the government has complete control over the ex ante distribution so that ex ante welfare weights (marginal welfare of a dollar) can be and are equalized (and we normalize so that the common value is unity).

Then, by differentiating the indirect utility functions (using the envelope theorem where appropriate) and aggregating, the welfare change from a first-order project may be written in the form

$$\sum_h \frac{\delta V^h}{\lambda^h} = \delta S_1 + \sum_h \left[\frac{E[\nabla_{c2}U^h(\omega)\,\delta d_2(\omega)]}{\lambda^h}a^h\right] + \sum_h \left[\frac{E[\nabla_{c2}U^h(\omega)\,\delta s_2^h(\omega)]}{\lambda^h}\right]. \tag{1.5}$$

[Capital letters (such as $S$ in this expression) always represent economy-wide aggregates of the associated allocation variable. Note that there is no term involving $\delta e$, because $\sum_h (a^h - \bar{a}^h) = 0$ due to asset market clearing.]

The rules associated with this expression can be discussed usefully both as is and with a further breakdown into risk components. We take up these approaches in turn.

### 1.1     *The Diamond–Dreze rules*

Let us focus on the valuation of asset returns $(d_2)$. The specific returns are evaluated by a *weighted Samuelson shadow price*. To see this, it is helpful to introduce new variables:

$$\eta^h(\omega) = \frac{\nabla_{c2} U^h(\omega)}{\lambda^h}, \tag{1.6}$$

where $\eta$ represents personalized shadow values on *Arrow securities* (hypothetical securities that pay off a dollar in a specific state of the world). They are personalized in that they will differ from household to household in the absence of actual Arrow securities. Should they somehow turn out to be equal for all households in each state of the world, then it is as if markets were complete. Note for future reference that if there exists a safe asset, (1.3) implies: $E_\omega \eta^h(\omega) = \rho$.

Now, firm $k$ should evaluate a small change in its output program using the coefficients of $\delta d_2^{\prime k}$ in (1.5). Labeling this vector of shadow prices $\Omega^k$, we have

$$\Omega^k = \sum_h \eta^h(\omega) a_k^h. \tag{1.7}$$

Thus, the firm's shadow price on state-contingent output is a weighted sum of the corresponding shadow prices of its owners, weights deriving from ownership shares. There is an analogy here [emphasized by Dreze (1974)] with the theory of pure public goods that yields important insights. All owners of a particular asset must share its common distribution of returns so that distribution is "public" to shareholders. Of course, owners need not share equally, so components of the Samuelson price are weighted by ex post share holdings. Note that the social objective of a firm issuing assets is well defined here even though our perspective is ex ante. Announced changes are revealed before people trade in our setup so the social objective takes into account anticipated reactions and weights using ex post holdings.

However, it is *not* clear that the optimal behavior can be decentralized as, for example, by letting the stockholders decide. Generally, the firm will not be able to simultaneously satisfy the desires of all its shareholders much less get them to agree on the socially desirable objective. Conflicts seem likely to arise as long as shareholders differ in their $\eta$; they will exhibit relative disagreements about those states of the world on which the firm should concentrate. What should we expect the firm to do in these circumstances? Clearly, we need to answer this question before we can prescribe public policy with respect to risk sharing. And, unfortunately, we do not have a very satisfactory general answer. However, there is a subclass of uncertainty structures that seem fairly general and for which the question has a simple answer.

## 1.2    *Spanning and ex post unanimity*

Suppose that proposed changes lie within the linear subspace of return structures spanned by assets available ex ante. [This section follows Grossman and Stiglitz (1980), who summarized the work initiated by Diamond (1967).] That is, if the changes are thought of as constituting a fictitious new asset, then this asset could be constructed as some linear combination of existing assets. Although this restriction may sound rather severe, there are a number of institutional settings where it seems to make sense [see Ekern and Wilson (1974) for some examples].

When the spanning condition holds, we ought to find that our change is valued in the same way as the associated linear combination of assets. We can see this formally as follows: First, we formalize the spanning condition as

$$\delta d_2(\omega) = d_2(\omega)X, \tag{1.8}$$

where the columns of matrix $X$ represent weights in the linear combination for the associated asset. (Naturally, these weights must be independent of $\omega$.)

Now, using (1.8) to substitute for $\delta d_2(\omega)$ in the Diamond–Dreze term, we find

$$\sum_h E_\omega[\eta(\omega)\,\delta d_2(\omega)]a^h = \sum_h E_\omega[\eta(\omega)d_2(\omega)]Xa^h$$

$$= eX\left[\sum_h a^h\right], \tag{1.9}$$

where the last step involves substitution from the first-order condition (1.3). Clearly, the change is valued at the market cost of the existing bundle of assets that spans it (that is, $eX$). Thus, for example, an asset spanned by an available arbitrage would be worthless, as we should expect.

Furthermore, stockholders now ought to agree that this social objective is the correct policy for the firm. *Regardless* of their personalized prices, a household can "undo" the change by selling the associated spanning portfolio and must be better off if the resulting net proceeds are positive. We can formalize this argument with one caveat. Carrying out the above analysis for the individual rather than society, we find

$$\frac{\delta V^h}{\lambda^h} = \delta S_1 - \delta e(a^h - \bar{a}^h) + eXa^h + E[\eta^h(\omega)\,\delta S_2^h(\omega)]. \tag{1.10}$$

Now, in evaluating a potential change in asset return, the household sees two considerations, one involving the risk sharing benefits from ex post holdings and the other involving capital gains (or losses) on transactions. As we can see, all stockholders *long* in a particular firm will agree on the sign of the first effect (for the reasons outlined in the previous paragraph). But they will *not* agree on the sign of the second; if the price of the asset is to go up, then those planning to sell some of their initial holdings will benefit, but those planning to buy will suffer losses. (From a social point of view, these effects cancel in the present context, which is why no capital gains terms appear in the social objective.)

Of course, if the proposed changes are revealed *after* (rather than before) trading takes place, then no one will be anticipating capital gains and we will observe *unanimity* on firm objectives by those stockholders long in the firm's equity. (Naturally, those *short* will have the opposite desires, but it is safe to assume they will not get to dictate firm behavior!) Thus, we only find stockholder unanimity for ex post announcements. Furthermore, in this ex post context, the social and private objectives agree.

These observations will have important implications for us later when we compare risk sharing potential for the government versus the private market. In particular, we see that (even accepting spanning) the stock market can only be expected to give correct allocations of *d given a* and vice versa. There is no obvious mechanism whereby a decentralized procedure will make both choices simultaneously. This fact has no particular significance in the present context of first-order projects but will become important when we deal with larger projects in Section 3.

However, if spanning fails (or, more generally, if the private and social production objectives differ), the analysis must change, even for small projects. Public *direct* projects will induce changes in private *d*. To the extent that these changes improve the social allocation, the project induces second-best benefits and vice versa. Generally, we will assume that these effects are not significant in the sequel.

## 2        Risk premiums in the Diamond–Dreze model

Let us turn now to the problem of measuring risk. One way of defining risk premiums involves the use of certainty equivalents. However, this method is not sufficiently general for our purposes here. Rather, we will define risk premiums in terms of differences between correct welfare measures and approximations based on simple expectations. Such measures are easy to evaluate here and serve to generalize the Arrow–Pratt measures of individual risk aversion. [Arrow's work on these measures is summarized in Arrow (1971, Chapter 3); see also Pratt (1964).]

We proceed by decomposing the measure (1.5) using the definition of *covariance* to substitute for expectations of products. For example, we write

$$E[\eta^h(\omega)\,\delta s_2^h(\omega)] = E[\eta^h(\omega)]E[\delta s_2^h(\omega)] + \text{cov}[\eta^h(\omega), \delta s_2^h(\omega)]. \tag{2.1}$$

Performing the requisite series of substitutions decomposes (1.5) as

$$\sum_h \frac{\delta V^h}{\lambda^h} = \delta S_1 + \sum_h [E[\eta^h(\omega)]E[\delta d_2(\omega)]a^h] + \sum_h E[\eta^h(\omega)]E[\delta s_2^h(\omega)]$$

$$+ \sum_h [\text{cov}[\eta^h(\omega), \delta d_2(\omega)]a^h] + \sum_h \text{cov}[\eta^h(\omega), \delta s_2^h(\omega)]. \tag{2.2}$$

We argue that the first line in our decomposition would represent the correct welfare measure in a risk-neutral world. The term $E[\eta^h(\omega)]$ represents a riskless (temporal) discount factor for household $h$. In fact, if there exists a risk-free asset, we saw that this term must equal the discount rate on that riskless asset. We label this term $\rho^h$ for future reference. Thus, the first line represents the expected present value of the marginal project with discounting carried out at the risk-free rate.

Consequently, the second line in equation (2.2) should be interpreted as a correction for risk, the first part associated with market assets and the second with direct government activity. These corrections are usefully interpreted as risk premiums the project must earn in its expected rate of return. To see this, assume we are looking at a marginal direct project with unit cost (so $\delta S_1 = -1$, $\delta d = 0$) and there is a riskless asset paying rate of return $r$ [so $\rho^h = \rho = 1/(1+r)$]. This project is socially desirable if the corresponding right side of (2.2) is nonnegative, that is, if

$$\sum_h E[\eta^h(\omega)]E[\delta s_2^h(\omega)] \geq -1 - \sum_h \text{cov}[\eta^h(\omega), \delta s_2^h(\omega)]. \tag{2.3}$$

Substituting the conditions for choice of the safe asset and rearranging somewhat, the condition for acceptance becomes

$$E[\delta S_2^h(\omega)] - 1 \geq r - \sum_h \text{cov}\left[\frac{\eta^h(\omega)}{E\eta^h(\omega)}, \delta s_2^h(\omega)\right]. \tag{2.4}$$

Thus, if we define the government risk premium for direct intervention $(RP_g)$ as

$$RP_g = -\sum_h \text{cov}\left[\frac{\eta^h(\omega)}{E\eta^h(\omega)}, \delta s_2^h(\omega)]\right], \tag{2.5}$$

the project should be accepted if its expected rate of return exceeds the risk-free rate by at least its risk premium. The corresponding analysis for market assets yields a risk premium $(RP_m)$ of the form

$$RP_m = -\sum_h \text{cov}\left[\frac{\eta^h(\omega)}{E\eta^h(\omega)}, \delta d_2(\omega)a^h\right]. \tag{2.6}$$

Examining these, we can answer such questions as (1) how do the social risk premiums relate to Arrow–Pratt measures of individual risk aversion and (2) should the government discount for risk differently than the private sector?

It is useful in our discussion to reintroduce the case of effectively complete markets as a benchmark. Of course, we do not need the present analysis when markets are really complete, but the benchmark still is useful in identifying the risk premium to associate with socially uninsurable risk. The principal implication of complete markets here is that the personalized shadow prices $(\eta^h)$ must be equalized across individuals (obviously this must occur if Arrow security markets exist and all complete market contexts are equivalent).

Note that when the shadow prices are equalized, all references to the individual disappear from the risk terms (and indeed from all terms in the welfare measure). Our risk premiums reduce to

$$RP_m = -\text{cov}[\eta(\omega), \delta d_2(\omega)\bar{a}] \tag{2.7}$$

$$RP_g = -\text{cov}[\eta(\omega), \delta S_2(\omega)], \tag{2.8}$$

where $\bar{a}$ is the vector of total asset supplies.

Our measures immediately suggest a precise definition of *fully insurable risk*. Namely, risk is fully insurable if $\eta$ is independent of $\omega$ (that is, if the marginal welfare of a dollar is state independent). When this independence condition holds, the risk premium terms disappear and our welfare criteria reduces to discounted expected value. As is well known, completion of the markets could be achieved in this case by a full set of insurance markets. [See Malinvaud (1972) for a development of these ideas.]

When some risks are socially uninsurable, the marginal welfare of a dollar will have to be higher in the "bad" states than it is in the "good" ones, and households must absorb this risk on balance. Our risk premiums then reflect the degree to which project net outputs correlate with the badness of state. These correlations are the natural generalization of asset betas in the CAP model and (as there) can be of either sign. A project that provides more net benefits (on balance) in the bad states than it does in the good ones naturally is more desirable in a risk-averse world than it would be in a risk-neutral one; for such a project, the risk premium will be negative.

Presumably, the typical project tends to confer its benefits in the good states and incur its costs in the bad ones, leading to an associated positive risk premium. However, it is interesting to note that projects whose distribution of benefits is independent from the goodness of state generate *no* risk premium. The reader may well be surprised by this result since we generally expect the addition of independent uncertainty to increase risk. Fortunately, there is no paradox here. Remember that our analysis is *first order* and that projects do not change the risk structure to a first order. Only a larger project adds independent risk.

Note that our discussion will apply equally well whether the project involves direct intervention or changes in private production. All that matters is the correlation of net returns with goodness of state. This observation may surprise readers who are familiar with the Arrow–Lind theorem on government discounting (Arrow and Lind 1971), since that theorem suggests conditions under which the government generally should discount less for risk than the private sector. But the theorem relies for its validity on differential capacities to provide risk sharing, so it does not apply in our present context of full insurance.

Let us return to the case of imperfect risk sharing where the risk premiums are measured as (2.5) and (2.6). What are the differences between these two measures now? Obviously, direct intervention involves more control. Although market assets constrain all holders to the same public return structure, the government is not necessarily so constrained. Direct intervention may have an advantage if the government is in a position to improve the degree of risk sharing (thereby giving more net benefits in state $\omega$ to those with especially high marginal valuations in that state and less to others).

However, there must be some limitations on the government's discretion in this regard. Otherwise, planners should provide full risk sharing (regardless of what else is done), and thereafter, we revert to the previous case in which public and private projects appear on equal footing. More-over, the Arrow–Lind theorem *still* does not apply. To see this, let us look more closely at their proposition. The original context was one in which project costs were distributed *uniformly* across households, and it was asserted that as the number of households got larger, the risk pre-mium would get smaller. This proposition fails here. Assuming (as seems appropriate) that we are comparing populations in which the ex ante de-gree of risk sharing is similar, our risk premium will be independent of the number of households: Spreading the costs means that each separate covariance term goes down at the rate $1/N$, but we sum $N$ of these. In-deed, for any direct project in which the net return (tax) structure is *fixed* across individuals, the government risk premium looks just like that for the private sector (where investors share returns in fixed proportions). We need to be talking about *larger* projects before the Arrow–Lind theorem will "bite."

If we are willing to impose some of the extra assumptions made in the CAP model, the risk premiums take more familiar forms. We confine ourselves here to a discussion of the direct intervention term, although the reader should have no trouble supplying the (similar) analysis for market assets. To begin, observe the following identity:

$$\eta^h(\omega) \equiv \rho^h \left[ \frac{\partial U^h(\omega)/\partial c_2}{E_\omega[\partial U^h(\omega)/\partial c_2]} \right]. \tag{2.9}$$

Then, define *certainty equivalent* second-period consumption $(c_{2*}^h)$ hold-ing first-period consumption fixed by the condition

$$\partial U^h(c_{2*}^h)/\partial c_2 = E_\omega(\partial U^h(\omega)/\partial c_2). \tag{2.10}$$

Now, suppose that we expand the marginal utility of income in a first-order Taylor series around the certainty equivalent income. Naturally, this expansion is "exact" only if utility is quadratic; otherwise, the fol-lowing expressions must be thought of as approximations. Utilizing the expansion, we can write

$$\frac{\partial U^h(\omega)/\partial c_2}{E_\omega(\partial U^h(\omega)/\partial c_2)} = -R_A^h(c_{2*}^h)[c_2^h(\omega) - c_{2*}^h], \tag{2.11}$$

where

$$R_A^h(\cdot) = \frac{\partial^2 U^h(\cdot)/\partial(c_2)^2}{\partial U^h(\cdot)/\partial c_2}, \tag{2.12}$$

the generalized Arrow–Pratt measure of absolute risk aversion for house-hold $h$, evaluated at the certainty equivalent income.

Finally, we assemble all these pieces to obtain the following expression for the risk premium:

$$RP_g = \sum_h \rho^h R_A^h(c_{2.}^h) \, \text{cov}[c_2^h(\omega), \delta s_2^h(\omega)]. \tag{2.13}$$

The covariance terms in this expression play the role of betas in the CAP model. They reflect the correlation of the project returns with the status quo ante and thus capture the degree of risk being borne by the associated household.

Consequently, we can think of the risk premium as a weighted sum of absolute risk aversion measures, weights being temporal discount rates times these betas. Of course, when there exists a risk-free asset, all the $\rho$'s will be equal and the weights simplify accordingly. [Wilson (1982) obtained somewhat similar measures (though without the betas) under more stringent assumptions.]

Before generalizing the model further, let us take stock of what we have learned so far about the social rate of discount and its relationship with the private rate. So far, the insights are roughly those of the capital asset pricing model. The rate of discount appropriate to any project (public or private) depends on its return structure, both with respect to its effect on risk sharing and with respect to the way it correlates with the ex ante socially uninsurable risk. Only if the government project *does better* in this regard than alternative private ones should the government use a *lower* discount rate.

Of course, a major argument for lower rates involves imperfections in capital markets and we have ignored these above. [Versions of this argument can be found in Arrow (1982) and Marglin (1963).] Indeed, we can see this argument immediately in the present context. Suppose there is a safe asset but investors face quantity constraints in borrowing. Then, it is well known that the private sector discount rate will exceed the price of the safe asset. [For a demonstration of this proposition in the present welfare context, see Starrett (1979).] Since the government should add its risk component only to the discount rate on the safe asset, it should discount less than would the private sector for this reason. However, it does not follow that government projects are to be favored. If private projects have more favorable return structures, the government should simply provide finance to the private sector (thereby "relaxing" the quantity constraints).

## 3      Larger projects and the Arrow–Lind theorem

We now consider government projects that are large enough to change marginal valuations. Clearly, when this is so, it is insufficient to work with a single social rate of discount since the appropriate rates before and after the project are likely to differ. Indeed, we must utilize some appropriate concept of surplus and find associated ways of comparing the evaluation of public versus private projects.

We do not have much new to say about the general difficulties in evaluating large projects; rather, we are interested in generalizing an important proposition due to Arrow and Lind concerning situations where (otherwise) large projects become small. Our proposed generalization is roughly as follows: Under certain restrictions (which will become clear later) on the nature of projects and the types of finance, all social projects become first order in character as the number of consumers in the economy becomes large. Other (private) projects may or may not become small in the same sense, depending on the nature of private risk sharing.

Consider the utility function of problem (1.1). It is well known that there is no ordinal (much less cardinal) transformation $F$ on $U^h$ that will put it in the form

$$F[U^h(\cdot)] = U_1^h(c_1) + U_2^h(c_2). \tag{3.1}$$

On the other hand, it is quite common to *assume* that such additive separability holds across time. Adopting this assumption, ex ante utility can be expressed as

$$\hat{U}^h = U_1^h(c_1) + E_\omega[U_2^h(c_2(\omega))]. \tag{3.2}$$

We develop the Arrow–Lind proposition first in the absence of private investment opportunities. Suppose the government has available an investment project $(\delta S_1, \delta S_2(\omega))$. These costs and benefits are to be divided in some way among the households. Arrow and Lind assumed these were always divided equally, but we can relax that assumption somewhat. Given a division, we can express the change in ex ante utility for household $h$ by the following second-order Taylor series formula:

$$\Delta \hat{U}^h = \nabla_c U_1^h \, \delta s_1^h + \tfrac{1}{2} \nabla_{c,c}^2 U_1^h [\delta s_1^h]^2 + o[[\delta s_1^h]^2]$$
$$+ E_\omega[\nabla_c U_2^h(\omega) \, \delta s_2^h(\omega)] + \tfrac{1}{2} E_\omega[\nabla_{c,c}^2 U_2^h(\omega) [\delta s_2^h(\omega)]^2]$$
$$+ o[[\delta s_2^h(\omega)]^2], \tag{3.3}$$

where all derivatives are being evaluated at the status quo, and the symbol $o[\ ]$ is used to represent terms that tend to zero when divided by the argument, as the argument goes to zero.

Now we hold the aggregate size of the project fixed and consider what will happen as the number of households ($N$) gets large. We focus on any measure of welfare change, which is some weighted sum of individual utility changes (with weights $w^h$ uniformly bounded in magnitude). Clearly, the number of such weighted terms goes up at the rate $N$. We want to argue that all second- and higher-order terms vanish from this sum in the limit. Suppose we make the following assumptions.

1. All moments of the project output distribution are finite.
2. All derivatives of individual utility functions are uniformly bounded away from infinity at the status quo.
3. There exists some number $K$ such that, for all $h$ and $N$,

$$|\delta s^{hN}| \leq K |\delta S|/N,$$

where $s^{hN}$ stands for the vector allocation to $h$ when there are $N$ households, and the inequality is interpreted to hold component by component.

The first two assumptions seem innocuous, although they can be violated in some examples. [Such an example is given in Wilson (1982).] The third requires that as the number of people served gets large, the allocation to any individual must become small relative to the whole at some uniform rate. This constitutes our weakening of the Arrow–Lind restriction.

These assumptions taken together will indeed imply that all terms of second or higher order "disappear" from our welfare measure as $N$ gets large. We demonstrate this for one particular term in the Taylor expansion above; the others are analogous and are left to the reader. We have the following sequence of inequalities:

$$\sum_{h=1}^{N} w^h E_\omega [\nabla_{c,c}^2 U_2^h(\omega)[\delta s_2^{hN}(\omega)]^2]$$

$$\leq N \sup[w^h] E_\omega [|\nabla_{c,c}^2 U_2^h(\omega)|[\delta s_2^{hN}(\omega)]^2]$$

$$\leq (K^2/N) \sup[w^h] \sup[|\nabla_{c,c}^2 U_2^h(\omega)|] E_\omega [[\delta S_2(\omega)]^2]$$

$$\leq M/N, \tag{3.4}$$

where $M$ is a constant independent of $N$. The first inequality follows from uniform boundedness of weights, the second from assumption 3, and the third utilizes both assumptions 1 and 2.

Given this insignificance of higher-order terms, we can use the following approximation to measure change in welfare ($\delta W$) when $N$ is *sufficiently large*:

$$\delta W \cong \sum_{h=1}^{N} \beta^h [\delta s_1^{hN} + E_\omega [\eta^h(\omega)\, \delta s_2^{hN}(\omega)]], \qquad (3.5)$$

where we have renormalized the welfare weights so that they represent the marginal welfare of a dollar (at the status quo) given to the associated individual. The reader should see that this formula is *exactly* the same as that derived in Section 1, given that we assume (as before) that the ex ante income distribution is optimal.

Before drawing further conclusions from this analysis, let us reintroduce the private sector assets. Could their presence alter our conclusions thus far? Clearly, households *will* adjust their private holdings in response to the government project. We know that we can safely ignore these adjustments in making *first-order* welfare evaluations due to the envelope theorem. And since our measures reduce to first order here, we can still ignore these effects. However, the project may also induce changes in $d$, and these could have welfare impacts of higher order if the private choice objective is different from the social one.

Therefore, we must add the following to our previous three assumptions:

4. There are no indirect second-best contributions from the government project.

Assumption 4 will be assured by the private equity markets if the ex ante income distribution is optimal, the public project induces (at most) first-order changes in $d$ for large $N$, our spanning conditions (from Section 1) hold, and associated rules of action are followed. Then

$$\sum_h E_\omega [\eta^h(\omega)\, \delta[d_2(\omega)][a^h + \delta a^h]] = eX\left[\sum_h a^h + \delta a^h\right] = eX\bar{a} = 0, \qquad (3.6)$$

the last equality following from the fact that any changes made in response to the project would have been privately desirable in the status quo.

Thus, we conclude that the approximation (3.5) holds generally under assumptions 1–4. The strongest version of Arrow and Lind derives from specializing (3.5) to the case of *no* uncertainty in the status quo. Then the Arrow–Lind theorem involves two statements: (1) The government objective criterion is *discounted expected value* (since $\eta$ is independent of $\omega$); there is no social risk premium. (2) Any second-order project is discounted for risk. The second statement follows from the fact that all risk-averse individuals prefer a certain return to any random prospect with the same expected return.

The first part of the proposition generalizes easily to cases where there is risk in the status quo but the government project return structure is *independent* (so that the project has a zero beta and no risk premium). However, the second part does not; small private projects whose return structures correlate negatively with underlying uncertainty will be preferred to government projects with the same expected return.

The Arrow–Lind theorem frequently is interpreted as saying that the government should discount for risk less than the private sector. Is this conclusion justified on the basis of our analysis? Certainly not always. For example, when there is uncertainty in the status quo, public projects with high social betas should be discounted more than private ones with lower social betas. But suppose we confine ourselves to projects that are uncorrelated with ex ante uncertainty. Then, with a sufficiently large population, we know the government can diversify away all "large" project risk. Thus, if the private sector is not as successful in this regard, the above interpretation would be correct.

But why should it be that private sector projects are second order whereas the government project is first order? The issue is capacity to diversify across people. Arrow and Lind show that the government always has "enough" of this capacity through its power of taxation. Can the private sector similarly diversify away the risk on large projects? Equity markets are commonly believed to be "good" at this function, but we will now argue that this perception is incorrect and that there is a proper context for the Arrow–Lind theorem after all.

Recall the "myopic" feature of private asset markets discussed earlier. Decisions on asset distribution functions had to be made *conditional* on ownership patterns. Dreze (1974) pointed out that this fact might lead to stockmarket inefficiency. Here we give an example that shows how it might generate insufficient diversification of large project risk. In the example, there are two states of the world, two firms, and two types of individuals (distinguished by preferences); there are fixed, equal numbers of the two types. The firms are producing $d^1 = (1, 1)$ and $d^2 = (\frac{5}{8}, \frac{3}{2})$ in the status quo (per dollar invested). Each individual has one dollar of ex ante income. Referring to Figure 1, we see that there is a status quo equilibrium in which firm 1 is owned exclusively by type I individuals, and firm 2 by type II.

Note that spanning must hold in the example (existing assets span the entire space), and clearly there is no divergence of interest among stockholders of each company. Now suppose that firm 1 has a large project that will move it to $\hat{d}^1 = (2, \frac{1}{2})$. Referring again to Figure 1, we see that owners would like "small" moves in the direction of this project, but find

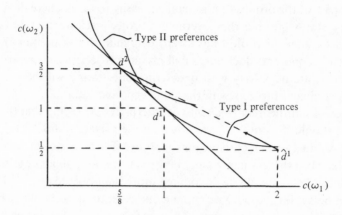

Figure 1.

the project as a whole too risky. Consequently, with ownership taken as given, $\hat{d}^1$ will be rejected. However, $\hat{d}^1$ clearly is desirable in conjunction with $d^2$ once optimal adjustments in ownership patterns are taken into account. The arrows indicate a pattern of trade (involving full diversification) that will leave everyone better off. Private investors will discount project $d^2$ for risk even though they should not. Assuming that the government cannot correct for the market inefficiency, then it should discount "less" than the private sector.

We close with a brief discussion of some earlier criticisms of the Arrow and Lind point of view. It was pointed out that as the number of people gets large, the government will want to add projects roughly at the rate $N$. And clearly, the totality of projects does not get small as $N$ gets large. [This critique was made by James (1975).] The problem here is that the sum of first-order projects is not first order. However, marginal analysis will still be appropriate as long as each separate project is small relative to the economy. All we must do is to reevaluate the status quo after each project is introduced. This means that even when we start from a riskless situation, we will not stay there. Thus, although the naive version of the Arrow–Lind theorem does not apply for a sequence of projects, the second version (discussed above) may. Of course, the conditions of the second version will be satisfied only if the returns on the various projects are independently distributed (otherwise risk from a new project will correlate with underlying uncertainty generated by previous projects). [Clearly, the independence condition is quite strong. It has been criticized by Foldes and Rees (1977), among others.]

A similar critique focuses on the nature of publicly provided goods (Fisher 1973). Suppose these are "pure" (uncongestible) public goods. Then, as the number of people sharing goes up, the benefit per person does not fall, so the project does not become first order. True, but this implies that project benefits grow with $N$ while costs are constant. In other words, the Arrow–Lind theorem for pure public goods takes the following form: *Every* pure public goods project becomes desirable relative to any private goods project as the number of people sharing grows without bound.

## REFERENCES

Arrow, K. J. (1965), *Aspects of the theory of risk-bearing,* Jahnssonin Lectures: Helsinki.

Arrow, K. J. (1966), "Discounting and public investment criteria," in A. V. Kneese and S. C. Smith (Eds.), *Water research,* Baltimore: Johns Hopkins University Press, pp. 13–32.

Arrow, K. J. (1971), *Essays in the theory of risk bearing,* Amsterdam: North-Holland.

Arrow, K. J. (1982), "The rate of discount on public investments with imperfect capital markets," in *Discounting for time and risk in energy policy,* Washington, D.C.: Resources for the Future.

Arrow, K. J. and R. C. Lind (1970), "Uncertainty and the evaluation of public investment decisions," *American Economic Review,* 60: 364–78.

Diamond, P. A. (1967), "The role of a stock market in a general equilibrium model with technological uncertainty," *American Economic Review,* 57: 759–76.

Dreze, J. (1974), "Investment under private ownership: Optimality, equilibrium and stability," in J. Dreze (Ed.), *Allocation under uncertainty: Equilibrium and optimality,* New York: Wiley, pp. 129–66.

Ekern, S. and R. Wilson (1974), "On the theory of the firm in an economy with incomplete markets," *Bell Journal,* 5: 171–80.

Fisher, A. (1973), "A paradox in the theory of public investment," *Journal of Public Economics,* 2: 405–8.

Foldes, L. P. and R. Rees (1977), "A note on the Arrow–Lind theorem," *American Economic Review,* 67: 188–93.

Grossman, S. and J. E. Stiglitz (1980), "Stockholder unanimity in making production and financial decisions," *Quarterly Journal of Economics,* 94: 543–66.

James, E. (1975), "A note on uncertainty and the evaluation of public investment decisions," *American Economic Review,* 65: 200–5.

Lintner, J. (1965), "The valuation of risk assets and the selection of risky investments in stock portfolios and capital budgets," *Review of Economics and Statistics,* 47: 13–37.

Malinvaud, E. (1972), "The allocation of individual risks in large markets," *Journal of Economic Theory,* 4: 312–28.

Marglin, S. A. (1963), "The opportunity costs of public investments," *Quarterly Journal of Economics,* 77: 274–89.

Pratt, J. W. (1964), "Risk aversion in the small and in the large," *Econometrica,* 32: 122–36.

Sharpe, W. (1964), "Capital asset prices: A theory of market equilibrium under conditions of risk," *Journal of Finance,* 19: 425–42.

Starrett, D. A. (1979), "Second best welfare economics in the mixed economy," *Journal of Public Economics,* 12: 329–50.

Starrett, D. A. (forthcoming), *Foundations of public economics.*

Wilson, R. (1982), "Risk measurement of public projects," in *Discounting for time and risk in energy policy,* Washington, D.C.: Resources for the Future.

CHAPTER 9

# A problem of financial market equilibrium when the timing of tax payments is indeterminate

*David F. Bradford*

## 1 Introduction

This chapter concerns an aspect of the question: When do government deficits matter? It takes as a starting point previous work (1981) showing how endogenously generated deficits might have no real effect, a result obtained under an assumption of perfect substitutability between government and private debt. The extension to a world of risky debt where the latter no longer holds turns out to involve new elements that may be of some general interest. In particular, the conditions for neutrality seem less likely to be fulfilled in a practical context.

The underlying idea is that it should not matter when taxes are paid provided there is an appropriate compensating interest element in the postponed liability. This notion conflicts with the assumption often employed that it is the government's cash flow balance that counts, even though current deficits may be offset by correspondingly larger liability for future tax payments, and surpluses may reflect drawing down liabilities for future taxes. This issue arises especially strongly in the context of analysis of proposals for consumption-type taxes, where there is a choice between a literal consumption tax and a tax on wage and transfer receipts. Typically, the two approaches generate the same liabilities in a present-value sense but very different cash flows. In some systems [for example, the Cash Flow Tax analyzed in Bradford et al. (1984)], the taxpayer has wide latitude to choose between the approaches.

The specific case analyzed here presents the same issues in a particularly clear way. It involves a tax on distributions by corporations to equity

I would like to express my appreciation for the helpful discussions with Pete Kyle, David Starrett, Joseph Stiglitz, and seminar participants at the National Bureau of Economic Research and at the Workshop on Economic Structural Change of the International Institute for Applied Systems Analysis.

177

holders, in essence, a dividend tax. If such a tax is assessed at a flat rate that is not expected to change, and if negative distributions (sales of new equity) are included (i.e., subsidized), the case is quite compelling in a partial equilibrium setting that the level of the tax should have no influence on real or financial transactions of a corporation acting in the interest of its stockholders. The reason is simply that the flat tax changes proportionately the consequences of all decisions as far as stockholder outcomes are concerned. In particular, the trade-off in after-tax dollars for the shareholders between a larger distribution today and the consequently smaller distribution at some future time is unaffected by the rate of tax.

In the absence of all taxes (and transactions costs), the various versions of the Modigliani–Miller (1958) theorem tell us the corporation will be indifferent between debt and equity finance. An implication is that the timing of dividend payments is a matter of indifference. Since, as I have just argued informally, a flat tax on dividends has no effect on the optimal financial policy, something like the Modigliani–Miller theorem should continue to hold. However, the choice of pay-out affects the government's cash flow. Government receipts will be determined by the whims of corporate managers; private wealth-maximizing calculations are insufficient to fix the path of revenues. Will the consequent fluctuations in tax receipts have real effects?

In Bradford (1981), I spelled out an overlapping-generations model in which government debt does generally influence the rational expectations equilibrium path, but in which variations in government debt attributable to variations in distribution tax receipts do not matter. The indifference about financial policy at the level of the firm, in spite of the tax on distributions, carries over to neutrality of the economy's path to the choice of financial policy, even though the flow of tax receipts is affected.

The key question is whether there are general equilibrium effects on the rate of interest. The basis for the neutrality conclusion may be sketched as follows: The capital investment level chosen by the firm is governed by the going interest rate. Therefore, a decision to issue an extra dollar of debt implies a decision to distribute an extra dollar to shareholders. This in turn implies extra tax receipts of $t$ dollars (where $t$ is the rate of tax). If real government spending is fixed, the extra $t$ dollars are devoted to reducing the public debt. The result thus far is a net addition of $1 - t$ dollars to the supply of financial assets. There remains, however, the equity interest in the corporation, the value of which is predicted to fall, not by one dollar, as a result of the extra debt cum distribution, but by $1 - t$ dollars, in reflection of the government's claim to a fraction $t$ of all cash flows to shareholders. As a consequence, all markets continue to clear. The firm's decision has no real effect, even though tax receipts are increased.

The foregoing analysis supports two conclusions. First, a tax on corporate distributions may not have the often-assumed incentive effects with respect to real and financial allocations. And second, variations in government receipts attributable to changes in corporate distribution policy may have no effect on the real path of the economy. The present investigation concerns how the neutrality results are affected if the perfect substitutability among financial assets used in the argument above and attributable to the assumption of certainty is replaced in the context of an explicit treatment of uncertainty.

As it turns out, the earlier results carry over without significant complication when only equity is risky at the margin, whereas corporate debt and marginal public debt are risk free and therefore perfect substitutes. The restriction on government financial choices is a special case of the requirement that applies when the risk characteristics of corporate debt are unrestricted. In the more general case, the neutrality conclusions require that the government policy be describable as one of issuing a certain prespecified risky debt together with the purchase of a fraction of the private debt supply equal to the tax rate.

These conditions on government behavior are not as arbitrary as might appear. As stressed elsewhere (Bradford 1981), the proportional tax on corporate distributions in effect gives the government a fractional ownership in the firm. Neutrality will follow if the government uses the tax revenue incident upon an incremental distribution to purchase bonds of the firm. This is just what is needed to preserve the predistribution portfolio of the government, taking into account its implicit ownership of corporate equity. In other words, the government behavior that implies neutrality is just what we would – in Modigliani–Miller fashion – expect of a shareholder that receives a dividend.

In Section 2, I review the certainty results as a way of introducing the basic model. The extension to a model with uncertainty is presented in Section 3. Section 4 contains concluding remarks.

## 2    Review of the certainty model

The model underlying the analysis is in the Samuelson (1959) consumption loan tradition. Individuals live for two periods in an infinite time horizon world. In the first life period, each individual works (offering one unit of labor inelastically), consumes, and saves for retirement. "Retirement" describes the second life period, when each individual dissaves and consumes, leaving nothing to his or her heirs.

All production takes place in the consolidated corporate sector, which is modeled as a single price-taking firm. Production conditions are described by a neoclassical production function of capital and labor employed, with constant returns to scale. The capital available to the corporation in any period is inherited from the previous period and is thus fixed in amount before the time of actual production. The output of a period may either be consumed or frozen into infinitely durable capital. Investment is regarded as reversible.

Savings may be held in three forms, bonds issued by the corporation, shares of its common stock, or bonds issued by the government. A given generation of individuals acquires these financial assets at the end of its first life period, after production for that period has been completed, and after the investment and financial plans of the corporation have been realized.

The holders of its common stock "own" the corporation. The owners at the beginning of a period control that period's production and the real investment that determines the amount of capital that will be available for use in production at the beginning of the next period. The owners of the firm at the beginning of a period specify as well the financial policy for that period, which means they set the amount of funds to be distributed to themselves as dividends and the amount of corporate borrowing. At the end of the period, the current owners sell the equity to the young generation of savers.

The government's real spending program is assumed fixed, for simplicity at a zero level. The government is thus modeled as a mechanical cash flow manager: In each period, the inherited debt obligation must be paid off, with any shortfall of tax receipts covered by the issue of new debt. Since the distribution tax is the only tax, there is nothing else for the government to do. Note that by allowing the government to make lump-sum transfers, the model could be used to permit the government to engage in (preannounced) intertemporal redistributions. This would involve issue of government debt in amounts larger or smaller than the difference between old debt obligations and distribution tax receipts.

**Notation.** To describe the results of the analysis formally, I use the following notation (involving minor changes from that of the 1981 article to facilitate extension to incorporate uncertainty):

$L$:    Total number of labor units available for application during the period (equals the number of individuals born in the period, exogenously given)

$K$:    Stock of corporate capital at the beginning of the period (used for production during the period)

$B$:    Total stock of corporate indebtedness at the beginning of the period, which must be repaid during the period

$F(K, L)$:    The production function, characterized by constant returns to scale

$D$:    Total distribution made by the corporation during the period

$B^g$:    Total stock of government indebtedness at the beginning of the period, which must be repaid during the period

$t$:    Rate of tax on corporate distributions (which may be negative) to stockholders

There are two ordinary prices in the model (current output is *numéraire*) and one pricelike "valuation function":

$w$:    Wage

$d$:    The discount factor, the current-period price of a bond paying one dollar next period

$V(K_+, B_+)$:    A function relating the "ex-dividend" value of equity, that is, the value at the end of a period, after production is complete, to the financial and investment decisions of the current owners

For any variable $X$, let $X_+$, $X_{++}$, and so on, represent its value in succeeding periods; $X_-$ represents its value in the preceding period. In order to determine how to value the firm's equity, individuals must form expectations about the prices and valuation function one period hence. Let $w_+^e$ denote the value of $w$ expected to obtain in the next period, and similarly for $d$ and $V$. It is assumed that everyone agrees about $w_+^e$, $d_+^e$, and $V_+^e$; forecasts more than one period into the future are not needed.

There are three classes of agents in the model, two displaying maximizing behavior. The "young" try to maximize $U(c^1, c_+^2)$ (labor is supplied inelastically), where $c^i$ is consumption during the $i$th period of the life cycle. The "old" manage the corporation to maximize $c^2$, which means maximize the sum of after-tax distributions and the proceeds from sale of the equity, $(1-t)D - V(K_+, B_+)$. The third agent is the government, which simply manages the cash flow according to $dB_+^g = B^g - tD$. (Reminder: $d$ is a price, not the differential operator.)

### Evolution of the economy

The situation inherited from the past is described by $(K, B, B^g, L)$, with $L$ evolving exogenously along a known path. The requirements placed on the model world are that the evolution to $(K_+, B_+, B_t^g, L_+)$ be determined by clearing of competitive "spot" markets for labor, corporate bonds, government bonds, corporate equity, and goods and that the price expectations on which the value of the firm depends be "rational." The general notion of rational expectations, attributed to Muth (1961), here encompasses two properties: Expectations are correct, and they are determinate, in the sense that they are governed by knowledge of the economic structure and the current state of the economy. For rational expectations to make sense, there must be an appropriate degree of determinacy of the model as a whole, including its expectations formation. Solving the model involves showing that the endogenous variables, including prices and expectations, can be expressed as stationary functions of the state variables $K$, $B$, and $B^g$ given the known path of $L$. Properly, there should also be a demonstration that the proposed equilibrium path of prices is at least locally unique – otherwise, why should the economic agents pick the required expectations-forming rule?

My previous paper (1981) described an equilibrium path of the economy sketched out above. (I did not succeed in demonstrating local uniqueness.) The neutrality result concerning the rate of tax on corporate distributions followed from the conclusion that the valuation function on the equilibrium path is given by

$$V(K_+, B_+) = (1-t)d(F_+(K_+, L_+) - w_+^e L_+ - B_+ + K_+).  \quad (1)$$

The objective of the owners of the firm is to set employment together with $K_+$, $B_+$, and $D$ to maximize $(1-t)D + V(K_+, B_+)$. If we substitute for $D$ in the objective function, using accounting relationship (2) among the outlays by the firm, $B_+$ drops out:

$$D = F(K, L) - wL - B + K + dB_+ - K_+.  \quad (2)$$

Maximizing values of the other variables are independent of $t$; the financial structure of the firm is indeterminate.

Indeterminacy of financial structure corresponds to indeterminacy of government tax receipts. The reason the equilibrium path of the economy's real variables and prices is nonetheless determinate is suggested by equilibrium condition (3), which describes equality between the value of demanded and supplied claims to future consumption:

$$dc_+^2(d,w)L = dB_+ + dB_+^g + (1-t)d(F_+(K_+,L_+) - w_+L_+ - B_+ + K_+).$$
$$(3)$$

Here $c_+^2(d,w)$ is the retirement-period consumption (which will take place next period) demanded by a representative young person, the values of $K_+$ and $B_+$ are set by the current owners of the firm, and I have taken for granted $w_+^e = w_+$. The expression on the left is the value of claims demanded on the basis of life cycle optimization by members of the young generation. The first two terms on the right are the values of bonds supplied by the firm and the government, and the third term is the value of corporate equity. Exploiting the government's budget constraint $dB_+^g = B^g - tD$ and the already mentioned accounting relationship (2) between $D$ and the other variables allows us to write condition (3) as

$$dc_+^2 L = B^g - t(F - wL - B + K - K_+)$$
$$+ (1-t)d(F_+(K_+,L_+) - w_+L_+ + K_+). \qquad (4)$$

Once again, $B_+$ has been eliminated, so the condition is independent of corporate financial policy.

Equation (5) expresses a further reformulation of the same condition, taking advantage of Euler's theorem:

$$dc_+^2 L = K_+ + B^g - t(F(K,L) - wL - B + K). \qquad (5)$$

The left side of (5) is, as before, the demand by the young generation for assets. The right side, the economy's net supply of assets, is the sum of the capital stock and the difference between government bonds carried over from the past and the tax receipts that would be generated if the corporation were to be liquidated in the current period. The last term affects the real equilibrium path like an anticipated tax receipt "asset" of the government, offsetting explicit government debt. Through this relationship, one obtains a clear sense of why deficits or surpluses due to variations in corporate distributions have no effect on the real path of the economy, even though government debt does matter. An increase in distributions simultaneously reduces government debt and the anticipated tax receipt asset by equal amounts.

## 3    Introducing uncertainty

There are various ways one might introduce uncertainty to this model. Taking advantage of the framework pioneered by Kenneth Arrow (see Arrow and Hahn 1971), suppose that future production conditions depend on the particular state (e.g., weather conditions) occurring. Specifically, assume that the investment decision is fixed in the current period, but the actual production function is determined in the next period.

Let $S$ be the set of possible states that might obtain in the current period, $S_+$ the set of possible states in the next period, and so on. The larger dimensionality of the problem requires some new notation. The following describes my compromise between comprehensiveness and mnemonics. In general, variables are now understood to have a subscript to designate the state and time with which they are associated. Thus, $w_i$, $i \in S_+$, refers to the wage rate realized in state $i$ in the next period. Since the story starts with a known current state, we can let variables with no subscript refer to the values currently realized.

It will be assumed that $S$ is finite in each period and that an ordering has been agreed upon for the states in each period, so we can use the subscript $+$ to refer to the vector of values of a variable potentially obtaining in the next period. (An exception is made for $K_+$ and $L_+$, which keep their previous scalar interpretation.) Thus, $w_+^e$ refers to the vector of wage rates presently anticipated for next period, with components $w_i$, $i \in S_+$, and has dimensionality equal to the number of states in $S_+$.

The firm and the government must now specify, instead of the single-dimensional bonds, vectors of state-specific claims. To simplify matters, assume that markets exist for each of the possible one-period contingent claims. A unit of type $i$, $i \in S_+$, pays one dollar next period if state $i$ is realized, and zero if another state is realized. To issue a riskless bond is equivalent to selling one unit each of claims of all types $i$, $i \in S_+$. The firm's bond financing is described by the vector $B_+$, the $i$th component of which $B_i$ ($i \in S_+$) is the amount the firm will owe its bondholders if state $i$ is realized next period.

Instead of the single discount factor $d$, we now have a vector of prices of unit claims contingent on the next period's state. Like the discount factor $d$ in the certainty case, the vector $d$ is understood as representing prices actually ruling in financial markets. (The prices of unit contingent claims might be observable only by appropriately packaging available financial instruments.) If $e_+$ is a vector of 1's of appropriate dimension, the inner product $e_+ \cdot d$ is the price of a riskless bond. Since we shall want to continue to use the ordinary subscript to refer to the state and time in which a particular variable is realized (for example, $d_i$, $i \in S_+$, is the vector of discount rates, applicable to claims on output two periods hence, realized if state $i$ occurs next period), I shall use parentheses when I wish to identify a particular element of $d$. Thus, $(d)_i$, $i \in S_+$, is a scalar, namely, the present price of a claim to one unit if state $i$ occurs next period. The symbol $d_+$ refers to the matrix of discount factor vectors, one for each possible state that might be realized next period.

We are now in a position to study the analog in the world of risk to the temporary equilibrium relationships discussed earlier. Of particular importance is the valuation function for corporate equity corresponding to (1) given by

$$V(K_+, B_+) = (1-t)d \cdot (F_+(K_+, L_+) - w_+^e L_+ - B_+ + e_+ K_+). \quad (6)$$

This is simply the value of the vector of payoffs, contingent on the state realized, that the purchaser of the equity expects to obtain next period in the form of distribution plus proceeds from the sale of the equity interest.

To analyze asset market clearing in this case, it is not sufficient to look at the aggregate value of present claims, as we did in (3) above. We must now look for the state-by-state equality of supplies of and demands for contingent claims. Recall that $c_+^2(w, d)$ is now to be interpreted as the vector of consumption plans by the representative young person for the retirement period, contingent on the state realized. Asset market clearing now requires the vector equation

$$c_+^2(w, d)L = B_+ + B_+^g + (1-t)(F_+(K_+, L_+) - w_+ L_+ - B_+ + e_+ K_+)$$
$$= tB_+ + B_+^g + (1-t)(F_+(K_+, L_+) - w_+ L_+ + e_+ K_+), \quad (7)$$

where, as before, we are taking for granted the determination of $K_+$ and $w_+$ via other equilibrium relationships, given $w$ and $d$.

In the certainty case, we were able to use the government budget constraint, $d \cdot B_+^g = B^g - tD$, together with the accounting relationship between $D$ and $B$, to eliminate both $B_+^g$ and $B_+$ from the asset market-clearing condition. Under uncertainty, the combination of these two relationships is no longer sufficient. Whereas before, constraining the value of the government's bond sales or purchases determined the quantity (given $d$), the government now may choose among various combinations of state-contingent claims (i.e., deal in bonds of different risk characteristics). Moreover, the same can be said of the firm. Thus, if we take as a starting point that the government only issues riskless bonds (buys riskless bonds in the case of negative government debt), we have still not pinned down temporary equilibrium because the risk characteristics of the firm's debt have not been determined.

If the corporation is restricted to riskless debt and the government is restricted to riskless debt at the margin, the argument goes through much as it did in the risk-free analysis. In that case, extra bonds issued by the corporation generate not only the exact withdrawal in value of government bonds (as a consequence of extra taxes paid) required to maintain financial market equilibrium but also the matching change in the state-by-state contingent claims. We can see this by inspection of equilibrium condition (7). If the firm issues another unit of bonds, it adds directly one dollar to each component of the vector $B_+$ of claims supplied on the right side but subtracts an amount $(1-t)$ from the anticipated recovery from owning equity in each state that might occur. If the government reduces its issue of bonds so as to deliver $t$ less in each state, the set of financial claims supplied will continue to balance the claims demanded.

Note that the condition calls for riskless bonds to be issued by the corporation but for the government to issue riskless bonds "at the margin." The requirement specifies the way the government must react to variations in distribution tax receipts. The government retains, however, freedom to set the risk characteristics of what we may call its basic debt issue, which we might specify as the debt issued if there were no corporate distributions in the period. The total value of the debt issue is determined by the budget constraint (which could itself be lifted by addition of, say, lump-sum taxes to the fiscal repertoire).

This freedom cannot, however, be unpredictably exercised. In order for the agents of the model to be able to formulate rational expectations, the risk characteristics of the basic government debt issue must be specified in advance (e.g., by a formula relating to the characteristics defining the different states of the world). This is a distinct addition to the model introduced by the extension to uncertainty. In the certainty case, the government was wholly predictable because it had no degree of freedom within the budget constraint. Uncertainty brings with it a range of options in each situation. Government policy will influence the course of the model economy (because the overlapping generations are, by assumption, not linked through bequests. In this case, the main effect of policy is to influence the choice among risky alternatives. It might be interesting to explore the question of optimal fiscal policy in this model; however, for present purposes, the point to stress is the requirement for predictability, involving prespecification of the characteristics of the basic debt and the rule for responding at the margin to variations in distribution tax receipts.

The latter requirement has thus far been spelled out for the case in which the corporation issues only riskless debt. However, we can readily formulate a more general rule relating private and marginal public debt to preserve the property of the model whereby the firm's financial policy has no real effect.

The investment and employment decisions in the model are essentially determined by the path of $w$ and $d$, wages and contingent dollar claim prices. Suppose we had a path of $w$ and $d$ such that (7) is continually satisfied when the firm is restricted to riskless debt and the government to riskless debt at the margin. Then equilibrium condition (7) provides us with a general condition on government finance that assures that the path is unaffected by other choices of private financial behavior, namely,

$$B_+^g = c_+^2(w,d)L - (1-t)(F_+(K_+,L_+) - w_+L_+ + e_+K_+) - tB_+. \tag{8}$$

In words, in order for corporate financial policy to have no real effect, government policy must be effective to issue basic debt, consisting of a predetermined package of contingent claims,

$$c_+^2(w,d)L - (1-t)(F_+(K_+,L_+) - w_+L_+ + e_+K_+),$$

and to *purchase* $tB_+$, that is, a fraction $t$ of the bonds issued by the firm. The requirement (7) of equilibrium implies that if any other government policy is followed, private financial policy will have real effects, and hence further restrictions on behavior are required to close the model.


## 4    Concluding remarks

With respect to the narrow question of whether the neutrality results obtained earlier in an all-certainty model carry over to a world of uncertainty, the analysis yields a clear conclusion. Uncertainty introduces degrees of freedom to government choices that must be balanced by restrictions. In particular, if corporate distributions are not to have real effects, the government must use the distribution tax proceeds to purchase the debt of the distributing firm (or, equivalently, buy back a set of government-issued contingent claims to generate the same effect on the supply of each type in the market). As suggested in the introductory section, there is an economic rationale for such a policy on the part of the government. It really is the same policy that we would expect shareholders to follow in rebalancing their portfolios following a distribution. The distribution by the corporation changes the characteristics of the equity claim. The portfolio can be restored to its predistribution characteristics by using the dividend to buy the firm's bonds. When we recognize that the government is an implicit equity owner, by virtue of the distribution tax, the restriction called for by the theory seems wholly reasonable.

However, it is hard to imagine any actual government carrying out this program. The systems used to account for government are typically weak in the dimension of measuring either liabilities to make future payments or claims to payment of taxes in the future already established by existing policies. To take an example, existing accounting conventions in the United States record the loss in tax revenue due to contributions to tax-favored retirement plans and make no allowance for the resulting increase in the present value of future liabilities implied by the same transaction [Kotlikoff (1984) develops this general theme more fully].

Unfortunately for the model described here, if the government does not follow the specified behavior, incremental distribution tax revenues will have real effects. The problem this presents is not simply to describe these effects but rather to understand how it is that equilibrium is determined at all. For the argument that corporate distributions are not determined in the model holds generally – it is simply a consequence of price taking by private agents in financial markets. As a result, corporate distributions cannot be predicted. If an unpredictable aspect of the model has real consequences, how can agents have rational expectations? Thus I must conclude this paper on a note of puzzlement.

REFERENCES

Arrow, K. J. and F. H. Hahn (1971), *General competitive analysis,* San Francisco: Holden-Day.
Bradford, D. F. (1981), "The incidence and allocation effects of a tax on corporate distributions," *Journal of Public Economics,* XV: 1–22.
Bradford, D. F. and the U.S. Treasury Tax Policy Staff (1984), *Blueprints for Basic Tax Reform,* 2nd ed., Arlington, VA: Tax Analysts.
Kotlikoff, L. J. (1984), "Taxation and savings: A neoclassical perspective," *Journal of Economic Literature,* XXII: 1576–1629.
Modigliani, F. and M. H. Miller (1958), "The cost of capital, corporation finance and the theory of investment," *American Economic Review,* XLVIII: 261–97.
Muth, J. (1961), "Rational expectations and the theory of price movements," *Econometrica,* XXIX: 315–35.

CHAPTER 10

# The shadow price of capital: implications for the opportunity cost of public programs, the burden of the debt, and tax reform

*Robert C. Lind*

## 1    Introduction

The concept of the shadow price of capital was developed in the context of the debate over the appropriate rate of discount for use in the economic evaluation of public projects and programs. However, the concept and the magnitude of the shadow price of capital have important implications not only for evaluating the cost and benefits of public investments but also for evaluating the opportunity cost of any public expenditure whether it be for public investment, public consumption of goods and services, publicly financed transfer payments, or programs in the private sector mandated by the government, such as pollution control. Furthermore, using the concept of the shadow price of capital, it can easily be shown that the opportunity cost of these programs depends critically on how they are financed and on the nature and rate structure of the tax system. Similarly, the concept of the shadow price of capital can be used to provide a first-order estimate of the burden of the debt and has important implications for tax policy and tax reform.

In this chapter, we develop the concept of the shadow price of capital and compute its values under varying assumptions about tax and savings rates. We then use these results to analyze the opportunity cost of public programs and the cost of "crowding out" private investment, to analyze the burden of the debt, and finally, to explore some implications for tax reform. The following section of this first essay traces the development of the concept of the shadow price of capital in the context of the social rate of discount and relates it to the work of Arrow and others in this field. The third section develops the concept and the basic mathematics of the shadow price of capital and computes the values of the shadow

I am indebted to David Bradford and David Starrett for their careful review of the manuscript and for their helpful comments and suggestions.

price of capital under various marginal tax and savings rates. The fourth section uses these results to analyze the opportunity cost of different public expenditures and programs.

The fifth section uses the concept and estimates of the shadow price of capital to analyze the burden of increasing the national debt and some of the implications of alternative proposals for tax reform. Although it is generally accepted that the major burden of the deficit is related to the crowding out of private investment, what is surprising is that the cost of crowding out in terms of the present value of future consumption foregone may be several times the value of the investment foregone. Related to taxation, the case is made for financing public expenditures through taxation but against using taxes on the return to investment such as taxes on interest, dividends, and corporate profits.

The final section discusses the underlying assumptions and the basic methodology of the analysis. It points out that although this essay is clearly in the "second-best" tradition, it does not attempt to analyze the costs of all of the distortionary effects of taxes on the earnings from capital investment nor does it attempt to derive a second-best solution that is optimal given some set of constraints as is typically the case in the literature on optimal taxation. Rather the focus is on the first-order magnitude of the cost of taxes on capital income and the displacement of private investment in terms of foregone future consumption. The justification for focusing on this cost alone is that it is very large and that even if some of the critical underlying parameters would change within reasonable ranges given policy changes, the basic results would still hold. Given that this is the case, the analysis of the cost of the deficit and alternative tax policies remains valid as a first approximation. This section also compares the results presented here with other results in the literature.

The fundamental result is that if the tax system is such that the shadow price of capital is high, and if the financing of public programs comes largely at the expense of private investment, then the opportunity cost of these public programs is likely to be several times their dollar cost to the government. This is true even for straight transfer programs, meaning that the provision of a dollar of additional income or benefits to a recipient may cost two or three dollars in terms of the present value of the future consumption foregone by the members of society at large. Therefore, the method of financing public expenditure and the tax structure may in many cases be the most important factors in determining the social cost of a particular program and therefore in determining whether or not a program should be undertaken.

## 2        The shadow price of capital and the social rate of discount

The concept of the shadow price of capital was motivated by the need to separate the question of the opportunity cost of private capital formation displaced by a public investment or program from the issue of the social rate of time preference. Depending on how a particular project or program was financed and the macroeconomic state of the economy, it would in part come at the expense of private capital formation and in part at the expense of private consumption. On the one hand, if public investments were to displace private investments on a dollar-for-dollar basis or if private and public investments were competing head to head in a particular sector of the economy such as steel production or electricity generation, many economists would argue that the rate of discount used to evaluate public investments should be the same as in the private sector and that this rate should equal the before-tax rate of return of a marginal private investment. The argument for this position is that we should not undertake public investments that produce a lower rate of return than alternative private investments.

On the other hand, another group of economists would point to the fact that because of the corporate profits tax, the personal income tax, and other possible sources of imperfections in the capital markets, individuals can only earn an after-tax rate of return on their investment that is much lower than the pretax rate of return on private investment. Put differently, the typical consumer's rate of interest has been less than half the pretax rate return on private corporate investment. Since it is the consumer's rate of interest that governs his or her savings and investment decisions, that is, intertemporal consumption decisions, they would argue that the appropriate rate of discount for evaluating public investment decisions should be a rate approximating the consumer's rate of interest. Others, combining these two lines of arguments, have taken the position that the appropriate discount rate for evaluating public investments should be a weighted average of the marginal before-tax rate of return on private investment and the consumer's rate of interest, with the weights being determined by the relative percentage of the project's resources coming, respectively, from private investment and private consumption.

Against this background, Kenneth Arrow made a major contribution to the debate over the appropriate discount rate for discounting the benefits and costs of public investments and more generally about the methodology for evaluating public programs and policies (Arrow 1966) by modeling the problem as one of optimal economic growth. Perhaps equally important, he noted that although public investments may draw resources from private investment, public investments may also stimulate future private investment and consequently that all of these effects on present and future private investment must be taken into account to properly evaluate public investment decisions.

Arrow assumed, in his initial paper on this subject, that the percentage of private investment displaced by taxes to pay for a project is the same as the percentage of future returns or benefits that go into future investment. Under these assumptions, the effects on private investment of the costs and the benefits of a public investment are essentially offsetting, and the appropriate rate of discount for evaluating benefits and costs is the social rate of time preference, which, if equated with the typical consumer's rate of time preference, would equal the consumer's rate of interest.

The result was remarkable in its practical simplicity in that regardless of the complex impacts that a public investment might have on private investment over time, these effects can be ignored in performing benefit–cost analysis, and the appropriate rate for discounting benefits and costs is the social rate of time preference for consumption, however determined. This result was of practical interest to policy analysts because it greatly simplified the problem of determining the appropriate rate of discount for use in benefit–cost evaluations of public investments and programs.

Although the approach taken by Arrow represented a very important advance and fundamentally changed the way that economists looked at this problem, the simple and easily applied result regarding the choice of the rate of discount depended on the special assumption about the symmetry between the impact of the financing of public projects on private investment and the impact of future benefits on private investment. This symmetry, as further analysis has demonstrated, cannot in general be assumed to hold, and therefore, the problem of accounting for the impact of public investments and programs on private investment is still with us. One could, of course, use the basic approach developed by Arrow and set up an optimal growth model incorporating the important market imperfections, macroeconomic conditions, and characteristics of the public investment under consideration and then solve for the appropriate discount rate; however, as a practical matter, this is a very difficult assignment.

Even in the hands of the most skilled economic theorists, complex models of optimal economic growth are not child's play. And although such a formulation allows for the explicit analysis of investment and reinvestment, focuses attention on alternative consumption paths, and builds into the analysis macroeconomic considerations, all of which are its great strengths, it presents serious difficulties for specific applications. In order to make the analysis tractable, we have to deal with a highly simplified economy, and it is difficult to do this and to be sure that we capture all of the critically important real-world complexities. This difficulty, along with the fact that the conditions of optimality are often exceedingly difficult to interpret and measure in terms of a consumption rate of interest, make this procedure, at best, of limited use to the practical application of benefit–cost analysis. And finally, there is the problem that, depending on a number of parameters, including the state of the economy and the nature of the public project, a different rate of discount may well have to be calculated for every project.

During the same period that Arrow (1966) and subsequently Arrow and Kurz (1970) were developing their approach to the problem of evaluating public investment decisions, and in particular the choice of the discount rate, an alternative approach using the concept of the shadow price of capital was being developed. This approach was first suggested by Eckstein (1958), was more fully stated by Diamond (1968) and Feldstein (1970), and was further developed and related to the earlier work of Arrow by Kay (1972) and Bradford (1975), who computed values for the shadow price of capital under alternative economic assumptions. Subsequently, Bradford's results were modified by Mendelsohn (1981) and extended and reinterpreted by this author (1982).

The shadow price of capital was defined as the present value of future consumption generated by one dollar of private investment discounted at the social rate of time preference for consumption. Most economists would agree that if all the consequences, that is, all benefits and costs, of a project could be stated in terms of consumption over time, the appropriate rate of discount for evaluating a public investment would be the social rate of time preference for consumption. If we believe that individual preferences as revealed by market behavior should be honored in public sector decision making, as is assumed by the basic benefit–cost methodology, then the appropriate rate of discount in this case should be the consumer's rate of interest.

What the concept of the shadow price of capital allows us to do is to capture the value of the consumption equivalent of one dollar of private investment at a given point in time. In the context of the debate over the social rate of discount, the concept of the shadow price of capital made it possible to separate the issue of the opportunity cost of private capital displacement from the question of the social rate of time preference. The opportunity cost or benefit from reduced or increased capital formation could be calculated in terms of its consumption equivalent by multiplying the changes in private investment associated with a public program or project by the shadow price of capital, and then the adjusted benefit and cost streams could be discounted at the social rate of time preference for consumption, however determined.

Bradford, in a pioneering paper (1975), was the first to develop the mathematics for computing the shadow price of capital and to calculate its value under varying assumptions. However, Bradford found that, under a wide range of values for $r$, the rate of return on private investment, $i$, the social rate of discount, and $s$, the marginal propensity to save, the shadow price of capital was not significantly different from unity. In fact, allowing $r$ to vary from 5 to 15 percent, $i$ to vary from 2 to 8 percent, and $s$ to vary from 0.1 to 0.3, he found that the shadow price of capital, $V$, was in the range $0.96 < V < 1.19$.

From this, he concluded that, as a practical matter, the opportunity cost of capital was not significant and therefore concluded that in the context of cost–benefit analysis for public investment decisions, one would get results that were approximately correct by simply taking the benefits and costs without any adjustments for the impact of the project on private capital formation and discounting at a rate equal to the social rate of time preference. Because the shadow price of capital was, for a wide range of parameter values, so very close to unity, one might have concluded that the whole issue of crowding out was not as significant as many had argued.

However, as important as Bradford's paper was in developing the concept, in formulating the expression for the shadow price of capital, he failed to distinguish between that part of the payout of an investment that was a return of capital, or depreciation, and that part that was a return on the investment. He assumed that all of the payout would be treated as current income and that the fraction reinvested would be $s$, the marginal propensity to save. Thus, in his model, where both the principal and the interest are returned every year, a one-dollar investment earning 10 percent would return $1.10 at the end of a year. In terms of this example, Bradford's calculation of the shadow price of capital assumed that the quantity reinvested the next year would be $s(\$1.10)$ with $(1-s)(\$1.10)$ being consumed.

As Mendelsohn (1981) and this author (1982), independently noted, the appropriate assumption would have been that $\$(1 + s(0.10))$ would have been reinvested and $(1-s)(0.10)$ would have gone into consumption. Put differently, the return of capital would have been reinvested and would not, in general, have been treated as current income. Mendelsohn recalculated all of Bradford's values for the shadow price of capital making this correction, and the recalculated values, $V$, range $0.5 < V < \infty$. From this, he concluded that the social present value of a dollar of private investment is sensitive to (1) the market rate of interest, (2) the social rate of time preference, and (3) the rate of savings from income and that no single discount rate can act as a satisfactory rule of thumb under all circumstances. While Mendelsohn's results are correct, he does not attempt to determine what the correct shadow price of capital might be nor to significantly narrow the range of possible values.

This author (Lind 1982) extended the work of Bradford in two ways and developed a different expression for computing the shadow price of capital. First, this author noted, as did Mendelsohn, that the original capital that is returned through depreciation must be treated differently than the earnings on that capital with respect to reinvestment. In addition, Lind also noted that some part of the invested capital will remain invested over more than one year. This in effect is like having some portion of the capital invested and reinvested over a number of years at the pretax, private rate of return, $r$, which increases the value of the shadow price of capital. And finally, it shows that based on reasonable assumptions about the relationship of the pretax rate of return on private capital and the after-tax rate of returns on investment to the individual investors, the shadow price of capital will be finite and lie in the range $0 \le V \le 6$. However, this work, like that of Bradford (1975) and Mendelsohn (1981) did not properly take taxes into account in computing the reinvestment rate. As a result, its estimates of the shadow price were higher than they would have been had taxes been properly accounted for. This will be remedied in the next section of this essay.

If we can establish a reasonable estimate of the shadow price of capital, it follows that this estimate has significance for evaluating the social opportunity cost of government expenditures, the cost of alternative methods of financing, and the cost of crowding out, which in turn is related to the burden of the debt. In the next section, we develop, demonstrate the convergence of, and derive the expression for the sum of the series that represents the shadow price of capital. We also compute its value under alternative assumptions about taxes and savings rates and compare these results with previous computations.

## 3    The shadow price of capital

Begin by considering one dollar of private investment in a typical project with a life of $N$ years. Assume for simplicity that the one dollar of private investment earns a pretax rate of return $r$ and that the capital and returns are paid out in an even stream of payments over the life of the invest-ment. In other words, a typical one-dollar investment can be seen as pro-ducing an $N$-year annuity of payments $A$ that come at the end of each year over the life of the investment. If we use straight-line depreciation, these payments of $A$ dollars can be divided into a component that repre-sents depreciation, $D = 1/N$, and another component $(A - D)$ that repre-sents the earnings or return on the invested capital.

From this, it follows that for each payment $A$, the amount that will be reinvested will be $D + s(1 - t)(A - D)$, where $s$ is the marginal propensity to save out of disposable income and $t$ is the total marginal tax rate on the earnings from capital. Therefore, the rate of reinvestment of the pay-ments $A$ is equal to $z = D + s(1 - t)(A - D)/A$. Note that the difference be-tween this formulation and Bradford's is essentially that Bradford equated $z$ to $s$ in his model where $N = 1$.

Put differently, one dollar of investment will yield a stream of $N$ equal payments of $A = r/1 - (1 + r)^{-N}$ occurring at the end of each year over the life of this investment. Each one of these payments $A$ will lead to the reinvestment of an amount $zA$ that in turn will result in a new series of $N$ payments of $zA^2$ starting the following year. The reinvestment rate $z$ is the fraction of each payment that represents depreciation $D$ plus the part of after-tax earnings that is saved and reinvested. Thus a one-dollar investment will generate a series of $N$ payments of $A$ that in turn will generate a series of $N$ additional investments of $zA$, each of which in turn will generate a series of $N$ payments equal to $zA^2$, and so on. We will demonstrate that the present value of the sum of all payments gener-ated by this investment and reinvestment process when discounted at a social rate of time preference (consumers rate of interest) $i$ is equal to $Ax \sum_{t=0}^{\infty} (Axz)^t$, which equals $Ax/1 - Axz$ for $Axz < 1$. Here $x$ is de-fined as the present value of an annuity of $N$ payments of one dollar at the end of each year, that is, $x = 1 - (1 + i)^{-N}/i$. Since private consump-tion and public consumption represented by taxes is the fraction of this stream of payments that is not reinvested (i.e., $1 - z$), the shadow price of capital or the present value of private and public consumption gen-erated by one dollar of private investment is equal to $Ax(1 - z)/1 - Axz$, namely, the present value of all payments multiplied by $1 - z$.

To prove this, we need several definitions. First, define $C_0$ as the set of dated payments generated by the initial one dollar of private investment. Second, define $C_1$ as the set of dated payments generated by the reinvest-ment of the fraction $z$ of the payments in $C_0$. And more generally, define $C_t$ as the set of payments generated by the reinvestment of the fraction $z$

of payments in $C_{t-1}$. Then, by construction, $C_0, C_1, \dots, C_n$ is a sequence of disjoint sets of payments such that their union $C_0 \cup C_1 \cup C_2 \cup \cdots \cup C_n$ is the set of payments from the investment and reinvestment process described above resulting from an initial one dollar of private investment.

Now we will demonstrate that the sum of the present values of payments in $C_t$, $P_v(C_t)$, equals $Ax(Axz)^t$. However, to do this, we first demonstrate that the sum of the present values of the dated payments in $C_{t-1}$, $P_v(C_{t-1})$, equals the sum of present values of the dated payments in $C_t$, $P_v(C_t)$, multiplied by $Axz$, that is,

$$P_v(C_{t+1}) = P_v(C_t)Axz.$$

Let $\{b_1, \dots, b_M\} = C_t$. Then for any $b_m \in C_t$ occurring at time $q$, $zb_m$ will be reinvested at time $q$ and generate a stream of $N$ payments $zb_m A$ starting at time $q+1$ and ending at time $q+N$. The present value of these payments as of time $q$ is $zb_m Ax$ so that the present value of $zb_m Ax = Axz P_v(b_m)$ for every $b_m \in C_t$. Because each element of $C_{t+1}$ is of the form $zb_m A$ and was generated as an $N$-period annuity by some dated payment $b_m$ for some $b_m \in C_t$, it follows that $P_v(C_{t+1}) = P_v(C_t)Axz$.

Now, by induction, it follows that the present value of $C_t = Ax(Axz)^t$. For $t = 0$, clearly $P_v(C_0) = Ax$. It then follows from the result derived in the preceding paragraph that

$$P_v(C_1) = Axz P_v(C_0) = Ax(Axz),$$

and continuing in this manner, we get $P_v(C_t) = Ax(Axz)^t$. Since the sequence of sets $C_0$, $C_1$, $C_n$ is disjoint, the present value of their union, $P_v(C_0 \cup C_1 \cup C_2 \cup \cdots \cup C_n)$ is equal to

$$\sum_{t=0}^{\infty} P_v(C_t) = \sum_{t=0}^{\infty} Ax(Axz)^t = Ax \sum_{t=0}^{\infty} (Axz)^t = \frac{Ax}{1 - Axz} \quad \text{for } Axz < 0.$$

This is the present value of the infinite stream of payments generated by one dollar of private investment earning a rate of return $r$ discounted to its present value at the rate of discount $i$. Since $1 - z$ is the amount withdrawn from each payment for private and public consumption, the present value of the private and public consumption stream generated by one dollar of private investment is $V = Ax(1-z)/1 - Axz$. Note when $i = r$, $Ax = 1$ and $V = 1$; that is, the shadow price of capital diverges from unity if and only if the pretax rate of return on private investment, $r$, differs from the social rate of discount $i$ and exceeds unity if and only if $r > i$.

The basic idea behind the shadow price of capital and its computation can be seen as follows. The initial investment of one dollar generates a stream of payments equal to $A$. These are shown in the second line of

Table 1

| $t=0$ | 1 | 2 | 3 | $\cdots$ | $N$ | $N+1$ | $N+2$ | $N+3$ | $\cdots$ | $2N$ |
|---|---|---|---|---|---|---|---|---|---|---|
| | $A$ | $A$ | $A$ | | $A$ | | | | | |

$$
N \text{ rows} \left\{
\begin{array}{l}
zA^2 \cdots\cdots\cdots zA^2 \\
\quad zA^2 \cdots\cdots\cdots\cdots zA^2 \\
\qquad \vdots \\
\qquad\qquad zA^2 \cdots\cdots\cdots\cdots\cdots zA^2
\end{array}
\right.
$$

Table 1. The series of dated payments $A$ shown in the second line of Table 1 constitutes the set $C_0$ and the sum of the present values of these payments is equal to $Ax$. Each of the payments in $C_0$ gives rise to a series of $N$ payments of $zA^2$, which are shown in the next $N$ rows, and these dated payments comprise the set $C_1$. If we multiply $zA^2$ by $x$, we get the present value of each of $N$ rows of payments as of the time of the corresponding payment $A$ that generated the sequence. We now have a sequence of payments $zA^2x$ running from $t=1$ to $t=N$. Multiplying this sequence again by $x$ gives us the present value of this sequence as of $t=0$. Thus, we have $zA^2x^2 = P_v(C_1) = Ax(Axz)$.

Given this formulation and the equation for the shadow price of capital, the next step is to compute the value of $V$. Given that

$$V = Ax(1-z)/1 - Axz,$$

we must know $N$, the life of the typical or average investment project; $r$, the marginal pretax rate of return on capital; $t$, the total effective tax rate on earnings from capital investment; $s$, the marginal propensity to save; and $i$, the social rate of discount, which we will argue should be the consumer's rate of interest and equal the after-tax rate of return on capital investment.

Following the earlier work by this author (1982) estimating that the average life of a capital investment to be fifteen years, we will let $N=15$. This is an estimate made by comparing the book value of corporate assets to depreciation using U.S. Treasury data (1973, 1974, 1975).

With regard to the real pretax rate of return on investment, most estimates lie in the range 10–15 percent. One study by Holland and Myers (1979), which is particularly useful for this analysis, estimates that the real rate of return on capital over the period 1946–76 averaged 12.41 percent and that the real after-tax rate of return to claimants on this income

Table 2. *Values for the shadow price of capital given different r, t, i, s.*

| | | | *r* = 5% | | | *r* = 10% | | | *r* = 15% |
|---|---|---|---|---|---|---|---|---|---|
| *t* | *i* | *s* | Shadow price of capital | *i* | *s* | Shadow price of capital | *i* | *s* | Shadow price of capital |
| 0.54 | 2.3% | 0.06 | 2.412 | 4.6% | 0.06 | 2.485 | 6.9% | 0.06 | 2.571 |
| | | 0.10 | 2.548 | | 0.10 | 2.563 | | 0.10 | 2.657 |
| | | 0.20 | 2.701 | | 0.20 | 2.781 | | 0.20 | 2.903 |
| 0.40 | 3% | 0.06 | 1.771 | 6% | 0.06 | 1.832 | 9% | 0.06 | 1.878 |
| | | 0.10 | 1.830 | | 0.10 | 1.871 | | 0.10 | 1.922 |
| | | 0.20 | 1.885 | | 0.20 | 1.989 | | 0.20 | 2.054 |
| 0.30 | 3.5% | 0.06 | 1.494 | 7.0% | 0.06 | 1.532 | 10.5% | 0.06 | 1.558 |
| | | 0.10 | 1.516 | | 0.01 | 1.552 | | 0.10 | 1.586 |
| | | 0.20 | 1.580 | | 0.02 | 1.627 | | 0.20 | 1.665 |
| 0.20 | 4% | 0.06 | 1.280 | 8% | 0.06 | 1.303 | 12% | 0.06 | 1.323 |
| | | 0.10 | 1.290 | | 0.01 | 1.317 | | 0.10 | 1.340 |
| | | 0.20 | 1.329 | | 0.02 | 1.354 | | 0.20 | 1.517 |

has averaged 5.77 percent. This takes into account both corporate and personal income taxes. Therefore, in terms of the parameters of our model, $r = 12.41$ percent, $i = 5.77$ percent, and $t = 0.54$, where $t$ is the combined tax rate on the earnings of corporate capital investment. Note that if the difference between $i$ and $r$ is caused by the combined effects of corporate and personal income taxes at the rate $t$, then $i = (1-t)r$. Certainly, it is reasonable to assume that most of the divergence between $r$ and $i$, where $i$ is taken to be the consumer's rate of interest, is caused by taxation.

If one accepts the permanent income hypothesis, then the marginal savings rate equals the average savings rate, and in the United States, this rate has historically been about 0.06 of disposable income. In this essay, we will calculate the shadow price of capital assuming $s$ equal to 0.06, 0.10, and 0.20. What we find is that the value of the shadow price of capital is not highly sensitive to the savings rate in this range.

Table 2 shows the shadow price of capital, $V$, for various parameter values for $r$, $i$, $t$, and $s$. We have computed $V$ for values for $r$ of 5, 10, and 15 percent. For each value of $r$, we have chosen a corresponding $i = (1-t)r$. We have computed $V$ for $r$ equal to 5, 10, and 15 percent to show that whatever the value of $r$, the value of $V$ is virtually unchanged over this range for the corresponding value of $i = (1-t)r$. What this shows is that $V$ depends largely on $r/i$, which measures the wedge that taxes have driven between the pretax and after-tax rates of return on capital.

Let $t$ be 0.54, 0.40, 0.30, and 0.20. We begin with $t = 0.54$, which is the Holland and Myers estimate made before the Reagan tax cuts were in effect. Although we do not have comparable estimates for the effective tax rate on corporate earnings for the last couple of years, if the tax reduction reduced the effective combined rate by 25 percent, which was the percentage reduction in the personal income tax rate, the new combined rate would be $t = 0.40$. We have also computed $V$ for $t = 0.30$ and $t = 0.20$ to show how the shadow price of capital declines as tax rates on the earnings from private investment declines and the wedge between the pretax and after-tax rates of return narrows.

First, note in Table 2 that for $t = 0.54$, the shadow price of capital is about 2.5 if $r$ is in the range 10–15 percent as most estimates indicate assuming that the marginal propensity to save is 0.06. If the marginal propensity to save were as high as 0.2, the value of the shadow price of capital rises to about 2.8, but one of the relationships that Table 2 illustrates is that within a reasonable range for the parameters involved, the shadow price of capital is not highly sensitive to changes in the savings rate. A second relationship that Table 2 illustrates is that as we vary $r$ across each row holding $t$ and $s$ constant and keeping $i = (1-t)r$, the shadow price of capital rises only slightly with increases in $r$. The critical relationship is the wedge between $r$ and $i$, which is determined by $t$. Economists have long been concerned about this wedge and its negative impact on efficiency, but the concept of the shadow price of capital makes clear how costly this wedge can be.

As we decrease $t$, $V$ falls as one would expect. However, for the period 1946–76, estimates indicate that the shadow price of capital was about 2.5, and even with a 25 percent effective tax reduction on investment income, the shadow price of capital would be in the neighborhood of 1.85 which is still high. It is equally interesting that even if marginal tax rates on the returns from private investment were reduced to 20 percent, the shadow price of capital would be about 1.3, which can be highly significant for evaluating public policies and programs.

We can also compare the estimates in Table 2 with previous estimates of the shadow price of capital. As we noted earlier, Bradford's estimates of $V$ based on an incorrect formulation of the reinvestment process are very close to unity for a wide range of values of $r$, $i$, and $s$. In all cases,

$|V| \leq 1.19$. From this, Bradford (1975) concluded that considerations of the impact of public investment and policy decisions on private investment, whether negative or positive, were not very important.

Mendelsohn (1981) corrects Bradford's reinvestment formulation to account for the reinvestment of returned capital and recomputes the shadow price of capital for the same values of $r$, $i$, and $s$ that Bradford uses, namely, $r = 5$, 10, and 15 percent, $i = 2$, 5, and 8 percent, and $s = 10$, 20, and 30 percent. He gets values for $V$ that range from 0.5 for $r = 5$ percent, $i = 8$ percent, and $s = 30$ percent to infinity in a number of cases such as where $r = 15$ percent, $i = 2$ percent, and $s = 3$ percent. Given this range of estimates for $V$, it would be extremely important to know precisely the parameter values of $r$, $i$, and $s$, and under many circumstances estimating these parameters with precision would be very difficult, if not impossible.

However, much of this variability in the value of $V$ is resolved if we equate the social rate of time preference to the consumer's rate of interest, which is the correct procedure for use in benefit–cost analysis. Using this approach, the relationship between $r$ and $i$ is determined by the effective tax rate on the earnings of private investment. In the case just cited, where Mendelsohn gets $V = \infty$, the marginal rate of taxation implied by $r = 15$ percent and $i = 2$ percent is given by $(1 - t)0.15 = 0.02$ or $t = 0.87$. For such a large wedge between $r$ and $i$, one would expect a large shadow price of capital; however, part of the problem with the computation of $V$ by Bradford (1975), Mendelsohn (1981), and the previous work of this author (1982) is that taxes on the return to capital were ignored in computing the reinvestment rate. Using the procedure developed in this essay for computing the shadow price of capital in the case just cited, the shadow price would be 14.9, which is a relatively large but finite number.

When Table 2 is compared with the earlier estimates of $V$ by this author (Lind 1982), the numbers in Table 2 are lower. This is because, in this earlier work, the reinvestment rate $z$ did not take taxes into account. In this previous work, $z = D + s(A - D)/A$ instead of $z = D + s(1 - t)(A - D)/A$. This had the effect of raising the earlier estimates of $V$. For example, for $t = 0.54$, $r = 0.10$, $i = 0.46$, and $s = 0.2$, the earlier estimate by this author was $V = 3.67$, whereas in Table 2 the comparable estimate is $V = 2.78$. Clearly, the importance of including the effect of taxes on reinvestment increases with the tax rate. Therefore, estimates for the shadow price of capital under the assumptions of this author's prior work should have been approximately 2.8 rather than 3.8.

## 4    The opportunity cost of public programs

In this section, we will not address the implications of the shadow price of capital for the evaluation of public investment decision as that has been thoroughly discussed previously (Lind 1982). What we want to focus on here are its implications for other public expenditure decisions and public policy decisions that affect private investment.

The main point is that although a great deal of attention has been paid to appropriately accounting for the impact of public investment decisions on private capital formation, it is equally important to consider the impact of any public expenditure or policy decision on private capital formation. A dollar of public expenditure has to be raised somehow whether it goes into a public investment, pays for public consumption, or is paid out as a transfer payment. Raising money for these expenditures will almost certainly have some impact on private investment, and that impact will depend on how it is raised. Although this point is obvious, it is not one that has been acted upon in evaluating the benefits and costs of public expenditures generally, except in the case of public investments. Perhaps this omission has occurred because the issue of the opportunity cost of private capital formation has been focused on the discount rate, which is only applicable in cases of public investment.

The concept of the shadow price of capital properly focuses on the value of an incremental dollar of private investment and therefore makes it clear that private capital displacement must be of concern in evaluating any public expenditure decision, and it gives us a measure of the cost of private capital displacement. Unlike the case of public investments, which in most cases will displace private investment when the costs of the project are incurred but will stimulate investment when the benefits materialize, most other public expenditures, such as for public consumption and transfer payments to individuals, will not stimulate significant amounts of investment.

In addition, how public expenditures are financed is critical to their impact on private investment and, therefore, to their social opportunity cost. There are two alternative, and very different, models of the public expenditure process that economists might assume. The one most often encountered in the economics literature is that incremental increases or decreases in expenditures correspond to incremental increases or decreases in taxes. Whereas few would argue that this would happen precisely, still most economic analysis of public programs has been based on the assumption that, at the margin, they will be paid for by taxes.

Now suppose that this is true and that the marginal savings rate is $0.1. Then for every incremental dollar of public expenditure, there would be an incremental dollar of taxes, $0.90 of which represents consumption foregone and $0.10 of which represents private savings and investment foregone. If the shadow price of private capital formation is 2.5, then the opportunity cost of the expenditure in terms of present and future consumption foregone is $(0.9)(1) + (0.1)2.5 = \$1.15$. If we were to make this computation based on the assumption that the marginal saving rate were 0.2, this opportunity cost would be $1.30. Thus, the impact on private capital formation means that the social cost of raising one dollar through taxation in these cases are $1.15 and $1.30, respectively. This is significantly higher than one dollar, but not earth shattering. Note that for the time being we are ignoring any possible effect of a rise in the tax rate on the shadow price of capital itself.

Now consider a second model of public tax and expenditure decisions that this author believes corresponds much more closely with what actually occurs. In this model, tax policy and tax rates are fixed and infrequently changed. Taxes certainly are not incrementally adjusted to increases and decreases in expenditures. In the second model, incremental increases or decreases in expenditures result in corresponding increases or decreases in the deficit. Certainly, U.S. experience appears to support the position that marginal increases and decreases in expenditures will be reflected in the deficit.

The implications of this for the social cost of public programs are obvious. First, the opportunity cost of public expenditures will depend on the degree of crowding out. If crowding out is complete, then for every incremental dollar of expenditure, the cost in terms of the present value of current and future consumption foregone as evaluated by consumers is simply the shadow price of capital. Therefore, the cost of one dollar of current public consumption or of making a one-dollar transfer payment in terms of the present value of foregone current private consumption and foregone future private and public consumption is $V$. Conversely, every one dollar of expenditure cuts, and therefore deficit reduction, is worth $V$. Obviously, there is an important question as to the degree to which marginal increases in the deficit results in crowding out. However, even if crowding out is only partial, say 0.5, the opportunity cost of one dollar of public expenditure is $1.75, assuming $V = 2.5$. With the larger deficits and high interest rates that we are experiencing in the United States, marginal increases in the deficit almost certainly cause some significant displacement of private investment.

It is also interesting to consider the opportunity cost of government programs that mandate actions in the private sector. Even though these programs never show up as a government expenditure nor do they directly affect the deficit, they may be exceedingly costly. Consider, for example, government requirements for pollution controls that necessitate billions of dollars of private investment. To the extent that the investment in pollution controls is substituted for other private investments, the social cost of these environmental controls will equal their dollar outlay multiplied by the shadow price of capital.

To summarize, the social cost of any public expenditure will depend on how it is financed and the extent to which it draws resources from private consumption and private investment. To the extent that it draws resources from or reduces private investment, the social cost of this depends on the shadow price of capital, which in turn depends primarily on the marginal tax rate on the earnings from private investment. However, even for relatively low values for $t$, $V$ is significantly greater than zero and therefore is highly significant for the evaluation of public expenditures. Finally, whether either a reduction in savings or an increase in the deficit has an impact on private investment is of critical importance for determining the social cost of public expenditures. This in turn depends on the macroeconomic state of the economy.

## 5    The burden of the debt and tax reform

The concept of the shadow price of capital also has some straightforward implications for the analysis and measurement of the burden of the debt. Although this concept does not capture all dimensions of the social cost of continuous deficit financing and the ever-increasing national debt that such deficits have produced, it does capture and provide a tool for measuring to a first-order approximation the dimension of the social cost of associated displacement of private investment that has always been of central concern. It turns out that this dimension of the cost is extremely large.

Government deficits that become part of the national debt may impose social costs both by displacing private investment through crowding out when the deficit is incurred and through crowding out in all subsequent years when the interest on the debt has to be paid. The case of crowding out by deficit financing is straightforward. For every dollar of private investment that is crowded out, the social cost will be equal to the shadow price of capital, $V$. Obviously, this social cost will depend on the amount of the reduction (or for that matter increase) in private investment, $\gamma$, for each dollar of the deficit. Here $\gamma$ will, in fact, probably be a function of the size of the deficit. Assuming, however, that each additional dollar of the deficit is accompanied by a dollar reduction in private investment, then the initial social cost of a dollar of the deficit is just the shadow price of capital.

However, the social cost does not stop there. By incurring an additional dollar of deficit, the national debt has been increased by a dollar. As a result, we are faced with options that range from paying off the debt in the next year to paying interest on the debt in perpetuity with a continuum of combinations in between. The most realistic assumption is that we will opt to pay the interest in perpetuity.

Now let $g$ be the government borrowing rate. Then incurring one dollar of additional debt requires that we raise an additional $g$ dollars of government revenue every year in perpetuity. The social cost of this commitment will again depend on how it is financed, that is, by incurring additional future deficits or by raising future taxes. Let us take the first case first and assume that the deficit causes a one-to-one reduction in private investment. Then the social cost from deficit financing to pay these interest payments each year will be $gV$, and the present value of this infinite sequence of costs discounted at the social rate is $gV/i$. If $g \approx i$, then the burden or social cost of the interest payments is $V$. Therefore, in the case where crowding out is complete and where future interest payments are financed by increased future deficits, the social cost of increasing the deficit by one dollar is approximately $2V$, and more generally it would be $2\gamma V$, that is, two times the shadow price of capital multiplied by the private investment displaced per dollar of deficit. Given a value for $V$ of 2.5, the social cost of incurring an additional dollar of debt given full crowding out would be about 5.

It is also straightforward to see that the social cost of paying the interest on each additional dollar of debt is different if funded by increased taxes. Following the line of argument in the last section, the social cost of one year's interest paid for by taxes is $g(1-s+sV)$, and the present value of these costs discounting at the social rate $i$ is $g(1-s+sV)/i$. The total social cost of incurring the initial debt and paying the interest with increased taxes, assuming $g \approx i$ and full crowding out, would be $(1+s)V+(1-s)$. Asuming, as before, for purposes of numerical illustration, that $s=0.1$ and $V=2.5$, the social cost when the interest on the debt is paid for by increased taxes would be $(1.1)(2.5)+(0.9)=\$3.65$.

To summarize, the social cost incurred as a result of incurring additional national debt is affected by its impact on private investment, on how the interest payments on the debt are financed, and on the value of the social rate of discount, which in turn depends primarily on the effective marginal tax rate on the income from investment. In addition, the relationship between the government's borrowing rate $g$ and the after-tax rate of return on investment $i = (r - t)$ could in some cases be important to the computation of the social cost of increasing the national debt.

The preceding analysis and that in Section 4 also have some immediate implications for tax reform. It follows directly that the social costs or benefit from tax reduction, given an initial deficit position, depend on what happens to the effective marginal rate of taxation on investment income and on how much the deficit increases or decreases. To the extent that the tax reduction lowers the marginal rate on capital income, it lowers the shadow price of capital and therefore the social cost of running deficits. However, to the extent that the tax rate reduction increases the deficit and, by implication, crowding out, it raises the social cost of the deficit. How the two balance out is an empirical issue.

However, using Table 2, we can construct an interesting numerical example. Suppose, initially $t = 0.54$ so that $V = 2.5$. Then, assuming complete crowding out and $g \approx i$, the initial social cost of incurring an additional dollar of debt would be $5, but it would drop from $5 to $3.70 if we were to reduce the effective tax rate investment income by 0.25 percent.

A second point is that except for very low rates of crowding out, it is socially less costly to raise additional revenues through taxation, provided it does not occur through a large increase in the effective marginal rate of taxation on the income from investment. Again, assume $V = 2.5$ and $s = 0.1$. Then the social cost of raising a dollar of additional government income through taxation is approximately $1.15, whereas, the social cost of raising the same dollar by deficit financing is approximately $5\gamma$ dollars, assuming the interest on the debt is financed by increased future deficits. Therefore, if $\gamma > 0.23$, the social cost of taxation is less than the social cost of deficit financing. However, as the effective tax rate on investment income goes down, the value of $\gamma$, which equates the social cost of taxation with the social cost of deficit financing, goes up.

In summary, the social cost of raising government revenue through taxation and deficit financing both increase as the effective tax rate on capital income increases. The social cost of the deficit and the national debt depends on both $t$ and on $\gamma$, and when $\gamma = 1$, this cost is three to five times the cost of the money raised. This is true even for relatively low values of $t$. Therefore, this analysis supports the conclusions that (1) tax financing is less socially costly than deficit financing except where there is very little crowding out; (2) all public financing is less socially costly the lower the rate of taxation on investment income, $t$; and (3) for both tax and deficit financing, the social cost of raising one dollar can significantly exceed the dollar of expenditure it pays for, and in the case of deficit financing, it may greatly exceed one dollar. From this, one can conclude that, except in circumstances where deficits do not significantly reduce private investment, government expenditures should be financed by taxes, and as a general proposition, tax rates on capital income should be lowered subject to the caveat that an optimal second-best tax plan that takes accounts for all tax-induced inefficiencies may not reduce taxes on the earnings of capital to zero. This would, in the context of the current U.S. tax reform debate, suggest that tax reform should include a general increase in taxes to reduce the deficit and the elimination or reduction of taxes on corporate profits, dividend payments, and interest.

## 6 A postscript on the methodology and conclusions

Clearly, the magnitude of the costs that have been shown to be associated with the crowding out of private investment is large and has significant implications for the evaluation of public expenditure decisions, tax policy, deficit financing, and the burden of the debt. However, the reader may well have some lingering questions about the methodology on which these conclusions are based and therefore on the conclusions themselves. For example, such questions arise as: Can one justify or is it important that the savings rate be assumed to be constant? Does the analysis imply that the optimal tax rate on capital income is zero? To answer such questions it is important to put this analysis in methodological perspective and then to consider what one can and cannot conclude from it.

First, the analysis is clearly in the second-best tradition. The starting point is that firms and households optimize in an economy with imperfect markets including imperfections in capital markets caused by personal and corporate income taxes on the earnings from capital. This drives a wedge between the before-tax rate of return $r$ earned by firms and the after-tax rate of return $(1-t)r$, that is, the consumer's rate of interest earned by an individual investor. We assume that consumers optimize and adjust their savings and investment to the point that their marginal rate of time preference just equals their rate of interest. It is this initial second-best situation that is the starting point of the analysis, and to simplify the analysis, we assume that the conditions of this initial equilibrium would, in the absence of a policy change, continue to hold into the future.

At this point, the concept of the shadow price of capital, $V$, is developed to capture the first-order effects of a one-dollar increase or decrease in private investment on the present value of the consumption stream in the economy when discounted at the consumer's rate of interest. The value of $V$ depends critically on $t$ and $s$ and much less importantly on $r$ and $N$, where $r$ and $s$ will be determined simultaneously by the interplay of the demand and supply for investment funds, $t$ is a policy variable, and $N$ is a historical average.

The basic question is whether one can take these first-order results and use them to analyze policy changes that are of significant magnitude such as sizable changes in tax or expenditure policy. The answer to this question depends first on whether the policy changes will have a significant impact on the variables that determine the shadow price of capital and second on whether, given the range of possible changes in these key parameters, there will be a significant impact on the value of the shadow price of capital. If many significant changes in policies and the state of the economy do not greatly affect the magnitude of the shadow price of capital, then it can be used to measure the social cost of significant changes in public policies accompanied by other comparable changes in the state of the economy. The question is, Does the concept of the shadow price of capital and its use in this paper meet this test?

The magnitude of the shadow price of capital depends primarily on the combined tax rate $t$, on capital income, which is a policy variable, and on the marginal propensity to save, $s$. With respect to the latter, in the U.S. economy, the marginal propensity to save has remained very stable over a long period of time under many changes in the economy and economic policy. However, even if it were to go up significantly, we observe from Table 2 that $V$ is not highly sensitive to changes in the value of $s$ and, further, that as $s$ rises, the value of $V$ rises. This means that if a policy change caused a relatively large increase in $s$, the change in $V$ would not be relatively large, and the impact would be in the direction of increasing the benefit and cost measures based on the concept and the measurement of $V$. The latter would generally strengthen the policy conclusions that have been drawn.

The insensitivity of $V$ to changes in $s$ is important. One might object that the underlying methodology equates people's marginal rate of time preference with their after-tax rate of return, which is only appropriate if one assumes people freely vary their savings in response to changes in their rate of return and that at the same time it uses a constant savings rate for computing $V$. Does this not reflect an internal contradiction in the methodology? The answer is no for two reasons. First, even if individuals vary their savings in response to changes in their rate of return, there is considerable, but not conclusive, evidence that their marginal savings rate is not highly sensitive to these changes. Therefore, the assumption of a constant marginal savings rate may be a good approximation even in a world where consumers freely adjust their consumption and savings in response to changes in their rate of return.

Second, even if the marginal savings rate were reasonably sensitive to changes in rates of return, the value of $V$ is not very sensitive even to relatively large percentage changes in $s$. Although a fixed $s$ is used in the computation of $V$, the results, which are based on the value of $V$, are not dependent on a particular fixed value for $s$.

With regard to policy changes that affect $t$, we can immediately compute the impact on the value of $V$ and therefore on the cost or benefit, respectively, of displacing or stimulating additional private investment. It is true that decreases in $t$ might result in increases in $s$, which would in part offset the impact of the decreasing of taxes, but Table 2 suggests that this offsetting impact is not likely to be highly significant.

The point of this discussion is that the concept of the shadow price of capital provides a good first-order approximation of the social costs of increasing or decreasing private investment that is relatively insensitive to changes in other economic variables that might occur as a result of policy changes. Therefore, it can be used to measure the costs or benefits of programs that affect private investment such as public expenditures financed either by deficits or by taxation.

Another important aspect of the shadow price of capital for the analysis of such policies is that it demonstrates that to a first-order approximation, the costs of crowding out under the present U.S. tax system or a similar tax system are very high. The importance of this cannot be stressed too strongly, and in fact, it is the magnitude of the inefficiencies caused by the wedge between the before- and after-tax return on capital that makes focusing on this single dimension of inefficiency important. These inefficiencies become particularly significant when we pursue social policies such as deficit financing that displaces private investment.

This method of analysis also demonstrates that the social cost of the distortions and the resulting inefficiencies from taxes on capital income are not limited to the period in which they occur but play out over time and therefore that the process of compounding must be taken into account in computing these costs. The reason for this is that any action that affects private investment now affects private investment and reinvestment into the future. If the rate of return on private investment is different from the consumer's rate of interest, then this generates a stream of social costs or benefits that have to be accounted for. This is closely related to the point made by Arrow (1966) in his initial paper.

Although a strength of this method of analysis is that it focuses on the investment and reinvestment process, it is obvious that personal and corporate income taxes produce many other inefficiencies such as by affecting the labor–leisure choice, the trade-off between capital and labor, and so on. The shadow price of capital does not address or capture any of these costs but simply focuses on social cost associated with the displacement of private investment. As a result, one cannot conclude that the optimal second-best tax plan would reduce the tax on capital income to zero because other dimensions of the social cost of taxation have to be taken into account in determining the optimum plan. Although it would be ideal to integrate and fully develop the results obtained here in terms of a model of optimal taxation, that is a future paper.

It is interesting to compare the results obtained here with those of two recent contributions to the literature that have used different approaches to compute the social cost of raising revenues through increases in existing nonoptimal taxes. The most recent of these (Ballard, Shoven, and Wholley 1985) uses a general equilibrium model of the economy to simulate a series of static equilibria in order to compute the *marginal excess burden* of increases in alternative U.S. taxes. These computations are made under varying assumptions about savings and labor supply elasticities. The estimates that are most comparable to those of this chapter are for the income tax. The estimates by Ballard et al. (1985) are that for every marginal dollar of revenue that is raised through increased income taxation, the social cost is between $1.163 and $1.313 depending on savings and labor supply elasticities. Earlier in this chapter it was estimated that the social cost of raising one dollar by an income tax was $1.15 and $1.30 for $s = 0.1$ and $s = 0.2$, respectively. If one takes their case where both the saving and labor supply elasticities are zero, which corresponds most closely to the assumptions used in the computations in this essay, they get a marginal social cost from income taxation of $1.163 compared with the $1.15 computed here using what we believe is the more realistic assumption regarding the value of $s$. Clearly, their study and this one yield very similar numerical results that are slightly higher than those obtained in an earlier paper by Browning (1976).

Although there are a number of differences in the underlying methodology used by Ballard et al. (1985), Browning (1976), and this one, the numerical results with regard to the marginal social cost of income taxation are encouragingly similar. What this essay does, which the other two do not, is to estimate the marginal social cost of deficit financing and the impact on the burden of the debt. It may well be that for most marginal public expenditures, this is the relevant cost, and our estimates indicate that, depending on the degree of crowding out, it may be much higher than the marginal social cost of raising money through increased income taxes. In fact, if we use the estimates of the marginal social cost of a variety of different types of taxation computed by Ballard et al. (1985), which range from about $1.15 to $1.60, the marginal social cost of deficit financing may be much higher than the marginal social cost of all these taxes.

Finally, it is important to point out that in any study designed to compute the marginal social cost of different methods of raising public revenues, the marginal social cost of raising these funds cannot be equated with the net social cost or benefit of the programs they are used to finance. The net social benefit or cost is the marginal social benefit of the program minus the marginal social cost of financing it. This point is obvious but bears repeating.

What emerges from this analysis using the concept of the shadow price of capital is that benefits as well as costs that take the form of increased private investment are worth several times more than benefits that go directly into public or private consumption. For this reason, one has to take the impact on private investment into account in computing both the costs and the benefits of a public expenditure. This is the fundamental point that Arrow (1966) made; however, he did not consider, in that paper, the fact that the impact on investment of financing a public expenditure may be very different from the impact on private investment of the program resulting from that public expenditure.

## REFERENCES

Arrow, K. J. (1966), "Discounting and public investment criteria," in A. V. Kneese and S. C. Smith (Eds.), *Water research,* Baltimore: Johns Hopkins University Press.
Arrow, K. J. and M. Kurz (1970), *Public investment, the rate of return, and optimal fiscal policy,* Baltimore: Johns Hopkins University Press.
Ballard, C. L., J. B. Shoven, and J. Whalley (1985), "General equilibrium computations of the marginal welfare costs of taxes in the United States," *The American Economic Review,* 75: 128–38.

Bradford, D. F. (1975), "Constraints on government investment opportunities and the choice of discount rate," *American Economic Review,* 65: 887–95.

Browning, E. K. (1976), "The marginal cost of public funds," *Journal of Political Economy,* 84: 283–98.

Diamond, P. (1968), "The opportunit cost of public investment: Comment," *Quarterly Journal of Economics,* 82: 686–8.

Eckstein, O. (1958), *Water resource development: The economics of project evaluation,* Cambridge, Mass.: Harvard University Press.

Feldstein, M. S. (1970), "Choice of technique in the public sector: A simplification," *Economic Journal,* 80: 985–90.

Holland, D. M. and S. Myers (1979), "Trends in corporate profitability and capital costs," in R. Lindsay (Ed.), *The nation's capital needs,* New York: Committee for Economic Development, pp. 103–189.

Kay, J. A. (1972), "Social discount rates," *Journal of Public Economics,* 1: 359–78.

Lind, R. C., K. J. Arrow, G. R. Corey, P. Dasgupta, A. K. Sen, T. Stauffer, J. E. Stiglitz, J. A. Stockfisch, and R. Wilson (1982), *Discounting for time and risk in energy policy,* Washington, D.C., Resources for the Future.

Mendelsohn, R. (1981), "The choice of the discount rate for public projects," *The American Economic Review,* 71: 239–41.

U.S. Department of the Treasury, Internal Revenue Service (1973), *Corporation income tax returns: Statistics of income,* Washington, D.C.: Government Printing Office.

U.S. Department of the Treasury, Internal Revenue Service (1974), *Corporation income tax returns: Statistics of income,* Washington, D.C.: Government Printing Office.

U.S. Department of the Treasury, Internal Revenue Service (1975), *Corporation income tax returns: Statistics of income,* Washington, D.C.: Government Printing Office.

# Author index

213